Ruins

and Rivals

Published in cooperation with the William P. Clements Center

for Southwest Studies, Southern Methodist University

Ruins

and Rivals
The Making of Southwest Archaeology

James E. Snead

The University of Arizona Press   Tucson

First paperbound printing 2003
The University of Arizona Press
© 2001 The Arizona Board of Regents
All rights reserved
∞ This book is printed on acid-free, archival-quality paper.
Manufactured in the United States of America

06 05 04 03 6 5 4 3 2

Library of Congress Cataloging-in-Publication Data

Snead, James Elliot, 1962–
Ruins and rivals: the making of Southwest archaeology / James E. Snead.
p. cm.
Includes bibliographical references and index.
ISBN 0-8165-2138-7 (cloth: acid-free paper)
ISBN 0-8165-2397-5 (pbk: acid-free paper)
1. Indians of North America—Southwest, New—Antiquities.
2. Archaeology—Southwest, New—History.
3. Southwest, New—Antiquities.
I. Title.
E78.S7 S53   2001
979'.01–dc21   00-010608

British Library Cataloguing-in-Publication Data

A catalogue record for this book is available from the British Library.

For Monica

Contents

Figures

Foreword

The depth of archaeological history in the American Southwest often confounds the modern researcher. We visit ruins in remote canyons and find inscriptions or silted-up trenches left by our predecessors. Our museums are filled with artifacts collected when our grandparents were young. In archives we search for field notes, journals, or sketch maps, struggling to decipher the ornate handwriting of nineteenth-century correspondence and the cultural context of Gilded Age America that produced the words we read. We are not, generally, trained as historians, but a feeling for the history of what we do is shared by many of us.

The impetus for this book was a change in direction in my graduate studies in the Department of Anthropology at UCLA. I was raised in the Southwest but on leaving for college had set my sights on the archaeology of another part of the world. Thus when the vagaries of opportunity brought me back to Santa Fe, I found myself ignorant of many of the basic texts and references that my colleagues had long before taken to heart. As a result I spent a considerable amount of time looking at original sources in the archives in order to get a feel for Southwest archaeology and its practitioners.

The picture of Southwest archaeology I assembled through this crash course, however, was significantly different from what I had expected. The stories told by telegrams, correspondence, and memoranda had less to do with things coming out of the ground than with political maneuvers and agendas. There was considerable dissonance between the standard disciplinary histories and the tangled reality of past days. As I read further, I crossed paths with several historians of anthropology who clarified many errors of fact and interpretation. But it also became clear from the richness of the archives that material for new histories of Southwest archaeology was readily at hand.

This history is a postdoctoral project based on those archival explorations. My purpose in examining in detail the activities of particular communities who took an interest in the southwestern past at the turn of the century is to identify patterns of interaction that set the stage for modern Southwest archaeology. Where possible, I prefer to let these individuals speak for themselves, and although there are theoretical points to be made, the logic of the argument is derived from the sources. As an archaeologist who also writes history, my concern for chronology has kept the narrative within relatively traditional bounds.

The majority of the research was conducted in 1996–97 while I served as Kalbfleisch Research Fellow in the Division of Anthropology at the American Museum of Natural History. David Hurst Thomas made my stay in New York possible and has promoted the project at every turn. Many other members of the anthropology staff, including Sumru Aricanli, Andrew Balkansky, Paul Beelitz, Robert Carneiro, Stan Freed, Martha Graham, Alvaro Higueras, Lori Pendleton, Annibal Rodriguez, Chuck Spencer, Lisa Stock, Nyurka Tyler, and Ann Wright-Parsons, contributed to the project. Belinda Kaye, in particular, welcomed me to the departmental archives. In the Museum library Mary DeJong arranged for loans and reference material, while the Special Collections staff of Tom Baione, Daryl Gammons, and Paula Willey provided access to the central archives.

Visits to archives throughout the country took place over several years and were supported in large part by a research grant from the American Philosophical Society. Archivists whose interest had a major impact on the course of my research include Sarah Demb, at the Peabody Museum of Archaeology and Ethnology at Harvard; Alison Jeffrey, at the National Museum of the American

Indian; Priscilla Murray, of the Archaeological Institute of America; and Kim Walters, at the Southwest Museum. Jack Focht, of the Trailside Museums at Bear Mountain Park, welcomed me to examine his unexpected cache of Talbot Hyde papers. In Santa Fe, Orlando Romero, Tomás Jaehn, and Hazel Romero at the Fray Angélico Chávez History Library provided access to the E. L. Hewett papers, while Willow Powers and Diane Bird King tracked down loose ends at the Museum of Indian Arts and Cultures. Other sites visited include the School of American Research; the New Mexico State Records Center and Archives; the Bancroft Library at the University of California, Berkeley; the Arizona Historical Society; Special Collections of the University of Arizona Library; Harvard University Archives; the Bentley Historical Library at the University of Michigan; the Century Association, in New York; the Hispanic Society of America; the always welcoming National Anthropological Archives; and the National Archives.

The opportunity to spend a fellowship year at the William P. Clements Center for Southwest Studies at Southern Methodist University allowed me to bring the writing to a conclusion. David Weber, that Center's director, offered sound advice at a critical stage, and many of the good things about the manuscript resulted from his suggestions. My colleagues in the Center, Steven Reich and Jane Elder, were unfailing sources of support, while David Farmer and his staff at the DeGolyer Library extended every courtesy. Being able to consult on a regular basis with David Meltzer in the Department of Anthropology was also quite valuable, as was the encouragement of Michael Adler. The panel assembled to discuss my work included Curtis Hinsley, Leah Dilworth, and Richard Francaviglia, all of whom made insightful comments. The students in Anthropology 5355 saw many of the ideas herein in development, and their patience with the process is appreciated. I also gratefully acknowledge the support of the Clements Center in making this publication possible.

Christine Szuter, director of the University of Arizona Press, has discussed the project with me since its early stages, and her positive attitude was a major incentive to finish the job. Among the dozens of colleagues whose comments and critique have helped to mold the work into its present shape I would like to list Don Fowler, Louis Hieb, Jim Hill, Bill Longacre, Joan Mathien, Bob Powers, Robert Preucel, J. Jefferson Reid, Douglas Schwartz, Jeff Thomas, Raymond Thompson, Bruce Trigger, Courtney White, Todd Wertheim, Steve Williams, and Monica Smith, whose insights always seem to come at the right moment. Finally, without the support of Jim and Georgia Snead and Bob and Jodie Phillips, none of my various projects would have a hope of completion.

Introduction

Competing for the Past

Always, incredibly, there lingers about these places, where once was man, some trace that the human sense responds to, never so sensitively as where it has lain mellowing through a thousand years of sun and silence.
　　—MARY AUSTIN,
　　　　Land of Journey's Ending

Pecos National Monument, a low ridge crowned with mud-brick ruins in the center of a wide river valley, is one of the first cultural landmarks visible to travelers entering northern New Mexico from the east. The high walls of a Spanish mission, abandoned since the early nineteenth century, stand adjacent to the sprawling remains of the pueblo village that served as the home of the historic Native American inhabitants of Pecos and their ancestors. Nearby are the ruts of a wagon trail, worn deep by the Spanish colonists who ventured eastward to trade with the Comanche of the Plains and by the Anglo-Americans who pushed west to Santa Fe. Today all of this can be glimpsed from the interstate highway, which replaced the old road and brings tourism as well as trade. Some of those who drive this route stop at Pecos National Monument, stroll the concrete pathways maintained by the National Park Service, and find themselves viewing a powerful symbol of the heritage and identity of the Southwest.

Less than a mile from the mission, still within the monument's boundaries, is another ancient pueblo, its adobe walls leveled and made nearly invisible by centuries of wind and rain. Parked in a grove of juniper and piñon pine at the center of this ruin is the wreck of a Model-T Ford once owned by the archaeologist A. V. Kidder. Left behind after a summer's excavations in the 1920s the pickup sits, gradually flaking into rust. Amidst a scatter of potsherds nearby and obscured by grass, a flat plaque marks the graves of Kidder and his wife Madeleine. Interred at Forked Lightning Ruin the Kidders, along with the truck they once called "Pecos Black," are now inextricably bound up with Pecos and its past, part of the archaeological record they devoted their lives to revealing. The symbolism of Pecos, its public monuments and the hidden record of its exploration, captures the complex relationship between archaeology, society, and identity in the American Southwest.

Ruins are as central to the modern image of the Southwest as are its mountains and deserts. Chaco Canyon, Mesa Verde, Bandelier, Hovenweep, Casa Grande, Montezuma Castle, and other relics of the past appear on calendars and coffee mugs and are major tourist destinations. The combination of stark landscapes and tangible reminders of a prehistoric past form visual touchstones of great power. Since the mid-nineteenth century this dramatic environment, together with the existence of Pueblo communities occupying the same terrain as their ancestors, has driven archaeologists to the study of the southwestern past. Artifacts have been excavated, settlements unearthed, and a wide array of information about ancient society assembled. In the process a set of methods and theories about ways to study the ancient Southwest have evolved, as have institutions and organizations designed to promote that pursuit. Southwest archaeology has emerged as a distinct scientific endeavor, a component of the broader fields of American anthropology and archaeology, but with its own traditions and goals. The contribution of archaeological research to our understanding of the prehistoric Southwest has been substantial, and much of our modern perception of this ancient heritage is directly related to this work.

But while Southwest archaeology as we know it today has shaped our perception of the region's past, it did not emerge as a field of activity simply from the convergence of scientific interests and significant cultural resources. Other communities have interpreted the remains of the ancient Southwest using their own frames of reference. To Native Americans, places where their ancestors lived remain part of an active cultural landscape, in ways to which latecomers are largely oblivious. The Anglo-American settlers who arrived in the region in the last century brought their own attitudes toward ruins.[1] Their firsthand experience differed from that of the public of the eastern United States, which saw southwestern antiquities through the filter of books and museum displays. Ultimately tourism brought people to the Southwest to visit the ruins themselves, an encounter that was structured by economics as well as expectations. Over time patrons, legislators, bureaucrats, museum administrators, writers, and activists all developed interests in southwestern antiquities, often with dramatically different motives.

As part of the social context within which antiquities have been perceived, these "other voices" played a critical role in the making of Southwest archaeology. The relationship between archaeology and society is discussed by the historian David Lowenthal, who argues that "relics," along with memory and history, are a primary source of knowledge about the past.[2] Humans respond more readily to "things" than to abstractions, and material objects thus become important links to what has gone before. The relationships between things and events, however, are complex and subject to multiple interpretations. In other words, whereas monuments and artifacts may "symbolize" the past, their particular significance depends heavily on the perspective of the observer. An ancient sarcophagus may serve as a symbol of fallen grandeur to one group, the sign of victorious cultural conquest to a second, or a watering trough to a third. Different interpretations of the histories attached to material objects have their roots in the sociocultural context within which the past is experienced. Ruins, as the cultural geographer J. B. Jackson has pointed out, have particular associations in American society, as symbols of both decay and the necessity for renewal. Other commentators, such as Susan Stewart, argue that artifacts provide a source of "authentic experience" under modern social conditions. The potential for multiple interpretations means that the past, and its harbingers, will always be contested ground.[3]

The symbolic utility of ruins and relics is fundamental to the context within which archaeologists established their Southwest work. In recent years historians of archaeology have acknowledged that social conditions define the way the past is used. In general, these scholars have focused either on the development of specific national "traditions" of archaeological research, or on the role of archaeology in constructing cultural identity in post-Renaissance Europe.[4] Institutional histories, which place scholarship in administrative and intellectual context, have grown increasingly sophisticated, with the benchmark study of this kind being historian Curtis Hinsley's *The Smithsonian and the American Indian*.[5] Despite this expanding body of research, however, the complex relationships between archaeology and society have often defied analysis. Few historians besides Hinsley have taken up the subject, while the breadth of the topic and the interdisciplinary nature of historical scholarship have made it difficult for archaeologists themselves to take a critical look at the evolution of their profession.

The problem facing students of the history of archaeology, then, is explaining how broad cultural themes related to antiquity and its material remains have played a role in shaping the scientific study of the past. Acknowledgment of the interaction between society and scholarship is simpler than defining ways to "capture" the process and make it explicable. The question underlying the different ways archaeologists and other visitors experience monuments such as Pecos is what shared history exists behind those divergent perceptions.

In this book I build a social context for the study of antiquity by adopting frames of reference that are particularly suited to examining the patterns of interaction among the different groups that have taken an interest in the subject. In looking at factors that influence the way disciplines form, I have been guided by several scholars. Both Hinsley and George Stocking have shown how the structure of institutions has shaped intellectual pursuits within anthropology generally. As yet there are few histories devoted to particular southwestern institutions, but their central role in organizing research and public interaction is increasingly recognized. Don Fowler's "Harvard versus Hewett," for instance, illustrates the complex networks of politics and personalities that control archaeological fieldwork and shape opportunities for scholarship within the Southwest itself. Studies of cultural concepts of the southwestern past to accompany these examinations of scholarly trends are also scarce, meaning that a broad picture of the role of southwestern antiquity in American society remains elusive.[6]

What is needed in a history of Southwest archaeology is the integration of social and intellectual perspectives on the past. In grappling with this issue I have emphasized particular "fault lines," areas where over time the interests of the scholarly community and those of the public have come together and clashed over the subject of southwestern antiquities. I have identified three critical elements of the history of Southwest archaeology within which scholarly-public interaction has been particularly important: *patronage, professionalism,* and *rationale.*

Introduction

To begin with *patronage*, it is obvious that the circumstances of funding, essential to the conduct of scholarship in all its aspects, have an inevitable impact on the research process itself. The institutions, governments, and private patrons that are called upon to support scientific and cultural endeavor have agendas that coincide with, but are not identical to, those of the practitioners themselves. The historian Howard Miller has demonstrated that the utilitarian, commercial interests of the nineteenth-century elite in the United States made it difficult for scientists to attract funding for "pure research" that had no practical application. The projects that did emerge were shaped to a significant degree by the desires of the patron.[7] In his influential study of antimodernism in the late nineteenth century, T. J. Jackson Lears documents the enthusiasm for art collecting that gripped the upper classes in the 1880s and 1890s, an activity that promoted museums that served as centers of display rather than of study or education.[8] Both Miller and Lears illustrate the critical contribution of patronage to the structure of scholarly inquiry in the United States.

The role of patronage in defining the social role of archaeology has been more thoroughly examined in Europe than in America, a strategy evident in Suzanne Marchand's recent study of German participation in classical archaeology from the eighteenth century to the present. Marchand argues that rising levels of state funding for the excavation of classical sites by quasi-governmental institutions promoted the increasingly prestige-based, competitive, and nationalistic aspects of archaeological fieldwork in the late nineteenth century. Within Germany, however, state patronage of prehistoric excavations was more limited, leading to domination of the field by associations of amateurs.[9] The contrast between minimal support of scholarship at home and abundant funding for work abroad, in part generated by conditions of patronage, had significant impact not only on the way prehistoric and classical societies were "understood" by their excavators but also on the social significance of archaeology itself.

Few studies of the links between patronage and archaeology have been undertaken on the American field.[10] State support of archaeological research in the United States prior to World War I was largely restricted to the activities of the Smithsonian Institution, which relied on congressional appropriation and was thus subject to political priorities. Archaeology was a rarity in universities, and scholars working outside governmental agencies depended on private patrons to support their work. Even within museums and similar institutional settings, external funding remained essential for the conduct of field research. Identifying and maintaining sources of patronage required that scholars take into account the interests and motivations of their supporters, which in turn reflected social priorities that often differed from those of science. The conflict that emerged over these divergent motivations inevitably shaped the conduct of archaeological research.

The second, related element is *professionalism*. In the early nineteenth century, American scholarship was dominated by generalists who conducted their studies as avocations rather than careers. Participation in scientific activity was constrained by wealth, facilities, and available time. With the gradual specialization of knowledge that characterized the years after the Civil War, scholarship subdivided into increasingly exclusive professions.[11] Overall, professionalization limited the participation of amateurs through legislation and the establishment of advanced degree programs, training regimes, specialized institutions, and professional societies. On an intellectual level, professionalization was an attempt to erect an orthodoxy of interpretation based on principles shared among what historian Thomas Haskell calls a "community of inquiry."[12] The evolution of professions was one of the major transformations of late nineteenth-century American life, considered a product of increasing interdependence and the resulting crisis of authority. Specialization was one means through which a society previously centered on small communities adapted to these changes, a process identifiable in all areas of work.[13]

American archaeologists in the late nineteenth century shared in this drive to establish a distinct profession for themselves. The historian Laurence Veysey has noted that what he calls "fields of effort" are not unitary but are instead composed of "multiple worlds, curiously isolated from each other."[14] Within archaeology, this multiplicity of interest groups was enhanced by widespread public curiosity over antiquities. Property rights made it difficult to establish control over archaeological resources, since any site could be legitimately excavated by its owner. In most cases a shovel was the only piece of specialized equipment required. The popular appeal of archaeology created a thriving market for artifacts, which archaeologists with limited resources had little success opposing. Resistance to the expanding professionalism of archaeology was expressed by individuals whose expertise (real or assumed) in matters of antiquity was not recognized in the new order. Local amateur groups, exhibiting what Tom Griffiths, an Australian historian, calls the "antiquarian imagination . . . a historical sensibility particularly attuned to the material evidence of the past, and possessing a powerful sense of place," developed throughout the United States. These societies formed the nucleus of public interest in archaeology and were centers of resistance to professionalization.[15] Archaeologists also faced difficulty in establishing institutional niches, since research agendas often conflicted with the education and policy orientations of museums, universities, and government agencies. The

vagaries of professionalization thus had a direct impact on the ability of archaeologists to establish themselves, develop research programs, and obtain funding.
Emphasis must also be placed, however, on the alternate strategies represented by
independent entrepreneurs and local societies. The interactions among Veysey's
"multiple worlds" was a key element in the making of Southwest archaeology, and
their analysis is important in understanding the process.

A third and more complex historical variable is *rationale*. The accessibility of
the archaeological record and its suitability for multiple interpretations has meant
that the acquisition or study of antiquities can be conducted for many different
reasons. Archaeology in the United States has been linked with anthropology
since the early nineteenth century, and in the modern day most archaeologists
specializing in the indigenous societies of the New World are trained as anthropologists. This is, however, an uneasy fit. Anthropology emerged as a scholarly
endeavor from the European expansion of the sixteenth and seventeenth centuries, addressing a need to account for the inhabitants of Asia and the New World
whose existence had not been suspected previously. In its emphasis on peoples
living under imperial rule, anthropology had a practical orientation distinct from
that of archaeology, which at the time was concerned with the material past of
Europe itself. While English antiquarians looked to Stonehenge and similar ruins
to construct models of their own heritage, the archaeological remains of the New
World, which pertained to the history of the indigenous inhabitants, were of little
interest to the new settlers. It was only in the nineteenth century that archaeology was harnessed to anthropology in an effort to study the Native American past,
but even then competing rationales for archaeological practice persisted. Classical archaeology, the product of a humanistic interest in the cultural heritage of
the Mediterranean, was well established in the United States after the Civil War,
and popular theorizing over "mound builders" and lost races flourished in the
American heartland.[16] The methods employed by practitioners of these different
forms of archaeology were in many cases indistinguishable, but the rationale for
the activity was quite different.

Other rationales for the conduct of archaeology include pecuniary interest,
since a commercial trade in artifacts is one product of the public interest in antiquity. Although modern archaeology has been defined to exclude "relic hunting,"
participants in the antiquities market have not been deterred. For other audiences, the educational applications of archaeology have greater value than abstract
theorizing. For archaeologists functioning as custodians of national monuments,
the rationale for archaeology might be quite different from that of the excavator.
The perspective of Native Americans must also be included, both because most
archaeology in the New World directly pertains to their heritage and because they

have served as observers, guides, excavation workers, and interpreters of archaeological remains. In examining the rationale for archaeology presented to the public by various interest groups, the perspective of women—largely absent from the professional ranks prior to the mid-twentieth century—must also be given a place.[17]

My point is not to argue that all perspectives on American antiquity and its study are equally important, but rather that archaeology itself has been influenced by these and other rarely acknowledged voices. Efforts to establish today's disciplines were accompanied by vociferous arguments over the nature of their proper subject matter. In the late nineteenth century, capturing the approval of the public and consolidating access to sources of funding were key concerns of the rival archaeological interest groups. This debate, the way in which archaeologists have over time rationalized their particular way of studying the past to suit different audiences, is a critical component of the social history of the discipline.

As a final element of this framework, I argue that the interplay of patronage, professionalism, and rationale in the study of antiquity is essentially competitive. The people who promoted archaeology in the southwestern states and territories were interested in more than the simple promotion of scholarship. Individual and institutional prestige required success, expressed in terms of sites excavated, strategies devised, artifacts acquired, funding obtained, museums built, public support achieved, and above all influence expanded. The promotion of one approach or project very often meant the failure of another. The participants in this decades-long struggle called on different allies at different times, of necessity incorporating parts of different agendas into their own. Compromises were inevitable but largely unacknowledged. Over time motivations for the conduct of archaeology and the parameters of its practice thus evolved, but rarely in a straightforward manner.

It is through this competitive process, the development of ideas and the implementation of programs in the course of struggle for prestige and dominance, that consensus emerges, and I contend that from the competition between scholarly and public interest groups over the study of southwestern antiquities at the turn of the century the modern paradigm for Southwest archaeology was created. This book illustrates the way broad cultural processes and attitudes toward the past were expressed and interpreted by different communities, often in opposition to each other, producing a frame of reference for the southwestern past that in the present day continues to structure archaeological research.

Introduction

Rather than attempt comprehensive coverage of 150 years of scholarship and contention over southwestern antiquities, I begin with the critical moment for public
and scholarly interaction over the ancient Southwest: the Columbian Exposition
in Chicago in 1893. By the early 1890s the results of southwestern exploration
conducted over the preceding several decades, with its dual themes of humanistic interpretation and scientific documentation, had established the basic parameters of southwestern antiquity. Government science, with its utilitarian focus
complemented by the romantic fascination with ruins, dominated the field of
southwestern antiquity in its formative stages. The subsequent thirty years saw
a dramatic expansion of archaeological fieldwork and for the first time the full
involvement of public museums and institutions outside the government. These
developments coincided with both the first serious efforts to establish anthropology and archaeology as professional disciplines and the acceleration of Anglo-
American settlement of the Southwest. This period was also marked by the
closing of the American frontier, a time in which public energy turned from
expansion to consolidation, bringing attention to formerly obscure corners of the
country. Popular interest in the Southwest increased dramatically in the 1890s;
in the American imagination the region was transformed from an obscure outpost into an exotic locale.[18] The Columbian Exposition, at which all of these forces
were on display, served as a catalyst for many of the subsequent developments
in Southwest archaeology. The early 1920s effectively mark the end of this formative stage in southwestern archaeology. On the national level, anthropology
had expanded significantly within the university system, a process of professionalization accompanied by the establishment of organizations, journals, and
institutions with educational and research mandates. This increasingly elaborate
structure made the discipline less susceptible to change and innovation than it
had been in previous decades. In the Southwest itself, what in 1893 had been a
freewheeling effort to exploit antiquities in a variety of ways was increasingly constrained by legislation and changing local priorities. Archaeological institutions
were fully established, and even for underdeveloped parts of the Southwest the
pattern had been set. Knowledge about the southwestern past was also becoming increasingly systematized. The publication in 1924 of A. V. Kidder's *Introduction to Southwest Archaeology* was both a landmark effort to pull together
information about the southwestern past and a symbol of the rise of a new generation of archaeologists for whom the challenges and opportunities of the era of
the Columbian Exposition were largely irrelevant.

Southwest archaeology was forged in the events and conditions surrounding
the turn of the century, and the story told here will be anchored in that era. While
the dozens of individuals and institutions that played roles in promoting south-

western research all had different motives, I focus on the activities of two groups of participants whose activities illustrate contrasting trends in scholarship and public interest: the Southwest expeditions of the American Museum of Natural History in New York, and the regional archaeological societies that developed within the West itself.

The southwestern program of the American Museum had its origins in events leading up to the Columbian Exposition and for thirty years was a dominant force in Southwest archaeology. The Museum's Department of Anthropology, founded in 1890, provided one of the first professional footholds for archaeologists outside government employ. The major public museums of eastern and midwestern cities were important niches for archaeologists in the 1890s, and created a particular set of opportunities and constraints. Educational outreach, the cultivation of patrons, and institutional competition were all prominent forces at the American Museum. Museum archaeologists, for their part, eagerly used this new base to stake their own claim to a field otherwise dominated by local relic hunters and federal agents. While the acquisition and collection of artifacts served to promote vague scientific goals, the enhancement of professional prestige also motivated these museum-based scholars.

The first program of southwestern excavations conducted under the auspices of the American Museum, known as the "Hyde Exploring Expedition," began at Chaco Canyon in northwestern New Mexico in 1896. Excavations at the famous site of Pueblo Bonito unfolded against a backdrop of shifting dynamics between patrons, professionals, and the lay audience. What began as an effort to establish scientific legitimacy and institutional prestige evolved into a lightning rod for competition, both in New Mexico and within the American Museum itself. Local interests, taking advantage of the uneasy blend of science and commerce that characterized the Hyde Expedition, fought to establish their own control over the archaeological resources of the Southwest. Ultimately the project was compelled to cease operations and withdraw to New York, where the ownership and proper use of the Pueblo Bonito collection became a source of conflict and intrigue.

Local southwestern interest in archaeology, rooted in a utilitarian philosophy toward the land and stirred by the machinations of the Hyde Expedition, flourished after the turn of the century. Regional archaeological societies—my second interest group—gained the support of large segments of the population, built alliances with national organizations, constructed museums, and dispatched expeditions of their own. Prominent among these were the Southwest Society in Los Angeles, the Santa Fe Archaeological Society, and the various western branches of the Archaeological Institute of America. The leaders of these organizations, with backgrounds in education and business rather than in the academic world, rationalized archaeology by touting its significance for regional identity. Their effort to classicize the Native American past and use it to construct a regional heritage, in essence an "invented tradition," was widely successful among local Anglo-Americans alienated from their cultural roots and insecure about their place in the Union.[19] Local museums, authorized by legislative action and funded by popular subscription, were stocked with artifacts from sites that were excavated by resident scholars and subsequently converted into tourist attractions. Common ground between eastern and western interest groups was established in the movement to protect antiquities, which all sides thought would further their particular interests. The School of American Archaeology in Santa Fe, founded as a national initiative with local sanction, was another place where eastern and western ambitions met.

The years that witnessed the high-water mark of the involvement of local societies in archaeology also saw the return of the American Museum to the southwestern arena. The Huntington Southwest Survey rose from the ashes of the Hyde Expedition and became the prototype for a new, integrated research strategy. In many ways a response to the crisis over archaeology's role within the broader discipline of anthropology, the new approach was explicitly oriented toward a professional audience, avoiding the entanglements both of patronage and public interest. The principal fieldwork of the Huntington Survey was in the Galisteo Basin near Santa Fe, where over four years several great pueblos were systematically unearthed. By establishing the chronological relationships between these sites and others across the Southwest, archaeologists of the American Museum managed to define a role for archaeology within anthropology, reinvigorate the prestige of their own institution, and present a model of scholarship to compete with that promoted by the local societies working nearby.

In addition to an emphasis on cultural nationalism and identity, however, the School of American Archaeology and similar southwestern institutions also made education part of their program for archaeology. The idea of field training, derived from a general effort to take students out of the classroom, evolved in the hands of the western societies from a means to develop professionals into a way to educate broad segments of society in the value of American antiquity. Initially based in archaeological camps in southwestern Colorado and amid the ruins of New Mexico's Pajarito Plateau, "summer schools" sprang up in urban areas from Colorado to southern California. Never making scientific research a priority, these conclaves instead continued the work of building constituencies for archaeology within the local communities themselves. The new antiquities legislation created a network of national monuments and parks throughout the region that also attracted a popular audience.

Figure I.1   Pecos Pueblo. (Courtesy Denver Public Library, Western History Collection)

By the First World War the chronological archaeology of the American Museum and the heritage-centered archaeology of the local societies had become dominant. In the tension between these two antithetical approaches to the study of the ancient Southwest lay the seeds of a new, synthetic approach. This agenda, which emerged fully in the 1920s, became by most definitions a research paradigm that has dominated Southwest archaeology over the intervening decades.

The making of this program, in essence the making of Southwest archaeology, is what I will discuss in this book. Patrons and professionals, Harvard students and Navajo laborers, patrician New Yorkers and Californians in corduroy suits, all played a role in building an image of the Southwest in which the relics of its past held a place of honor. This story is rarely apparent to the tourist who steps off the path to peer into the crumbling rooms of Pecos Pueblo and learn something of the people who once lived within them. But the people who first unearthed those ancient relics and dozens of others scattered across the region brought Southwest archaeology to the attention of the American mind and, in so doing, created both a discipline and a heritage.

Ruins

and Rivals

1

Relic Hunters and Museum Men

Southwest Archaeology in the Late Nineteenth Century

In the winter of 1891 Frederic Ward Putnam, curator at the Peabody Museum of Archaeology and Ethnology at Harvard and head of the Department of Ethnology at the upcoming World's Columbian Exposition, sent a letter to Conrad Viets, a farmer and itinerant laborer living in the town of Cortez, Colorado. Viets was also a relic hunter, supplementing his income by digging in the prehistoric ruins of the region for artifacts to sell to individuals and institutions. On this occasion Putnam was interested in procuring a set of specimens for the Exposition, to be held in Chicago in 1893. The small group of professional anthropologists and archaeologists in America, of whom Putnam was one of the most prominent, expected the World's Columbian Exposition to provide a forum in which the scientific achievements of their discipline would be displayed to a national audience. The material products of anthropological research would be presented to the public in educational displays, while the scholarly community would discuss the results of new research at associated congresses and colloquia.

Large collections of artifacts were required to promote education and scholarship, and new finds from the southwestern states and territories would be given a prominent place. Viets was ready to oblige, and quickly responded to Putnam's query. "In reference to plan of work," he wrote,

> I think we should ransack the cliff-houses as soon as possible before others carry off everything and secure some of the dried mummies, some of the dressed stone of the walls, stone door clubs, sections of the cedar beams of the buildings showing work of stone axes besides all other relics found. From the mounds fine collections of pottery, skeletons, stone implements & c. could be secured. In fact I should scour the country in all directions for 40 or 50 miles. If Chicago would furnish the money I do not think it impossible to take down a cliff house and rebuild it in that city.[1]

The relationships between eastern "museum man" and western relic-hunter, between scientific aspiration and economic motivation, between professional ambition and popular demand were at the heart of the relationship between Southwest archaeology and American society as the end of the nineteenth century drew near.

Science, Humanism, and Southwestern Antiquities, 1845–1890

From its beginnings in the 1840s Southwest archaeology was characterized by the interlocking rationales of utilitarian science and humanistic interpretation. Spanish chroniclers had recorded ruins in what would be Arizona and New Mexico as early as the seventeenth century, discoveries William H. Prescott introduced to the Anglo-American audience in his *History of the Conquest of Mexico*.[2] In the early nineteenth century, however, direct Anglo-American experience with southwestern antiquities was limited to the observations of a few traders and mountain men. These travelers' reports attracted the interest of some of the American officers and civil servants who traversed the region during the Mexican-American war, and out of the conquest of the Southwest for the United States came the first formal observations of ancient ruins.[3]

The military explorers who encountered southwestern antiquities in the

1840s and 1850s evaluated them with a blend of romanticism and empirical observation. Lt. William H. Emory, a military topographer who accompanied General Stephen Watts Kearny into New Mexico in 1846, wrote of his anticipation of the ruin on the Gila River now known as Casa Grande:

> We are now approaching the regions made famous in olden times by the fables of Friar Marcos, and eagerly did we ascend every mound, expecting to see in the distance what I fear is but the fabulous "Casa Montezuma." Once, as we turned a sharp hill, the bold outline of a castle presented itself, with the tops of the walls horizontal, the corners vertical, and apparently one front bastioned. My companion agreed with me that we at last beheld this famed building; on we spurred our unwilling brutes; restless for the show, I drew out my telescope, when to my disappointment a clay butte, with regular horizontal seams, stood in the place of our castle; but to the naked eye the delusion was complete.

After finally casting his eyes upon the fabled ruin, Emory made a phlegmatic and vaguely disappointed appraisal. "It was the remains of a three-story mud house," he wrote, "60 feet square, pierced for doors and windows."[4]

The conflicting impulses in Emory's perception of southwestern antiquities reflected both the uncertain status of archaeology and the cultural significance of ruins in early nineteenth-century America.[5] A small "community of interest" concerned with the ethnology of native peoples of the Americas had existed for decades, largely composed of armchair scholars. College "cabinets" included antiquities along with other natural history specimens, but archaeology was not a formal subject of study.[6] A small number of scholarly organizations, which considered archaeology to be a component of ethnology, were supported by their more affluent members. These groups, such as the American Ethnological Society of New York and the American Philosophical Society in Philadelphia, relied on the reports of correspondents for new information and did not directly promote fieldwork.[7] Interested members of the clergy and other literate residents of the midwestern states amassed private collections of antiquities and maintained loose affiliations with their colleagues on the eastern seaboard but were rarely able to undertake substantive projects of their own. Early initiatives of the Smithsonian Institution, founded in 1848, were directed toward publishing rather than direct sponsorship of research.[8]

In the absence of either a widely shared sense of the purpose of archaeology or an organizational setting for its promotion, documentation of southwestern antiquities remained a side benefit of the process of national expansion rather than a scientific endeavor. Relics of the past were one resource among others to be tallied in the newly conquered territory. Members of the Topographical Corps of the U.S. Army recorded ruins as they documented routes of travel, sources of water, and related aspects of the southwestern landscape. When the archaeologist Ephraim Squier summarized the new discoveries in the Southwest for the readers of *The American Review* in 1848, he based his account entirely on the reports of Lt. Emory and his fellow officers. Squier recognized, however, that scientific and utilitarian rationales for the study of the Southwest were not entirely compatible. Reviewing reports on the Hopi people, then called "Moqui," he predicted that they would be devastated by the forces of development, and that there would soon be a "*Moqui Universal Improvement and Land Investment Association,* No. __, Wall Street, New York!"[9]

In addition to their ill-defined material value, however, ruins had cultural value in Anglo-American society as touchstones for the imagination. Ruins and exotic locales were central to the art and literature of the romantic era, allusions which were readily associated with antiquities of the New World as well as the old. Many themes in nineteenth-century American culture were built on the romance and heritage of the past, grounded in the imagery of ruins. Ruins and "ruination" were important biblical themes as well as romantic tropes. Ivy-covered monuments depicted in paintings and poetry served as metaphors of loss and decay, while preachers thundered about the ruin of Nineveh from the pulpit.[10]

American artists traveled to the Mediterranean to depict the ruins of antiquity on their canvases. Archaeological discoveries in the Near East were of great interest to the nineteenth-century public because of their bearing on the historicity of the Old Testament and the *Iliad.*[11] In the 1820s and 1830s romantic associations attached to the newly discovered mounds and earthworks of the Ohio Valley had given rise to the myth of the Mound Builders. The idea that a civilized race had inhabited North America in some remote epoch and had subsequently been destroyed by hostile Indians sparked novels and epic poetry as well as scholarly discussion.[12] Emory's enthusiastic anticipation of Casa Grande and his invocation of romanticized associations with Aztec civilization, albeit eventually tempered by reality, were an indication that the romantic appeal of the mounds of Ohio was also found in the ruins of the ancient Southwest.

Humanistic interpretation of southwestern ruins was thus a second rationale for Southwest archaeology to emerge in the mid-nineteenth century, one that was also expressed in artistic renderings of the West. John Mix Stanley, a painter of western natives and landscapes, accompanied Kearny's expedition to New Mexico, and his lithographs appeared in Emory's published report.[13] Stanley's illustration of the Casa Grande, its massive character and associated relics evoking images of the Old World, was one of the first views of a southwestern ruin to come before an Anglo-American audience. Richard and Edward Kern visited Chaco Canyon with Lt. James H. Simpson in 1849, and the lithographs produced from their sketches depict the ruins encountered there with the same tottering walls and dramatic lighting accorded to medieval castles. Images such as these were derived from the lexicon of nineteenth-century education and esthetics and interpreted southwestern antiquities through traditional frames of reference.[14]

Following the Civil War the military's utilitarian documentation of southwestern ruins was gradually assumed by teams of civilian entrepreneurs supported by federal subsidies. These included the United States Geological Survey of the Territories, directed by Ferdinand V. Hayden; George M. Wheeler's Geographical Surveys of the Territories of the United States West of the 100th Meridian; and the various surveys led by John Wesley Powell. Although much of the survey work emphasized the Great Basin and the central Rockies, some parties entered the Southwest and were responsible for significant archaeological and ethnographic discoveries. Return visits were made to places like Chaco Canyon, and the ruins in southwestern Colorado dubbed "cliff dwellings" were discovered. The surveys shared the utilitarian ethic of their military predecessors but emphasized more explicitly the collection of practical information that would promote resource exploitation and settlement.[15]

Wheeler, Hayden, and Powell competed with each other for congressional appropriations and found it useful to stimulate popular interest in southwestern antiquities. New discoveries were an important source of favorable publicity, communicated to the eastern public by reporters who traveled with the survey teams. "Of late, blown over the plains," wrote Emma Hardacre in an 1878 *Scribner's Monthly*, "come stories of strange newly discovered cities of the far southwest; picturesque piles of masonry, of an age unknown to tradition."[16] William H. Rideing, a reporter for the *New York Times* who accompanied the Wheeler survey, and Ernest Ingersoll of the *New York Tribune*, who traveled with W. H. Jackson of the Hayden Survey on his explorations of cliff dwellings in southwestern Colorado, sent regular dispatches to their papers and subsequently compiled them in popular books. Art also continued to be an influential medium in the romaticization of the prehistoric Southwest. Hardacre's article, for instance, was illustrated with an engraving by the famous landscape artist Thomas Moran depicting a cliff dwelling under attack by a savage horde.[17]

The increasing public interest in Southwest antiquities in the 1870s did not immediately translate into opportunity for the few archaeologists working outside the government, a dilemma illustrated by the career of Frederic Ward Putnam. Like other scholars of his generation, Putnam came to archaeology from an eclectic background in the natural sciences. A student of the famed zoologist Louis Agassiz at Harvard, he rebelled against his mentor and spent several years pursuing other projects. Putnam returned to Harvard in 1874 to become curator of the Peabody Museum of Archaeology and Ethnology, which had been founded eight years earlier and was the first institution of its kind in the country. Despite the museum's significance for American archaeology, however, Putnam's position at Harvard was marginal. The university's administrators considered the study of the Native American past to be of little importance, and Putnam's own intellectual abilities were questioned. Institutional funding and support for archaeological work was thus scarce. A steadfast promoter of archaeological research and the prestige of the Peabody Museum, Putnam spent much of his career struggling against his own community's indifference to his work.[18]

As had Squier twenty years before, Putnam realized the opportunities the Southwest offered to archaeologists. Artifacts from the Southwest made their way into the collections of the Peabody Museum at an early date. In the late 1870s Putnam edited the archaeological reports of the Wheeler Expedition, which included descriptions of Chaco Canyon and various ruins in northern New Mexico. Criticizing the utilitarian rationale that characterized the archaeology of the surveys, Putnam argued instead for a strictly scientific strategy for the study of Southwest antiquities. He advocated "an expedition, properly equipped, with no other than ethnological and archaeological work to perform, with plenty of time allowed for the work," to answer questions about the southwestern ruins archaeologists and the public found so compelling.[19]

Putnam's ambitions to lead a southwestern expedition himself would take time to mature, but in 1879 two research parties entered the Southwest under circumstances that defined the complex motivations shaping the study of the region's antiquities. Journeys down the Colorado River in the late 1860s had stoked J. W. Powell's interest in Native Americans, and as support for the surveys diminished he lobbied successfully for the creation of a new agency to collect ethnological data in the interest of Indian policy. The new Bureau of Ethnology, subsequently (in 1894) renamed the Bureau of American Ethnology, was established under Powell's leadership as a unit of the Smithsonian Institution. The new agency was infused with the ethos of the surveys, with many of the same personnel.[20]

The Bureau thus wedded ethnology to government science and maintained a strong utilitarian cast, a structure in which the role of archaeology was ambiguous. Powell had a general interest in archaeological work but found the need to collect information from living Native American populations more pressing.[21] A mandate to acquire ethnological and archaeological specimens quickly developed, however. Spencer Baird, the Secretary of the Smithsonian and technically Powell's superior, was actively building up the Institution's collections, which in 1881 led to the founding of the U.S. National Museum. Baird's demand for artifacts to fill the museum's shelves and the popular appeal of archaeology led Powell to dispatch a collecting team to the Southwest as one of the Bureau's first initiatives.[22]

The expedition, led by James Stevenson, a veteran of the Hayden Survey, arrived in the Southwest in August 1879. In the course of several field seasons Stevenson's party, which included his wife Matilda Coxe Stevenson, the photographer J. K. Hillers, and the young ethnologist Frank Hamilton Cushing, visited many of the prominent ruins and pueblos of New Mexico and Arizona. Excavations were conducted with local assistance, but few records were kept. Large quantities of artifacts were obtained and sent back to Washington, where they were catalogued and incorporated into the collections of the National Museum.[23]

If the Stevenson expedition continued the tradition of government science and utilitarian documentation of southwestern antiquities, a more humanistic rationale was behind a contemporary effort to study the region. Charles Eliot Norton, a prominent cultural critic and professor of fine arts at Harvard, established the Archaeological Institute of America in 1879. In Norton's conception, the Institute would promote American participation in the archaeology of the classical world. "The conditions of American life," he wrote, "separating us in great measure from direct acquaintance with the works of past times . . . tend to beget indifference to one of the chief sources of culture," the ruins of classical antiquity.[24] Ancient Greece and Rome were the wellsprings of European civilization, and the surviving monuments of ancient society were a source of moral inspiration. Archaeological research at these sites would not only provide corrective lessons for the ills of the nineteenth century but would stake an American claim to a study dominated by European scholars.

The founders of the Institute were a formidable group of Bostonians who shared Norton's vision of classical archaeology as a source of national heritage. Some among them, however, also envisioned a role for the new organization in the promotion of American archaeology. Despite his derisive characterization of the antiquities of the New World as being of merely "scientific" rather than cultural importance, Norton sensed that American research would be an inexpensive way to promote the broader ambitions of the Institute. He consulted with Powell and with the prominent ethnologist Lewis Henry Morgan, who had recently traveled to the Southwest, and devised a plan for southwestern research that would increase the Institute's visibility while plans were being laid for establishing schools of classical studies in Rome and Athens and conducting excavations throughout the Mediterranean.[25]

Bypassing Putnam, who bitterly resented the slight, Norton engaged Morgan's protégé Adolph Bandelier to carry out the Institute's southwestern explorations.[26] The Swiss-born Bandelier, an Illinois businessman who was largely self-taught, eagerly accepted the charge. With instructions from Morgan he trav-

Figure 1.1   A Bureau of American Ethnology party documenting ruins in Chaco Canyon, 1880s. (Courtesy National Anthropological Archives, Smithsonian Institution)

eled to Santa Fe in August 1880 to begin several years of solo fieldwork. Bandelier was not expected to make large collections of artifacts, since the Institute had neither a museum to fill nor sufficient funds to support excavations. Instead he devoted his effort to ethnological study of the northern New Mexico pueblos and documentation of archaeological sites throughout the region. Despite coming to this new career at the age of forty Bandelier proved to be an indefatigable fieldworker. His reports, published in 1892, provided an important baseline for archaeological research in the region, and his journals are filled with detail about the peoples and places he encountered.[27]

The different character and the different legacies of the Stevenson and Bandelier expeditions illustrate the conflicting rationales for Southwest archaeology in the 1880s. Both were mounted as a matter of political expediency. From Powell's utilitarian perspective, studies of living peoples supported an agenda of social reform, for which the historical data supplied by archaeology were less relevant. To Norton archaeology *did* have social relevance, but only if it emphasized the historical and intellectual roots of American culture. The archaeology of North America was thus a lower priority, since it pertained to the ancestors of people who were being absorbed or annihilated by Anglo-American society and who had made no measurable contribution to modern life.

That both men involved their organizations in Southwest archaeology despite reservations as to its value is testimony to its growing popular appeal. But the opportunistic nature of the Stevenson and Bandelier expeditions provided an unstable foundation for future work. The demands of the National Museum for collections were satisfied, but there was no archaeological equivalent to the detailed vocabularies and grammars being constructed by the scholars of the Bureau. Stable federal funding guaranteed that the Bureau's expeditions would dominate the Southwest field for years to come, yet the utilitarian, government science agenda it represented had little room for the detailed studies required to solve archaeological problems. The Archaeological Institute quickly moved on, leaving Bandelier scrambling to find other sources of funding to continue his work. Its promotion of archaeology as a source of moral inspiration, however, would eventually have an impact on Southwest archaeology in ways that Norton could not have anticipated.

Southwest archaeology in the 1880s was thus characterized by conflicting rationales, weak institutional support, and uncertain patronage. Scholars functioning outside the umbrella of government science found that in order to participate in the study of Southwest ethnology and archaeology they had to search out new sources of support and build new intellectual frameworks for their activities. The most ambitious attempt to enter the Southwest field was the Hemenway Southwestern Archaeological Expedition, launched by Frank Cushing in 1886. Finding work with the Bureau too confining, Cushing gained the patronage of Boston heiress Mary Tileston Hemenway and spent nearly three years excavating ruins and conducting surveys with a large field team in Arizona and New Mexico.

The Hemenway Expedition attracted considerable attention from scholars and the public, but Cushing's dismissal in 1889 was a blow to the research program and his contemporaries viewed the project as a failure.[28]

But scholarship was not the only rationale enabling Southwest archaeology to take hold at the end of the nineteenth century. In general terms the public's interest in archaeological discovery was catered to only as a way to ensure financial support. As Bandelier, Cushing, and Putnam scrambled to promote their scientific vision, however, another group claimed southwestern antiquities for its own utilitarian purposes: the residents of the southwestern states and territories themselves.

Relic Hunters

By the 1870s the new Anglo-American residents of the southwestern states and territories had begun to encounter the antiquities of the region in their own way. When this new population first began to settle in towns such as Santa Fe, they regarded ruins as curiosities hidden in the more remote corners of the landscape. Exposure to relics of the past increased as settlement spread into more rural areas, however, and local interest grew. Casual investigation of antiquities by southwesterners, which came to be known as "relic hunting," reflected a new, utilitarian approach to the cultural resources of the Southwest, one that ultimately came to compete with the scientific strategies being developed by eastern scholars.[29]

Although receptive to the intrigue surrounding southwestern ruins, many of the farmers and ranchers who encountered them on a daily basis also perceived antiquities as a resource much like the lumber, minerals, and livestock that were central to the local economy. In the absence of a market for antiquities, their exploitation was at first spontaneous and undirected, driven mainly by a sense of curiosity about the ancient inhabitants of the landscape. One New Mexico resident, trying to drum up interest in his own collection of "relics," remarked that "the fascination is great. But fascination is not money."[30] T. Mitchell Prudden, a New York physician who traveled widely through the Southwest during the period, exaggerated only slightly when he wrote of a young woman on a Sunday outing, "cosily seated amid piles of broken pottery, darting lizards and dead men's bones," while her escort dug in a ruin nearby.[31]

Relic-hunting began to have a recognizable economic and cultural impact in the southwestern states and territories following the arrival of the railroad in 1879. Buying and selling artifacts became widespread in the Southwest, and by

Figure 1.2 Gold's Old Curiosity Shop, Santa Fe, ca. 1897. (Photograph by William Henry Jackson; courtesy Photo Archives, Fray Angélico Chávez History Library, Palace of the Governors, Santa Fe; neg. no. 16514)

the mid-1880s Indian traders like Thomas Keam at Hopi were already engaged in a thriving curio trade that included the sale of antiquities.[32] The practice received particular emphasis in Santa Fe, due to its status as capital of the territory, commercial entrepôt, a point of debarkation for visitors, and the hub of Anglo-American settlement in the region. When Adolph Bandelier arrived only months after the tracks were completed, he found himself in the midst of a thriving antiquities market. Curio dealers supplied artifacts to tourists and other interested parties; Gold's Provision House, operated by Aaron Gold, was an early center of the trade, and Jake Gold, Aaron's brother, was the leading local curio dealer in Santa Fe for much of the late nineteenth century (fig. 1.2). Bandelier returned to Gold's repeatedly throughout his residency in the Southwest to see new items, and sketched particularly appealing pieces in his notebooks.[33]

Tourists not only purchased relics but were encouraged to conduct their own excavations. A highlight of Ernest Ingersoll's 1884 visit to the hot springs at Ojo Caliente, New Mexico, was the opportunity to hunt for relics on his own:

> We heard that many skeletons and relics had been found there by casual excavating, and so went up to try our luck. . . . We could only "coyote round," as a western man calls desultory digging, but saw how rich a treasure to the archaeologist

would be exposed by systematic excavations. . . . We were told that a javelin-head of this material [obsidian], over a foot in length and exquisitely worked, had been dug up here by a fortunate prospector for relics, and that he had refused fifty dollars for it.[34]

Although most residents saw antiquities in terms of commercial value, awareness of their potential cultural significance increased as time went on. The railroads brought not only casual visitors but also a rising tide of immigrants who, as they made their homes in the towns of New Mexico and Arizona, had cultural as well as economic aspirations.[35] Some of these new residents saw antiquities as a source of local distinction, and amassed considerable artifact collections. Among Bandelier's many contacts in Santa Fe was the educator E. L. Cole, who had amassed a "handsome" collection of relics. Cole purchased artifacts and hired people to make excavations for him. After visiting a small ruin at Peñas Negras, near the city, Bandelier remarked that "Cole has completely cleaned it out, excavating every room."[36]

The most prominent citizen of New Mexico to take an interest in archaeology in the late nineteenth century was LeBaron Bradford Prince, an attorney and politician. Scion of an established political family in the Northeast, Prince came to New Mexico in 1879 and served in several governmental posts before being appointed governor of the territory in 1889 by President Benjamin Harrison. He married Mary Beardsley, another New Yorker, in 1881, and they quickly became leaders in the community in cultural as well as political matters. Later characterized by an opponent as "the most reckless handler of the truth west of the Mississippi River," Prince was a formidable force among the Santa Fe elite.[37]

The Princes represented the middle-class merchants and politicians who brought with them the values of their native communities and converted Santa Fe's Palace Avenue into a stately row of Victorian mansions. This new group of southwestern Anglo-Americans, however, was also separated from the sources of cultural inspiration and familiar points of reference of their previous homes. As they reproduced Gilded Age America in the architecture and institutions of Santa Fe, Las Vegas, Albuquerque, and other southwestern towns, they also began to construct distinct local identities from the resources and traditions they found there. Members of this prosperous community shared the humanistic perception of the antiquities of the Southwest that was developing in eastern audiences, but since these relics were local landmarks rather than distant rumors, their interest was keener.[38]

Local curiosity about the southwestern past was channeled into cultural organizations, and early in his years in Santa Fe Prince helped revive the New Mexico Historical Society. Originally founded in 1859, the Historical Society took as part

of its mission the collecting of antiquities, and the Princes were themselves indefatigable artifact collectors. The centerpiece of their collection was a group of what
they called "idols," anthropomorphic figures and figurines found on archaeological sites. Some of these items may have been excavated by the Princes themselves,
but they generally relied on friends and acquaintances throughout the territory
to obtain artifacts for them. Their network resembled others that developed in
the 1880s, linking relic hunters with collectors throughout the country. "The Indians from whom I purchased the images came in with several burros loaded with
them," reported one correspondent, and "said they came from a long distance.
Said they know you. The idea I received was that they had been dug up from some
ancient ruins but I could not locate the place."[39] The Princes cultivated a close
relationship with residents of the pueblo of Cochiti, one of whom, referred to by
the Princes as "Cleto," visited their home to exchange artifacts for cash and cloth-
ing in time of need. "He came before I was up this morning," Mary wrote Bradford, absent on a business trip to the East, "weary and worn . . . the weight [of the
artifacts] was more than I could lift." Mary made some effort to collect information on the provenience of finds such as these, but with little success. Cleto often
secured the sales by alleging persecution on the part of the Pueblo authorities, or
claiming that other Santa Fe collectors were bidding for his services.[40]

As the Princes' collecting activities expanded, so did their network. Other
enthusiasts, both in the United States and abroad, wrote desiring exchanges of
relics, or requesting details of their discoveries. Their correspondents ranged
from an Oklahoma dentist to British antiquarians and to members of local scientific societies and museums throughout the country. "Will you have the kindness
to give us the particulars as to the stone idols said to have been unearthed by you
in some Aztec ruins near Chace [sic] Canyon?" wrote C. W. Darling, correspondence secretary of the Oneida County Historical Society in Utica, New York.[41] In
the late 1880s a portion of the idol collection was placed on extended loan at the
Metropolitan Museum of Art in New York, where it remained on exhibit for more
than twenty years. During his tenure as territorial governor Prince gave an idol to
President Harrison, and one to the Secretary of the Interior, who responded that
he would "value it highly."[42]

These plaudits, while satisfying, did not carry with them either the sanction
of the scholarly community or the possibility of monetary reward for the Princes'
efforts, both of which they craved. In 1890 Prince made direct contact with
J. W. Powell, proposing to sell a portion of his collection to the Bureau for $2,000.
Powell passed the query on to the U.S. National Museum, which took no action.
Several years later arrangements were made to photograph the collection, and
some items appear to have ended up in Washington. Over the decades, the

Princes made a number of increasingly improbable attempts to dispose of the idols through agents and representatives, with the asking price going as high as $50,000. The loan to the Metropolitan was returned in 1911, together with a curt note from the curator indicating that "the Museum no longer includes American antiquities in its galleries." The ultimate fate of the collection is unclear, and it seems to have been largely dispersed by the time of Bradford Prince's death in 1922.[43]

The dilemma faced by the Princes concerning their "idols" and their role in archaeology typifies that faced by members of the southwestern public in the late nineteenth century. Their residence in the Southwest provided substantial opportunities to obtain collections and information about archaeological topics. This also meant, however, that they functioned outside the rudimentary edifice of professional scholarship that was being constructed in eastern institutions. Motivated by both a desire to contribute to an understanding of Southwest prehistory and the possibility of profit, these individuals consistently appealed to more established archaeologists for legitimation. In these encounters, however, the conflict between the goals of the two groups was apparent. Early on, scholars expressed doubts about the authenticity of the Prince collection, and the absence of provenience information for most of the finds limited their utility.[44] William Henry Holmes, a veteran of the Hayden Survey and a curator at the U.S. National Museum in the 1890s, reviewed Prince's offer to sell his collection to the Smithsonian. "I am not in favor of purchasing *any* object for itself *merely*," he responded, thereby underlining a growing divide between professional and public rationales for archaeological research.[45]

Unable to satisfy the scholarly audience but without other channels into which their efforts could be directed, private collectors occupied an uncertain niche in Southwest archaeology. Despite the cool reception given to Prince and other collectors, however, southwestern artifacts were increasingly desirable commodities for the scholarly audience in the East. Archaeological method in the late nineteenth century relied heavily on comparative analysis of material culture, and in the absence of funding for fieldwork the study of collections was an important way to generate information about ancient society. Artifacts were also a source of institutional prestige. Acquiring collections was a way to establish the right to participate in scholarly debates and to be considered full partners in the emerging professional community.

At the Peabody Museum, Frederic Putnam nurtured his modest funding and his network of contacts, expanding the archaeological collections and gradually enhancing the museum's reputation as a center of scholarship distinct from the Smithsonian. Rather than dealing with Prince and collectors of his ilk, however,

Putnam's preferred strategy was to work through local agents who would accept his direction. This type of arrangement had deep roots in American science. In the 1850s the Smithsonian had developed a wide network of correspondents who provided collections and scientific information for the new institution at a time when it was not equipped to dispatch expeditions of its own. Amateur scholars from all social classes participated, and over a thirty-year period the network had functioned quite successfully.[46] Putnam cultivated residents of important archaeological regions to conduct local fieldwork and ship the results to Cambridge, reserving for himself and his small staff the responsibility of analyzing the new collections. Payment for the work was modest, and the system relied heavily on the enthusiasm of its participants. With only the Smithsonian as a rival, the high national visibility of the Peabody meant that new opportunities frequently crossed Putnam's desk, and western relic hunters eager to attract new patrons inevitably saw him as a potential client.[47]

In early December 1888 Putnam received his first letter from Conrad Viets. "If your institution wishes to purchase any relics found or likely to be found here," Viets wrote, "I will dispose of mine or engage to make, or assist in making, exploration of these ruins, or make collections of relics." As proof of his sincerity Viets enclosed a testimonial from the local postmaster.[48] Putnam's initial response is not preserved, but that it was at least encouraging is evidenced by a series of letters and exchanges between the two men over the next four years.

Like many others, Viets's interest in southwestern antiquities was both personal and financial. He had read some of the reports of the Hayden Survey and was eager to expand upon the earlier discoveries. Without a farm of his own, however, Viets hired out his team of horses for income, and when that proved inadequate he turned to relic-hunting. "However much interest I shall take in the work, or how much pleasure and information I might derive from it," he wrote Putnam, "my situation compels me to ask a fair remuneration for my time and my labor." For $20 he was prepared to send a few items he already had in hand, or he would excavate a small "burial place" for $60–$75.[49]

The modest price suited Putnam's resources, and the work began at a small ruin near Yellowjacket Springs, Colorado, in late summer 1889. Even as he insisted upon rigorous recording of data, Putnam's lack of personal experience in the Southwest meant that he had little understanding of what sites looked like and what could be expected from them. Viets, for his part, was sufficiently familiar with the local environment to make a number of reasonable inferences both about preservation within the sites he was excavating and about the prehistoric occupation of the region in general. In his methods he was relatively thorough, but he had neither assistance nor equipment and was not versed in the comparative methodology promoted by museum archaeologists. The documentation provided with the shipment included maps identifying the location of the finds and sketches of burials and some of the associated objects, but little else. The money came in, $50 at a time, and digging continued at a desultory pace. Putnam was apparently satisfied, and the results of what ultimately was a three-year project were deposited without significant analysis in the Peabody storerooms.[50]

Despite their different social standing, Conrad Viets and Bradford Prince were both entrepreneurs who hoped that southwestern antiquities would bring them financial gain and personal satisfaction. Since the local market for their work was small, success was contingent upon the existence of a receptive audience outside the Southwest to purchase their collections and, at least in Prince's case, legitimate their intellectual contributions. Arrangements with Putnam and his colleagues could be made, but the relationships that emerged were unstable. Without direct knowledge of conditions in eastern institutions, relic hunters had difficulty identifying patrons and markets. Even in the late 1880s the professional network developing between scholars in the government and in universities was sufficiently rigid to make it difficult for outsiders to be accepted as equals. And yet, with popular and scientific demand high and funding scarce, acquiring artifacts from relic hunters and local collectors was one of the only ways archaeologists outside the Bureau could study Southwest antiquity.

The complex role played by relic hunters in the development of Southwest archaeology is fully exemplified by the career of Richard Wetherill. The most successful relic hunter of his generation, Wetherill relied on the trade as a source of revenue but also had higher intellectual aspirations. Astute in reaping the benefit of important archaeological discoveries and in developing his own network of patronage and support, Wetherill embodied the conflict between science and commerce, and between western relic hunter and eastern museum man, as the 1890s began.

In most respects the family of Benjamin Kite Wetherill resembled that of Viets or other western contemporaries, sometimes called "moving people," mobile entrepreneurs who subsisted upon ranching, farming, and mining throughout the mountain West. The Wetherill family began arriving in southwestern Colorado in 1879, where they established the Alamo Ranch near the town of Mancos. Perhaps due to their Quaker background and concern for education, the Wetherills took an interest in local antiquities, and exploration of ruins became a family pastime perhaps as early as 1883. The publicity surrounding the discovery

by the Hayden Survey of cliff dwellings in the Mancos area had stimulated tourism on a small scale, with visitors from throughout Colorado making their way to
the remote location to see the ruins for themselves.[51]

The trickle of visitors to the cliff dwellings provided a business opportunity
for the Wetherill family, and Richard Wetherill, the eldest son, assumed the lead
role in the enterprise. To supplement their ranching income the Wetherills provided lodging and guides for travelers, in the process excavating a large number
of artifacts in the Mesa Verde ruins. In 1886 a portion of this collection was purchased by one of the visitors, the wife of a Denver merchant named Chain—an
event that set the entire relic-hunting economy of southwestern Colorado in
motion.[52] Richard Wetherill, along with Conrad Viets and many other residents of
the region, quickly saw the potential in the artifact trade. Within months antiquities became yet another component of an economy based on resource extraction,
one accessible to anyone with shovels to do the excavating and a team of horses
to pack out artifacts.

What separated the Wetherills from their competitors, however, was their
use of the increasing tourist traffic to promote the relic-hunting business. Richard Wetherill's role as guide to the cliff dwellings brought positive publicity and
helped him build a network of clients throughout the United States. Many of
these were average citizens, such as John Jones and Allen Dunaway, two Ohio
businessmen who returned from Mancos with an artifact collection that Wetherill
had helped them to acquire and that was later described in the popular archaeology journal *The Antiquarian*.[53] More prominent guests included author Frederick
Chapin, whose 1892 *The Land of the Cliff Dwellers* provided more publicity for
the Wetherill operation. Advertisements promoting tours of cliff dwellings were
taken out in Colorado papers. Al Wetherill, Richard's brother, noted in his memoirs that more than a thousand people visited the Alamo Ranch and were guided
to the ruins of Mesa Verde between 1889 and 1901. The Wetherills sent new specimens and news of recent discoveries to their eastern clients after they returned
home. These clients in turn gave positive recommendations to their friends and
made repeated visits to the Alamo Ranch.[54]

In addition to promoting tourism, the Wetherills devoted considerable effort
to selling artifacts to larger buyers. In 1889 they joined fellow relic hunters
Charles McLoyd and J. Howard Graham to expand the Mesa Verde excavations.
The resulting collection was exhibited in Durango, Pueblo, and Denver, where it
was sold to the Colorado Historical Society for $3,000. Viets, who was at the
time collecting for the Peabody, reported news of the transaction to Putnam. "I
know you don't estimate such things by dollars and cents," he wrote, "but per-

Figure 1.3   Resting at Cliff Palace. Richard Wetherill (third from right) guiding the Sumner family through the ruins of Mesa Verde, August 1889. (Courtesy National Anthropological Archives, Smithsonian Institution)

haps it will give you an idea of quantity, at least." The regional market, however, was quickly saturated, and another Mesa Verde collection sent to Denver in 1890 attracted limited interest before it was eventually sold to entrepreneurs involved in an industrial exposition in Minneapolis.[55]

As he tapped the economic potential of the cliff dwellings to support his family, Richard Wetherill also gradually became conscious of the scientific opportunities they offered. Like other western relic hunters and collectors, however, his opportunities to interact with the scholarly community were limited. At the recommendation of Frederick Chapin, a member of the Hartford Archaeological Society in Connecticut, Wetherill wrote to Putnam, who does not seem to have responded. Letters written by other family members to Powell at the Bureau also failed to attract attention.[56] Exposure to the techniques of contemporary archaeology ultimately came in the summer of 1891, when the Wetherills dug in the Mesa Verde ruins with the Swedish traveler Gustav Nordenskiold. A natural scientist by training, Nordenskiold approached the work with greater rigor than many of his contemporaries and convinced his associates of the value of methodical excavation and careful note taking. After working with Nordenskiold Wetherill became more aware of the scientific importance of his excavations, and within a few years was publishing short notes in archaeological journals such as *The Antiquarian*.[57]

Wetherill's experience indicates that Southwest archaeology in the early 1890s was characterized by new opportunities and new constraints. Fueled by scholarly curiosity and increasing popular interest, demand for antiquities was on the rise. The relic-hunting economy that emerged brought income to western entrepreneurs and provided the material for scientific analysis and the promotion of institutional prestige. This relationship between science and commerce was uneasy, however—an indication that the multiple rationales that characterized Southwest archaeology were not entirely compatible. The flexibility of the mid-nineteenth century, which had allowed military officers, natural scientists, and amateur travelers to contribute to the study of the southwestern past, was giving way to a more structured professional system. This professionalizing trend promoted scientific and institutional priorities but took little account of local interests or concerns. While Wetherill's clients respected his abilities, they did not accord him the status of a scholar. The growing rift between the scholarly and public audiences for Southwest archaeology would result in resentment and resistance, and in efforts to construct new modes of archaeology that would accommodate different perspectives.

Southwest Archaeology and the World's Columbian Exposition

As the World's Columbian Exposition of 1893 reflected the contradictions of American society in the Gilded Age, so the collections of antiquities on display there mirrored the alternative rationales and competitive conditions of South-west archaeology.[58] Public interest, scholarly ambition, and utilitarian exploitation found expression in the exhibits on view and in entrepreneurs and audiences who met on the Midway. By the time the gates closed, these encounters had stimulated action that would give rise to new rationales for the study of southwestern antiquity, new avenues of patronage, and new settings for the clash between public and professional interests.

The theme and the timing of the Columbian Exposition favored a prominent role for exhibitions featuring native peoples. The fair presented a utopian vista in which modern achievements were presented as an orderly, classified whole. In this collective representation of 1893 America, advances in commerce and industry were displayed beside works of art and culture, all within the unified architectural setting of the "White City." In effect, the Columbian Exposition presented a model for social reform and cultural uplift. Such an exercise in organization necessarily included Native American peoples, whose roles in the expanding corporate system required definition. The coincidence of the four hundredth anniversary of the Columbian encounter with the final military defeat of the plains and western tribes offered an opportunity for the science of non-European peoples to broadcast its achievements. As public attention shifted from conquest to assimilation, the position of Native Americans in American society became ripe for reexamination.[59]

Prominent advocates for incorporating American ethnology into the fair's programs included Frederic Putnam, whose lectures on the subject caught the attention of the Chicago press.[60] Responding favorably, the fair's planners established a specific administrative branch, called Department M, "Ethnology, archaeology, progress of labor and invention, isolated and collected exhibits," to coordinate exhibits and associated events. Borrowing from the Paris Exposition of 1889, admired by many American scholars, the ethnological exhibits were planned to include model "villages" inhabited by native peoples brought in for the duration. The term "anthropology" was also brought from Europe, making its debut before the public in Chicago as a term for the general science of humanity.[61] "Ethnology" remained in use, but in the more specialized sense of the study of living peoples, joining archaeology as a subdiscipline of anthropology.

Putnam was made Chief of Department M in 1891 and was given a budget to coordinate exhibitions and bring in collections. More than $100,000 was spent, and at one point in the process Putnam had seventy-five assistants engaged in fieldwork and related preparations.[62] In addition to Conrad Viets, archaeologists engaged by Putnam included Warren King Moorehead, an Ohio-based scholar who was sent to the Southwest, and Edward Thompson, who made casts of Maya monuments from the Yucatan for display. Not all of the collecting efforts were directly funded by the fair, and not all achieved great success; Moorehead's work, for instance, was cut short by the collapse of the magazine that had funded his expedition.[63] In the face of heated competition for the space originally assigned to anthropology in the prominent Manufactures Building, an "Anthropological Building" was constructed, in a more peripheral area but with adjacent open space for outdoor exhibits. Among the highlights of the exhibition was an elaborate display of artifacts and entire structures brought from the Northwest Coast and arranged by Franz Boas, a young German ethnologist Putnam had hired for the purpose.[64]

Science and commerce were dual facets of the Columbian Exposition, and the Anthropological Building was not the only venue there to promote archaeology and ethnology. Displays sponsored by the Bureau of American Ethnology and the U.S. National Museum were located in the government building. In consultation with Putnam, the Smithsonian scientists emphasized archaeological and ethnological work not covered elsewhere. The Midway Plaisance, a mile-long thoroughfare of entertainments that was the obverse of the formal White City, featured many attractions of "ethnological" interest. Technically under Putnam's jurisdiction, the sights of the Javanese village and the belly dancing of "Little Egypt" presented another view of non-European culture, one that was exploited for profit by commercial entrepreneurs.[65]

Displays of southwestern antiquities were prominent in all of the anthropological venues at the fair, and they mirrored the scientific and commercial rationales that inspired their promoters. Putnam's Anthropological Building presented ethnology and archaeology as two aspects of the professional, scientific study of Native Americans, within which Southwest archaeology played a prominent role. Similar motivations lay behind the exhibits of the Bureau, although its association with federal policy provided a touch of the utilitarian philosophy that had long characterized government science.[66] Several of the western states and territories featured collections of prehistoric relics alongside other resources in their own pavilions. The state of Utah purchased a collection of artifacts owned by a resident of the town of Bluff, while Colorado hired Richard Wetherill to collect cliff dweller relics for its own exhibit.[67] The strictly commercial side of the relic-hunting business was also on display. The Wetherill collection that had been taken to Minneapolis was brought to Chicago and exhibited within a sixty-five-foot artificial cliff, with a mock ruin beneath its overhang. The "H. Jay Smith Exploring Expedition," which operated the model cliff dwelling, had also obtained photographs and sketches of the excavated sites, and these were displayed alongside scale models of the ruins. Admission tickets and souvenir photos generated a substantial profit of $87,366.28, although the aggressive tactics of the sales staff became a nuisance to some fair attendants.[68] The impact on the visiting public of southwestern antiquities at the Columbian Exposition was demonstrated in Henry Fuller's popular 1893 novel *The Cliff Dwellers,* which metaphorically compared upper-class Chicagoans in their apartments with Native American tribes living among the canyons of the desert Southwest.

The inclusion of Native American artifacts in exhibits sponsored by the southwestern states and territories marked a new rationale for Southwest archaeology, one that emphasized antiquities as a source of local pride and identity. What had been a source of individual accomplishment to Prince and other southwestern collectors in the 1880s was a decade later being perceived as an asset for entire communities. Regionalist sentiments about Southwest archaeology had been evident in southwestern Colorado since at least 1891, when Gustav Nordenskiold was detained in Durango and charged with making illegal excavations. "Americans would rather that cowboys, miners, etc. dig amongst their antiquities, than foreigners," he wrote, after establishing that his archaeological explorations had violated no laws.[69] Humanistic interpretations of the value of southwestern ruins were not devoid of utilitarian practicality, and a pamphlet on Colorado produced for the fair touts ancient ruins and relics as important touristic resources for the state. Expressions of interest in Native American artifacts by southwestern states and territories at the Columbian Exposition was not uniform, and many areas rich in antiquities emphasized agriculture and similar achievements in their own displays rather than relics.[70]

In addition to displaying the conflicting rationales for the conduct of Southwest archaeology, the Columbian Exposition was also a place of encounter between the different individuals with personal interests in the field. Putnam, in his capacity as chief of the Anthropological Building, was omnipresent. Design and implementation of the exhibits involved most of the anthropologists who had southwestern interests, such as Frank Cushing, who was involved in the government exhibition, and W. H. Holmes, whose archaeological work for the U.S. National Museum had gained him national prominence. An anthropological congress convened in association with the fair brought together the majority of the practicing anthropologists in the United States. Entrepreneurs, such as H. Jay Smith and his associate, C. D. Hazzard, were also in attendance. Members of the different interest groups coalescing around Southwest archaeology interacted in conference halls and around the tables of pubs along the Midway. Some, such as Cushing, flowed easily between these different groups, debating southwestern ethnology with Putnam by day and planning new expeditions with Hazzard and Smith by night.[71]

Richard Wetherill also came to Chicago, and his experience there illustrated both the limited professional options available to him and his entrepreneurial ability to solve the dilemma. Wetherill supervised the installation of the artifacts he had collected for the state of Colorado, and stayed on to view the other attractions and pursue new opportunities.[72] Having taken a hand in providing most of the cliff dweller material on display at the fair, he must have seen the event as a personal triumph. Whatever intellectual curiosity Wetherill may have felt at the fair, however, was tempered by his need to obtain new patronage in order to support his archaeological work. As had been the case three years before, his ultimate goal was to attract the attention of Putnam. At some point in the course of the fair the two men met, and Wetherill offered his services. "[I]f you should wish any work in this feild [sic] I should be glad to have the opportunity under your direction," Wetherill wrote later. Putnam seems to have taken the opportunity to dispense advice on archaeological methods, and to indicate his hope for a future visit to the Southwest, but there is no evidence that he regarded Wetherill as any different from the other relic hunters seeking commercial opportunities at the fair.[73] In the waning days of the Exposition Wetherill was not the only entrepreneur offering to sell artifact collections or lead new expeditions, and he came away from Putnam without a firm commitment.

The Columbian Exposition thus revealed three distinct communities of interest in Southwest archaeology, each with its own structure, rationale, and obstacles. Scholars used the occasion to demonstrate the scientific value of archaeology, a point emphasized by displays of artifacts from the Southwest and elsewhere as well as by congresses and meetings. The southwestern states and territories organized their own exhibits but presented antiquities as valuable local resources rather than as items of strictly scientific import. Entrepreneurs converted public curiosity about southwestern ruins into profit. None of these groups were exclusive, and relic hunters had provided most of the artifacts the three groups used to promote their own interests. This reliance on outside suppliers weakened professional attempts to make archaeology a scientific concern. Relic hunters and interested westerners, for their part, did not have access to the scholarly networks that would legitimate their participation in archaeology. Different dilemmas required different solutions, and when Wetherill and the other westerners returned home it was the scholarly community that took the initiative. The public interest generated by the Columbian Exposition created possibilities for building a professional discipline, and Southwest archaeology would be at the heart of these new developments.

"Museum Men" and the American Museum of Natural History

The most important new professional opportunities to arise for American anthropologists in the aftermath of the Columbian Exposition were in the large museums of natural history in the cities of the Northeast. The popular success of the anthropological displays in Chicago caught the attention of the directors of the expanding museums, who saw in the new discipline a means to promote their own educational programs. At a time when institutional competition was on the rise, archaeological and ethnological collections were also seen as a source of prestige. The new institutional niche promised to be a productive setting for scholarship, but also inaugurated a new relationship between anthropology, education, and the public.

The rapid growth of natural history museums was one of the distinctive features of mid-nineteenth-century America. Several factors drove this building boom, including a desire for new modes of public education, the reorganization of the scientific community, and the expansion of a middle class that perceived the accumulation of material objects as a sign of prosperity.[74] Museums evolved in different ways in different settings. In some instances scholarly societies of the 1840s and 1850s transformed themselves into educational museums as their original function became outmoded. In others, museums were founded as cultural adornments to showcase civic pride or as the personal projects of wealthy philanthropists. Some museums on college campuses grew out of the cabinets maintained by the professors of a previous generation, while others were built specifically to house new scientific endeavors and collections. The U.S. National Museum remained paramount, with more than two and a half million specimens in 1887. Among smaller institutions, the increasing need for topical displays fueled a commercial trade in natural history specimens. The entire process was supported, by and large, by the rising economic elite of American cities, who thereby linked their commercial achievements with scientific advancement and the natural order represented by neatly arranged geological, botanical, and anthropological specimens.[75]

The American Museum of Natural History was founded in New York in 1868. Initially housed in an armory in Central Park, the museum moved in the 1870s to a new facility on the West Side of Manhattan. The museum's founders were members of the established mercantile class of New York who saw a need for an institution that would provide practical knowledge of interest to the public. The new museum would be a vehicle for "popular education," rather than for the promotion of scientific research. Collections flowed in from the trustees and their associates, and over its first three decades the museum became one of the important cultural centers of the city.[76]

After a financial crisis in 1881 the museum's presidency was assumed by Morris K. Jesup, a philanthropist with holdings in railroads and banking. Supported by many among the elite of the city, he embarked upon a plan of expansion. Jesup was aware that a judicious combination of research and acquisition would enhance the Museum's educational programs, and he promoted this goal by hiring scholars who would support his agenda.[77]

In the early 1890s Jesup turned his attention to anthropology. An active social reformer, he was one of the founders of the Young Men's Christian Association and a supporter of the Protestant New York Mission and Tract Society. Like many of his contemporaries, Jesup saw increasing immigration as a threat to the cultural foundations of America.[78] Anthropology provided "scientific" informa-

Figure 1.4 The American Museum of Natural History under construction, ca. 1892. (Courtesy American Museum of Natural History Library)

tion on relationships between different societies and races, which in a museum setting could be transformed into educational displays. "Today," Jesup wrote, in the Annual Report of the museum, "the study of the human races—those of the remotest past and those approaching extinction—is engaging the keenest attention of scientists and the awakened interest of the public."[79] In order to promote the educational use of anthropology, collections of artifacts would be required and new exhibits would have to be mounted. The museum's first archaeological collection dated to 1873, but the process of acquisition since then had been piecemeal. Artifacts were donated by interested patrons, who also sponsored expeditions, but the effort was uncoordinated. Back at the museum the collections were lumped together with the general natural history specimens. Ultimately a Department of Ethnology and Archaeology had been created, but when a series of temporary curators proved inadequate Jesup decided to bring in a scholar of higher profile to organize the department and inaugurate a new program of anthropological research and exhibition.[80]

The person recruited to be the curator of the revamped Department of Anthropology was Frederic Putnam. Putnam recognized that the new museums of natural history provided opportunities for anthropology beyond the scope of the Peabody Museum, and he was deeply involved in the organization of the Field Columbian Museum in Chicago as a legacy of the Columbian Exposition. Animosity on the part of the new museum's administrators, however, prevented Putnam from establishing a permanent place for himself there.[81] A position in New York would be an even more prominent platform for his personal and professional ambitions, and Putnam responded to Jesup's queries with alacrity. An arrangement was made whereby he maintained his position at the Peabody, but agreed to spend one week a month in New York. By June 1894 Putnam, with his former student Marshall Saville as assistant curator, had set himself up in temporary quarters in New York and begun the job of overhauling the anthropological collections.[82]

Putnam's ambitions to make the Department of Anthropology a center of American research were the result of twenty years of planning and represented the beginning of a new phase of professionalism. His first report as curator promoted both scholarship and public education, and expressed the hope that "liberal men and women" from the community would provide financial support for an aggressive fieldwork program. His vision coincided with the desires of Jesup, who forwarded the report to the press for general dissemination and arranged to have it sent to prominent New York philanthropists.[83] An important test of Putnam's tenure at the American Museum would, in fact, be his ability to find patrons to support fieldwork. Funding shortages had been a hindrance at the Peabody, and while the opportunities for attracting patronage would be greater in New York than they had been in Boston the stakes were also higher. Nor were they alone in the search for patronage, since both the University Museum of the University of Pennsylvania and the Field Columbian Museum were entering the anthropological domain.[84]

As he began searching for patrons to support the American Museum's new anthropological agenda, Putnam also sought an appropriate project into which such support could be channeled. And it was inevitable that, as he began to execute his plans, his thoughts returned to his report on the Hayden Survey of 1879, to the shelves of artifacts in the Peabody sent by Viets, to the crowds that had swarmed to the model cliff dwelling in Chicago, and to the image they conjured of the opportunities for archaeology to be found among the deserts and mesas of the American Southwest.

In the forty-odd years between Lt. Emory's visit to Casa Grande and Putnam's arrival at the American Museum of Natural History images of southwestern antiquity had become objects of scholarly desire and public fascination. The dichotomy between utilitarian science and humanistic interpretation that had characterized the surveys and their publicity campaigns had by the time of the Columbian Exposition manifested itself in different interest groups and rationales. A fundamental constant, however, was the divide between scholars and the public over the significance of archaeological research. Relic-hunting derived from the utilitarian perspectives of early days and treated artifacts as a source of profit, but what had been a cooperative relationship in the preprofessional era would become a point of conflict when scholars sought to make archaeology their exclusive domain. The ambition of the professionals to exclude competitors was also a threat to the Southwesterners who sought local benefit from archaeology. Their approach was closely related to the humanistic perception of antiquities as a source of identity and was antithetical to the scientific aspirations of the new generation of "museum men" in eastern institutions. As these disparate rationales became more distinct in the years following the Columbian Exposition, competition among their proponents over funding, fieldwork, and collections grew more pronounced.

In an early report on the cliff dwellings of southwest Colorado, W. H. Holmes had remarked that "a rich reward" awaited the archaeologist who delved into "the masses of ruins, the unexplored caves, and the still mysterious burial-places of the Southwest."[85] To observers in the mid-1890s, the anticipation of such a reward was palpable. But what it would consist of, what shape the new Southwest archaeology would take, was very much open to question.

2

"Fires of Jealousy and Spite"

The Hyde Exploring Expedition and Its Competitors

As he prepared to take up his new position in New York in early May 1894 Frederic Putnam received a letter bearing news of an important advance in Southwest archaeology. "I have the pleasure of informing you," wrote Richard Wetherill, "of the discovery of a race of people . . . who inhabited this country before the Cliff or Valley dwellers." Frustrated at his failure to gain the sanction of the scholarly community at the Chicago exposition, Wetherill had returned to the network of clients who had backed his earlier work and found new supporters. His approach to the archaeology, however, was subtly different, and the brief report emphasized scientific detail and concern over the depredations of relic hunters. "I thought you should give this early attention on account of the terrible vandalism of collectors—I am powerless to stop this work and it would make your heart sick to see the vast amount of damage done by that kind of people—who care nothing for the result of their work except for the few dollars they get out of it."[1]

Wetherill's new endeavor, known as the "Hyde Exploring Expedition," was based in the Grand Gulch country of southwestern Utah and would become known to science for its discovery of the ancient culture dubbed the "Basketmakers." The advent of the Hyde Exploring Expedition inaugurated a period of keen competition over southwestern archaeological resources and archaeological collections. Wetherill's relationship with his sponsor, Talbot Hyde, was built upon traditional patron-client lines but would ultimately make it possible for Putnam and his "museum men" to establish their own foothold in Southwest archaeology. This opportunity for professional archaeologists would also have unforeseen impacts on entrepreneurs like Wetherill, and on the new southwestern interests that saw antiquities as resources with cultural as well as economic value. In the story of the Hyde Expedition can be discerned the complex interaction and competition between patrons, scholars, and the general public that paved the way for the emergence of Southwest archaeology in the modern sense of the term.

Grand Gulch, New York, and Chaco Canyon

Benjamin Talbot Babbitt Hyde, called "Talbot" by his family, was born in New York in 1872. His grandfather, Benjamin Babbitt, was an inventor and self-made industrialist whose "Babbitt's Best Soap" had made the family wealthy.[2] The elder Babbitt's daughter, Ida Josephine, married Frederick Erastus Hyde, a doctor who pursued interests in the natural sciences, and the couple raised their four children within the Babbitt household. Talbot was thus brought up in a privileged environment in which learning was valued, and was early exposed to "the facts of art and science, mechanics, religion and philosophy." Benjamin Babbitt's death in 1889 was followed by that of his daughter in 1890, after which Frederick Hyde retired from the practice of medicine and devoted himself to leisure and philanthropic pursuits. Talbot and his younger brother, Frederick Hyde Jr., were educated at St. Paul's, a military school on Long Island, where they excelled more at sports than in the classroom. Talbot in particular was drawn to the outdoors, where he preferred "tramping" over horsemanship. An accident prevented him from completing secondary school, perhaps a precursor to the nervous attacks he experienced in stressful situations later in life. Photographs of Talbot taken as a

young man show him to be tall and outwardly sturdy, with mustache and thin-
ning hair.[3]

Unable to gain admittance to MIT, Talbot at twenty-three entered the family
firm as a chemist, ultimately rising to the office of president.[4] He did not have an
aptitude for business, however, and a series of small enterprises he launched both
before and after retiring from the Babbitt Soap Company in 1913 were failures.
The image of Talbot Hyde that emerges from the scant biographical details available is of a man of kind temperament but unsteady judgment, who approached
projects with enthusiasm but limited ability and was rarely able to follow through.
At one point he confided to a friend that he had "to keep brakes down all the time
in order not to act too foolish."[5] One of the ironies of Hyde's life was that his
wealth and social position continually provided opportunities that lack of aptitude
made inadvisable.

The event that ultimately brought Talbot Hyde into Southwest archaeology
occurred in 1892, when on a trip around the world with his father and brother he
visited the Alamo Ranch and toured the Colorado cliff dwellings with the Wetherills. It is probable that the stop was recommended by family acquaintances who
had previously been to the Mesa Verde and were part of Wetherill's network of
clients. There is no evidence, however, that the Hydes were treated any differ-
ently than the other tourists who visited during that season, which for Richard
Wetherill was crowded with activity leading up to the Columbian Exposition. The
Hydes journeyed on, traveling through the Orient by steamship and spending
seventy days on horseback in Palestine and the Sinai in the course of their world
tour, experiences that whetted the younger men's appetite for travel and adven-
ture.[6] Upon their return they were caught up in the excitement of the Columbian
Exposition and went to Chicago to see it for themselves, a trip that renewed their
acquaintance with Richard Wetherill as he scouted the fair for new patrons.

No record has been preserved of the agreement concluded between Wetherill and the Hydes in Chicago, but Wetherill's expectations are fairly certain. The
economics of the Alamo Ranch deteriorated steadily through the 1890s, making
the family more dependent on the archaeology and tourism business. Wetherill's
arrangement with the Hydes would allow him to continue his involvement in
relic-hunting as an economic activity, but the hoped-for new discoveries would
also give him another chance to gain the attention of Putnam and his professional
colleagues.

As for Talbot and Fred Hyde, their role in the planned expedition was in
the established tradition of acquiring exotic goods as a symbol of social status.
As with previous patrons of the Wetherills, obtaining artifacts was the reason
for their sponsorship. Wetherill's early communications with Talbot Hyde often

evaluated the productivity of potential sites in terms of the number of artifacts obtainable versus the cost of gaining access to them. The fact that the Hyde brothers seem to have had only vague plans for their Cliff Dweller finds after they had been removed from the ground also suggests that possession was, for the time being, enough.[7]

The title selected for the new enterprise, "The Hyde Exploring Expedition," was in keeping with the practice of naming southwestern expeditions after their sponsors. The plan of research was also similar to that of previous endeavors. Acknowledging that the Mesa Verde region had been heavily damaged by relic-hunting, Wetherill shifted to Utah's Grand Gulch, where his competitors had met with considerable success. A party of eight departed from Mancos in November 1893 and worked throughout the winter from a base at the town of Bluff. Many of the areas they explored showed signs of previous excavation, although Wetherill's thoroughness meant that the Hyde Expedition found large quantities of artifacts at the same locales. He had organized the effort along scientific lines from the beginning, with plans for identifying artifacts and mapping ruins; "the work we do must stand the most rigid inspection," he had written Talbot Hyde, "and we do not want to do it in such a manner that anyone in the future can pick flaws in it." These recording strategies were poorly implemented, but Wetherill was able to discern the stylistic and stratigraphic differences between the artifacts being excavated and to understand their significance. Fieldwork was completed by April 11, 1894, by which time Richard Wetherill was back at the Alamo Ranch, organizing the season's finds.[8]

The archaeological importance of the first Hyde Expedition was Wetherill's discovery of previously undescribed antiquities buried beneath the more familiar cliff dwellings of the Utah canyons. As patron, Talbot Hyde was asked to name the newly discovered "race," which he called the "Basket Makers" on the basis of the preserved basketry found in the excavations. Wetherill, encouraging his sponsor, wrote that the name was "more distinctive than anything I have thought of." He also suggested that Hyde prepare an article on the discovery for the popular journal *American Archaeologist*. Hyde was enthusiastic about the results and arranged to inspect the sites with Wetherill in the summer of 1894, but did not follow through on the article; it was therefore a few years before a description of the Basketmaker finds became widely available.[9]

In fact, the more overtly scientific strategy Wetherill adopted for the Hyde Expedition did not have the desired effect of gaining the respect of the scholarly community. Seeking to capitalize on the expedition's success, Wetherill sent letters to interested parties describing the finds. "I have carried on the work this winter according to your direction," he wrote Putnam. "Had I not done so I could not have proven this discovery." Yet Wetherill's efforts to gain Putnam's sanction continued to be frustrated, since, preoccupied with his new assignment, Putnam does not seem to have found the news particularly noteworthy. A total of 2,118 "articles" from the Grand Gulch excavations were shipped east by September 4, 1894, and placed in storage pending the Hydes' decision as to their ultimate disposition. For the time being, no further work was planned.[10]

What ultimately changed the equation and brought Putnam, Hyde, and Wetherill together was the rising demand for Southwest artifacts for museum display. In the mid-1890s the need for collections to fill expanding museum galleries and the cliff dweller mystique fueled by the Columbian Exposition made southwestern antiquities a locus of institutional competition. At the conclusion of the Chicago fair many of the Southwest collections exhibited there were sold, some going to the new Field Columbian Museum.[11] C. D. Hazzard, who emerged as the principal impresario behind the artificial cliff dwelling, purchased the Colorado state collection and added it to his own. After seeking a buyer for the combined "Hazzard collection" from among the nation's most prominent institutions, Hazzard settled upon the University Museum at the University of Pennsylvania. The cliff dweller artifacts were placed in Philadelphia on loan, and while the collection was not formally purchased until 1896 its acquisition must have been immediately perceived as a coup by the museum's institutional rivals.[12]

Prior to Putnam's arrival the American Museum of Natural History's southwestern collections had consisted of only a few photographs and "three models of a cliff dwelling in Colorado" donated by a trustee.[13] In light of the recent acquisitions by its rivals and Morris Jesup's interest in promoting anthropology, Putnam was expected to rectify this situation. The escalating value of southwestern antiquities, however, made entry into the market prohibitive without a major patron. When the University Museum ultimately paid $14,500 for the Hazzard collection it was only able to do so through the generosity of Phoebe Hearst, a prominent supporter of the institution.[14] In New York anthropology remained untested, and until Putnam became fully established it was unlikely that the level of patronage needed to acquire a major Southwest collection could be achieved. Putnam was also interested in developing a research program, rather than simply buying artifacts. He had been critical of the Field Columbian Museum's southwestern acquisitions, writing to Franz Boas that "the same amount of money used in sending a man into the field . . . could probably secure a similar collection of thorough scientific importance" rather than a poorly documented amalgam of specimens.[15]

The solution to this dilemma was provided by Fred Hyde, who was enrolled in one of Putnam's anthropology courses at Harvard.[16] Through Fred, Putnam became aware of the circumstances surrounding the Hyde Expedition, and the brothers' vague plans for the collection. Wetherill was under the impression that the artifacts were destined for the Metropolitan Museum of Art, while Talbot Hyde later indicated that the two had planned to establish a new museum; Putnam's alternative, which the Hydes eagerly accepted, was to place the Basketmaker finds under his care in the American Museum.[17]

What had begun as an expensive souvenir of a southwestern excursion was transformed into an important asset for the museum and then into a new program of archaeological fieldwork. The American Museum's annual report for 1895 described

> the interesting collection from the cliff houses and burial caves of Utah, presented by the Messrs. Hyde, who have not only given their collection to the museum, but have arranged to continue their explorations in the Southwest for several years, under the general direction of the curator of the department, until the museum is supplied with an extensive and authentic collection from the cliff houses, ancient pueblos, burial caves and mounds of the Southwest. The interest taken in the museum by these gentlemen is most gratifying, and is suggestive of what others might do in the [other] departments of the museum.[18]

In the plans for the second Hyde Exploring Expedition the museum's need for collections and Putnam's ambitions for a major research project coincided. Entering the southwestern field would be a prestigious step for all interested parties, since only the Smithsonian had been able to maintain a consistent presence in the region. The new endeavor would strengthen the American Museum's claims to be a center of anthropological scholarship and would provide new exhibits to support its educational mission.

Hyde funding would also place archaeologists in control of the resource on which their scholarship was based. In order for archaeology to be fully established as a profession, archaeologists had to be the only people who could legitimately excavate and analyze antiquities. By relying on relic hunters to provide collections Putnam and his contemporaries were, in essence, supporting a rival camp. Putnam had also consistently argued that archaeology would be able to contribute to larger anthropological questions only when the context of finds could be reliably established. This was rarely possible using purchased collections. By putting an archaeological team directly into the field, control over the resource could be established, benefiting both the profession and its scientific aspirations.

In their effort to establish themselves in a position of authority, however, Putnam and his staff were themselves subject to control by their institution and their patron.[19] At the Columbian Exposition Putnam had spent much of his time trying to reconcile the promotion of science with the education-and-entertainment orientation of the fair's administration. His ultimate failure to negotiate this terrain and take charge of the Field Columbian Museum was a major personal and professional setback. For museum administrators such as Jesup and his colleagues in Chicago, scholarship was a means to an educational end, and they were skeptical about the value of research that had no direct utility. The fate of the expedition was also contingent on the shared vision of Putnam and Talbot Hyde. Hyde's financial role gave him the power to hinder, terminate, or redirect the project if it failed to meet his expectations. Putnam clearly saw the young Hyde as a genial and pliable patron, but his influence would nonetheless be a constant factor.

Notwithstanding potential conflicts of interest, the organization of the Hyde Expedition proceeded along with Putnam's consolidation of the Department of Anthropology. In the favorable administrative climate he hired several of his protégés, including Franz Boas, who after eighteen rocky months at the Field Columbian Museum had come to Putnam seeking employment.[20] To supervise the Chaco project Putnam nominated George Hubbard Pepper, a New Yorker who at twenty-three had already been involved with the American Museum for two years and had conducted excavations of his own on Long Island. Originally interested in a planned Peabody Museum expedition to Honduras, Pepper instead found himself organizing the artifacts of the Hyde collection and preparing for the upcoming Southwest field season. Pepper had not attended college, although he spent the fall of 1895 studying with Putnam at Harvard to acquire professional training. His salary, both in the field and at the Museum, was paid by the Hydes.[21]

Richard Wetherill also played an important role in the plans of Hyde and Putnam, although not in the way he desired. Putnam was reported to be "greatly astonished and pleased" by the careful numbering of the specimens in the Grand Gulch collection, but this did not mean that he was prepared to let the westerner lead the field party. Wetherill's local knowledge and ability to coordinate the excavations would be important, but intellectual control would reside with Putnam and his surrogate, Pepper. Since the end of the first Hyde Expedition Wetherill had spent much of his time traveling through the Southwest, gaining personal experience with antiquities far beyond his original territory. His income suffered, however, and his letters to Hyde included references to financial hardship and his hope that a new expedition would be organized. "I love the work and research," he wrote, "and for that reason I can stand almost anything."[22]

It was only in autumn 1895 that Hyde contacted Wetherill about the new project, which was vaguely described as a plan "to make a comparative study of the various branches of the Uto-Aztecan stock." Wetherill suggested a number of promising sites for excavation, including new locations on Mesa Verde and ruins he had recently worked on his own in the vicinity of Tsegi Canyon, Arizona. He had also visited the ruins of Chaco Canyon in summer 1895, and reported enthusiastically about their potential. The area was still remote from centers of population, making Wetherill's statement that the ruins were "practically unknown" accurate despite periodic visits by government survey parties and relic hunters.[23]

The decision to send the expedition to Chaco Canyon, based on Putnam's knowledge of the earlier surveys and Wetherill's firsthand account, was made in early 1896. After a final consultation, Talbot Hyde set out on April 28, 1896, with Pepper and supplies, meeting Wetherill in Mancos. Hyde, concerned about Pepper's competence, traveled on with the team to Chaco Canyon. In a letter written to his brother Fred during the journey, he remarked on the "advanced type of civilization" manifest in the ruinous masonry structures dispersed along the shallow canyon floor.[24]

Hyde soon returned to New York, and the 1896 excavations got under way. Conditions were as hot and dry as expected, with water and fodder in short supply. The leader of a fossil-hunting team from the American Museum that had worked near Chaco Canyon in 1891 remarked that the wind had been strong enough "to blow the hair off a dog."[25] The immense ruins were also quite different from the towers and alcoves of Mesa Verde and Grand Gulch, so it was some time before Wetherill became sufficiently familiar with their nature to develop a realistic plan of attack. In addition, labor was scarce, although Wetherill recruited Navajos living in the area to do the digging.

Wetherill quickly focused on Pueblo Bonito (fig. 2.1). Excavations commenced in the mounds surrounding the site, presumed to be the location of burials and associated grave goods, but when this proved unsuccessful work was expanded to include other sites in the vicinity and then interior rooms of the ruin itself. Burials were eventually found in the smaller mounds, while the rooms of Pueblo Bonito contained rich assemblages of stone and ceramic artifacts, carved wood, basketry, cordage, and even eagle feathers. In some cases roofing material had been preserved within the masonry structure, allowing the excavators to move from room to room underneath the rubble. Prehistoric workshops were identified, along with storage areas and large sections of the ruin that had been burnt prior to abandonment. The most spectacular cache consisted of one hundred and fourteen cylindrical vessels of a type not previously noted in the Southwest.[26]

Despite these successes, Wetherill resented his subordinate position. He clearly felt that Pepper's lack of experience was a detriment to the project and chafed at working under his authority. Pepper acted principally as record keeper,

Figure 2.1   Pueblo Bonito in the late 1890s (Courtesy
American Museum of Natural History Library)

but he also kept the accounts, at one point suggesting that Wetherill's contract
be modified in the interests of economy.[27] By acting as agent for the Hydes,
Pepper laid bare Wetherill's reliance on the Hydes' patronage, previously masked
by acknowledgment of Wetherill's authority in his own domain. In their rivalry
Pepper and Wetherill were proxies for a larger conflict between professionalizing
trends in American archaeology and the more open categories of earlier years.
Wetherill's ambition to step beyond the role of relic hunter and to recast himself
as an archaeologist was blocked by the desire of Putnam to promote his own protégés. Pepper, whose officiousness masked an insecurity with the setting and the
responsibilities of the job, needed success in order to establish himself in the
museum's hierarchy. The maneuvering between Wetherill and Pepper in what
seemed a remote and deserted corner of the Southwest took on ramifications
beyond their individual ambitions.

Despite such tensions, the success of the first season at Pueblo Bonito was
an important milestone in the establishment of the Putnam program at the
American Museum. It provided tangible evidence of the importance of American
archaeology and contributed substantial collections for exhibition. One of Hyde's
progress reports applauded Pepper for the large quantity of artifacts recovered,
which would "impress the trustees of the Museum more than simply extensive

field-notes and data." Part of the Grand Gulch collection was exhibited in the museum's new Ethnological Hall, and had been featured in an 1896 exhibition at the New York Academy of Sciences.[28] The collection from Pueblo Bonito, which filled an entire railroad car, provided an even more substantial and well-documented body of artifacts, which augured well both for future exhibitions and for the next season's research.

Science vs. Commerce at Pueblo Bonito

The 1896 excavations at Pueblo Bonito established a pattern for the ongoing work of the Hyde Exploring Expedition: collections-oriented research within a context of conflicting personal and professional agendas. In the four years from 1896 through 1899 more than one hundred rooms were excavated in the ruin, providing thousands of artifacts and an extraordinary trove of information about the ancient Southwest. Putnam, Wetherill, and Pepper clearly understood the stakes involved, and each took particular steps to maximize his individual success. Talbot Hyde rarely played a direct role in the project, but his influence was seen by all participants as the way to gain desired results. The conditions of patronage were central to the struggle between science and commerce that shortly emerged at Pueblo Bonito.

Richard Wetherill's response to his unsatisfactory position within the Hyde Expedition was to reestablish himself as an archaeological entrepreneur in the winter of 1896–97. Opportunities for relic-hunting remained in Utah and Arizona, and when Hyde declined to sponsor the work Wetherill sought the patronage of the Field Columbian Museum and the California Academy of Sciences. Failing at this as well, he turned to private sponsorship, arranging to take a Harvard student and his tutor recommended by Putnam into Grand Gulch and Tsegi Canyon. In his letters to Hyde Wetherill emphasized that the excavations were of importance largely for the "scientific data procured." Wetherill had married Marietta Palmer just before the expedition departed, and she had taken charge of the record-keeping. Unfortunately for Wetherill, the Harvard party showed little interest in the scientific results, preferring instead to see a financial return on their investment. Reverses at the Alamo Ranch and his new family responsibilities also placed Wetherill in need of funds. The artifacts were ultimately sold to Hyde at a loss and the entire affair only increased Wetherill's economic reliance on his fickle patron.[29]

During the 1897 season at Pueblo Bonito, Pepper's own reliance on his patron was revealed. As his confidence increased, Pepper felt free to complain to Hyde about political matters within the museum and about his wages, not realizing that Hyde was the one actually paying the salary. This prompted a letter of admonishment, and Pepper was faced with the loss of his position. "[W]hatever may be my faults," he wrote in hasty apology, "ingratitude may not be counted as one of them," and he labored to reestablish himself in Hyde's good graces.[30]

The realities of patronage, in some cases conflicting with the professional ambitions Pepper and Wetherill professed, thus increasingly characterized the operation of the Hyde Expedition. Wetherill's hope of achieving scholarly recognition was undermined by financial hardship, while Pepper discovered that his professional status was less relevant than his relationship with his patron. Neither man was helpless in the face of reality, however, and both worked steadily to protect their positions. Pepper ensured that his loyalty to Hyde would never again be called into question, while Wetherill pragmatically worked to create a new role for himself. Although each of these strategies proved successful in the short term, their ultimate impact on the Hyde Expedition's research agenda was negative.

Excavations continued in 1898, but during that summer the "Hyde Exploring Expedition" name was attached to a new mercantile operation at Pueblo Bonito, with Wetherill in charge. He and Marietta had left Colorado for good that spring, and with debts from their failed relic-hunting expedition the previous year still hanging over them the couple sought to establish a permanent source of income. Some small-scale trading had always been a feature of the Pueblo Bonito fieldwork, and Hyde later noted that in 1896 Pepper had kept goods in his tent that he sold to the local Navajos. In Wetherill's eye the new trading business would be an integral part of the Hyde Expedition, and he immediately requested financial backing from the Hydes. By the time Pepper arrived for the start of the field season, bringing with him another Putnam protégé, John R. Swanton, the store was under construction and business was already picking up. Talbot Hyde, immersed in the affairs of the Babbitt Soap Company, did not take an active role in the operation. Instead, it was Fred Hyde, who was visiting Pueblo Bonito that summer, whose personal interest in the new trading post made it a great success.[31]

According to witnesses interviewed much later, what was an economic necessity for the Wetherills became a sociological opportunity for Fred Hyde. Fred represents a more mysterious character for posterity than his older brother, with little in his own hand having been preserved. Unlike Talbot, he played no role in the family business, and there is no evidence that he was ever gainfully employed. The various Wetherill memoirs describe Fred as a highly eccentric young man, given to showing up unannounced out of the desert, hungry and wearing worn-out shoes but with substantial quantities of cash hidden on his person. He took a greater interest in the Navajo people than in archaeology, living in a hogan near Pueblo Bonito for extended periods of time. Herman Schweizer, who worked for the Fred Harvey Company, later recalled that "Fred Hyde . . . had some philanthropic ideas of stabilizing values" for Navajo weavings, believing that higher prices would translate into economic prosperity for the weavers. The trading-post business became a way for Fred to realize this ambition, and to establish better control over the commodity more trading posts were acquired. Ultimately more than a dozen were administered as part of the Hyde Exploring Expedition. Schweizer indicated that Clarence Hyde, Fred and Talbot's uncle, was the major investor in the project, although Fred made a substantial commitment from his own inheritance.[32]

Seeing the trading posts as a way to escape from debt, Richard Wetherill allied himself closely with Fred Hyde, and the business quickly became the economic mainstay of the entire Wetherill family. By the time the Alamo Ranch failed completely, in 1902, all of the Wetherill brothers and their wives were working for the Hyde Expedition in some capacity. "We are reaching out for the whole trade of the San Juan country and will get it," Wetherill wrote.[33] Financial transactions between the Hyde Expedition and the local Navajos seems to have been limited originally to the payment of salaries and small-scale trading, but the expansion of this relationship to include weaving, pawn, and other commercial transactions drew in larger numbers of people and increased the stakes for all concerned.

The marketing effort associated with the trading post's Navajo weavings had an even broader scope, since the Hydes tapped into the national demand for southwestern curios. For a time they served as suppliers to the Fred Harvey Company, and through them reached markets along the railroads and on the West Coast. Rugs and blankets were placed on consignment at the John Wanamaker Department Store in New York during the winter of 1899. The success of this arrangement prompted the Hydes to open their own store in autumn 1900, which was ultimately relocated to 42nd Street.[34]

With the Hyde Expedition name now attached to both an archaeological project and a trading-post empire, confusion of aims and intentions was inevitable. This was illustrated by the contentious issue of the sale of antiquities in Hyde trading posts. In later years Talbot Hyde went to considerable pains to deny accusations that the Hyde Expedition had sold relics from Pueblo Bonito. The truth was more complicated. The Navajo work force on the excavations had quickly realized that the Hyde team was willing to pay them for finds of turquoise and similar items. In some cases Wetherill found himself buying back small finds that undoubtedly came from Pueblo Bonito, but many of the artifacts came from other sites. Various commentators present in the Chaco region at the turn of the century observed ruins that had been worked over by Navajos looking for turquoise. The relic-hunting economy, entrenched in the local Anglo-American population, had spread to the Navajos as well.[35]

Most of the artifacts brought in by Navajos, being without provenience, were of limited use to archaeologists. They did, however, have commercial value, which in the context of the trading-post business was irresistible. The evidence indicates that many artifacts in this category—primarily ceramics—were purchased by Wetherill on behalf of his sponsors. "That cellarful of pottery that seemed to be an elephant on our hands," Wetherill wrote Talbot Hyde, "has proven to be the best seller that we have had; orders are coming in for $100. worth at a time." Hyde's own reconstruction of the practice was more circumspect, but it is apparent that some of the items being sold were the unprovenienced antiquities. Hyde's sensitivity to the issue reflects the fact that by selling artifacts the Hyde Expedition was opening itself to charges that the line between the scientific and commercial aspects of the project had become blurred.[36]

The trading-post business had an immediate impact on the Pueblo Bonito excavations. Despite Wetherill's assurances that Marietta would run the store while he supervised the work crew, by the middle of July 1898 only eight new rooms had been excavated. John Swanton described a situation in which the expedition's leaders generally left him alone to supervise the excavations, with mixed results. "At noon I was so tired that I took a sheepskin up to a crack in the overhanging cliff and lay down there until work recommenced," he recounted in an unpublished memoir. "We were in some danger from the collapse of walls while we were clearing a room . . . but the catastrophe occurred during the lunch hour and a shovel or two were the only casualties." According to Swanton, Pepper spent most of his time in the tent, cataloguing finds. He seems to have settled into an annual routine, his ambitions for the time being fluctuating along with those of his sponsors.[37]

Although Wetherill's new priorities and the corresponding distraction of the Hydes meant that the Bonito excavation slowly ground to a halt, related projects began to proliferate. In general these were sponsored by Putnam and served the purpose of exposing younger scholars to southwestern fieldwork. Pepper had been the first of these, followed by Swanton. Frank Russell, a rising star on the Harvard faculty, made a personal exploration of the Southwest by bicycle in 1898. "I rode 700 miles on my wheel to see the Snake Dance," he reported, "went alone, crossed desert, passed within 25 miles of Mr. Pepper but could not stop."[38] In 1899 Richard E. Dodge, a geographer on the faculty at Teacher's College in

Figure 2.2   A Navajo excavator at Pueblo Bonito in the
1890s. (Courtesy Museum of Indian Arts and
Cultures, Museum of New Mexico)

New York and a member of the New York Academy of Sciences, spent part of the
summer at Chaco Canyon studying the geophysical environment. He returned in
1900, and the results of his endeavors were described for Putnam in two brief
reports.[39] The 1901 season featured the participation of two Harvard students,
William Curtis Farabee and Alfred Marston Tozzer. The two men were assigned
their own sites to excavate and spent much of their time at Chaco working out of
a remote camp, although Tozzer's project was the collection of ethnographic data
from the local Navajos.[40]

The information generated by these small projects was relatively unsystematic and rarely reported to the scientific community. Despite the fact that Putnam
was the scientific director of the Hyde Expedition, he seems to have treated student efforts as an entirely separate matter. This was not, however, a field school in
any real sense, since the work seems to have progressed without any coordination
or significant oversight by senior members of the project.

Putnam himself began to make annual excursions to Chaco Canyon, making
the first of three visits in August 1899. Talbot Hyde paid for the excursion, and

Figure 2.3 Frederic W. Putnam at Mesa Verde, 1899. (Courtesy Peabody Museum of Archaeology and Ethnology, Harvard University)

Putnam was accompanied by his wife and Fred Hyde.[41] The journey was a kind of grand progress, taking Putnam through regions he had long been involved with but never seen. The reverse of a photograph taken of him at Mesa Verde, white-bearded and wearing a jaunty cummerbund, is inscribed "My first view of the cliff houses (Spruce Tree House) from opposite rim rock, Sept. 19, 1899" (fig. 2.3). Afterwards the party spent a few weeks at Chaco Canyon. To Boas, Putnam wrote "I have had a great treat here."[42] He seems to have been popular with the Wetherill clan as well, and when the trading post at Pueblo Bonito became a U.S. post office it was named "Putnam" in his honor. During his stay Putnam visited many of the sites and conducted modest excavations of his own, an activity which he described as "a study of the facts relating to the antiquity of the ruins and to the cause of the desertion of this ancient pueblo by a once numerous and agricultural people."[43]

The most substantive research sponsored by the Hyde Expedition during this period was not archaeological at all. Aleš Hrdlička, who would become the most prominent physical anthropologist in America in the first half of the twentieth century, made a series of Southwest trips under Hyde sponsorship to collect skeletal and anthropometric data under the umbrella of the Hyde Expedition.[44] Hyde funds also supported the publication of a famous study of Navajo ceremonialism, Washington Matthews's "Night Chant." Ironically, "Night Chant" may represent the major scholarly achievement of the Hyde Expedition, although it had no relationship to the fieldwork central to the project, and it is conceivable that Talbot Hyde and Washington Matthews never met.[45]

The blend of science and commerce, the interaction between eastern scholars, western ranch hands, Navajo weavers, and others, made Pueblo Bonito the crossroads for many ways of life during the heyday of the Hyde Expedition.[46] Strange juxtapositions were the result. One season Aleš Hrdlička set up a "laboratory" within the ruins of Pueblo Bonito. He tried to convince members of the local Navajo population to allow him to make casts of their faces, but because of their relative prosperity, a product of Hyde Expedition wages, the small gifts he brought as incentive attracted little interest. Hrdlička's European sensibilities ran counter to the more relaxed attitudes of the other residents of Putnam, as he observed: "Had induced Mr. Hyde to buy in Denver a music box and of this I am the master. Take the box outdoors and have it play every one of the seventeen lovely classic tunes we brought with it. The Whites here like music, they say, yet they will talk about the commonest things during such exquisite pieces as William Tell, Aida, or Il Trovatore."[47]

Another who wrote about life in Chaco Canyon was Alfred Tozzer. In letters home over a two-month period in 1901, the young Harvard anthropologist drew a detailed picture of the little community of "Putnam." The informality of Tozzer's letters, filled with references to new sights and experiences intended for people who knew him well, makes them a critical source for filling out the context within which the events of those years took place.

Tozzer traveled to the Southwest by train in the company of Putnam and his wife, William Farabee, Talbot Hyde, and George Pepper. He had high praise for Pepper and Hyde, whom he described as "simply fine, so kind and so interested in our work." The party dismounted at the railroad hamlet of Thoreau and were immersed in the southwestern landscape and the expanding enterprise of the Hyde Expedition. After spending the night amidst what he estimated to be $10,000 worth of stock in the company "blanket house," Tozzer and the others traveled on to Putnam, passing Hyde Expedition freight wagons en route and stopping at the company station at Pintado. After fifty-odd miles what he called the "city of Putnam" came into view, identifiable by the "huge American flag flying from the store."[48]

By the time he arrived at the company headquarters Tozzer had garnered much superficial knowledge about the Hyde Expedition. He described it as an enterprise built around philanthropic principles, almost accidentally commercial. He also noted other aspects of the business, such as the encouragement of weaving standards and the use of specially made aluminum "scrip" in company transactions. By 1901 several buildings had been erected at Putnam, including a boardinghouse, storeroom, and the Wetherill residence. As at the Alamo Ranch, tourism was also a function of the Hyde Expedition. Against his will Tozzer was called upon to entertain a party of women from Colorado, who, on their departure, carted away "whole timbers from the ruins, boxes on boxes of fragments of pottery, weaving sticks, spindles, and even looms." Later in the year more elaborate preparations were called for to welcome the president of the Santa Fe Railway, Edward Payson Ripley, who toured the area with a substantial entourage. Days spent excavating in mounds or grappling with the complexities of Navajo linguistics were leavened with parties, dances, and picnics. By his own account Tozzer was well regarded by the Navajos, and he finagled his way into some of the ceremonial events and "sings," which were part of the fabric of life in the Pueblo Bonito community.[49]

The central event of the season came in late September, when after the departure of the rest of the anthropologists Tozzer found himself assisting in the transport of most of the expedition's stockpile of goods, a herd of horses, and 135 people from Chaco Canyon to the New Mexico State Fair at Albuquerque. Most of those in the party were Navajos, going along to dance at the fair in exchange for food and fodder. Nearly thirty wagons, emblazoned with "HEE" banners, made the journey to the Rio Grande in five days, where they were joined by dozens more from other Hyde Expedition stations; ultimately the whole procession entered the city escorted by "a troop of cavalry and a colored band." A vacant block near the fairgrounds was rented as a campsite. Tozzer divided his time between assisting at the Hyde Expedition store and fair exhibit and other tasks, such as preparing a float for the parade. He describes the Navajo dancing as "a glorious climax to the whole week. The main street was roped off, the cavalry were there to keep off the crowd, huge bon-fires were built at frequent intervals along the street, and four squads of twelve each danced and sang."[50]

Tozzer's letters capture a brief window of time when the Hyde Exploring Expedition exerted an influence far beyond the bounds of its original conception. Wetherill ingenuity, in combination with Hyde financing and philanthropy, had created an enterprise that bore little resemblance to the sober archaeological project of a few years earlier. Although Putnam remained the benevolent figurehead, it was clear that scientific schemes laid in New York were no longer of particular relevance to the activities at Chaco Canyon.

To the residents of New Mexico, the Hydes represented an expansive and flamboyant commercial enterprise. By virtue of its setting and origins, however, the Expedition was still linked to archaeology. And it was in the ascendance of commerce over science that some local observers spied a weak link in the control of the Hyde Expedition over what remained its central asset: Pueblo Bonito.

Competition

There is no record that in their preparation for fieldwork at Pueblo Bonito either Hyde or Putnam asked for permission to conduct the research. Chaco Canyon was ostensibly on federal property administered by the General Land Office, which in the late 1890s had yet to establish regulations governing archaeological resources on its lands. It was also sufficiently remote, both from the center of Cliff Dweller interest in southwestern Colorado and from the capital of the New Mexico Territory at Santa Fe, to insulate it from public or private inquiry.

Local distrust of the Hyde Expedition, however, was expressed early on. In May 1896, while Hyde and Pepper were preparing to begin work, an article from a Denver newspaper was reprinted in the *New York Times*. It described those working in the cliff dwellings as "despoilers" who destroyed the ruins and sent the artifacts overseas. Even the involvement of the Smithsonian in Southwest archaeology was criticized in the article, which ended by ominously foretelling the arrival of "a second representation from the East"—clearly a rumor of the Hyde Expedition.[51] In similar, but less emphatic ways, resentment over the destruction of the ancient ruins and the removal of artifacts to distant museums and collections was being expressed by local residents throughout the Southwest. The traditional, utilitarian attitudes toward antiquities persisted, but the perception of archaeological sites as sources of regional pride that had begun to emerge at the Columbian Exposition was in the late 1890s spreading throughout the region. The social environment into which the Hyde Expedition was entering was in flux, the conditions of which Talbot Hyde, Frederic Putnam, and their representatives would shortly be made aware.

Putnam's first concern about competition over the Pueblo Bonito discoveries pertained to his professional colleagues. Since rights of access to antiquities on the public domain were poorly defined, there was little to hinder other groups, sponsored by individuals or institutions, seeking to investigate Chaco Canyon for themselves. In the 1880s the Bureau of American Ethnology had planned a program to map the ruins of Chaco Canyon. Although the project had never been completed, in some eyes a prior claim to the area had been established. In 1895 the Bureau launched an aggressive new Southwest expedition under the direction of Jesse Fewkes, who like Putnam had been trained by Louis Agassiz at Harvard but was also a protégé of Smithsonian Secretary S. B. Langley. Putnam perceived Fewkes's activities as a threat to the Hyde Expedition, and responded by downplaying the significance of the finds from Pueblo Bonito. Most of the spectacular items from the 1896 season went immediately into storage. Although the ostensible reason was a lack of exhibit cases, Pepper wrote Wetherill that Putnam seemed "to fear the Washington people."[52]

The threat of competition was realized in April 1897 when Warren K. Moorehead, who after the end of the Columbian Exposition had formed an alliance with the philanthropist Charles Singleton Peabody, conducted his own exploration of Pueblo Bonito when Wetherill and Pepper were absent. While this action was ethically dubious, there were no legal restrictions to prevent Moorehead's incursion. Some of the six hundred pounds of specimens collected by the party were advertised for sale the following summer in the Ohio-based archaeological journal *The Antiquarian*.[53]

The Hyde expedition thus found itself competing with real and potential rivals within the profession. Archaeologists and their sponsors sought to safeguard their own territorial interests or to establish new beachheads. Scientific interests coexisted uneasily with institutional rivalries, circumstances that were repeated throughout the Southwest as the years wore on.

Conflict over professional goals was also beginning to surface within the American Museum, where the energy and ambition of Franz Boas was filling the leadership vacuum left during Putnam's long absences. Since his arrival from Germany in the late 1880s Boas had been seeking an institution from which he could promote the professionalization of anthropology. In addition to his post as assistant curator he had also gained a faculty appointment at Columbia, and he would use the two positions to promote both research and the training of graduate students. Like Putnam, Boas was conscious of the importance of coordinated field projects, which required patronage; unlike Putnam, he focused on the opportunities available in New York for the funding of expeditions. Despite a contentious relationship with the museum's administration Boas attracted the attention of President Jesup, who in 1897 agreed to underwrite personally a major anthropological expedition to the North Pacific. By the next year seven different parties had taken the field as part of the "Jesup North Pacific Expedition." The project, and its sponsor, received accolades in the press. The *New York Times* editorialized that Jesup had "set a commendable example for men of wealth who are willing to employ a part of their fortunes to increase the stock of human knowledge."[54]

As a prototype for the multidisciplinary, professional anthropological expeditions of the early twentieth century, the Jesup North Pacific Expedition quickly made the Hyde Expedition appear anachronistic. The processing and cataloguing of the Jesup Expedition's collections required an expansion of the department's staff, a need filled in part by Boas's Columbia students. As the department expanded Putnam's influence began to wane, since he still spent most of each month at the Peabody Museum.[55]

The growing rift between research and education was another source of conflict within the American Museum. The museum's administration regularly faulted the Department of Anthropology for ignoring its responsibilities to the public. As early as 1896 Putnam and Boas were accused of disregarding procedures and leaving exhibits unfinished. Jesup also found that the department's expressed concern for making exhibit labels intelligible to the average visitor was often not translated into action.[56] Boas was not averse to public education, and in a letter to Jesup he remarked that "the two prime objects of the museum being, First: Public instruction, and Second: Advancement of science, the interests of both must be equally borne in mind." Boas's vision of museum education, however, was hierarchical, one in which exhibit design would be coordinated around a single broad theme designed to have influence "upon schoolteachers."[57] Exhibits that appealed to the broad mass of museum visitors were secondary in the minds of both Boas and Putnam.

One ardent proponent of the use of anthropology in education was Talbot Hyde, who prevailed upon Pepper to give public talks during the winter months. In the spring of 1899, for instance, Pepper made presentations on Southwest archaeology to the New York Boy's Club and the Young Ladies Auxiliary of the Women's Foreign Missionary Society. Church organizations and "working girl's clubs" were also on his circuit. The "150 attendees despite bad weather" at an American Museum program the same spring testified to the popularity of the topic.[58] The Hyde Expedition itself may have been left behind by shifting professional currents, but Hyde's support of educational programs gained him allies that helped to insulate the project from criticism within the museum.

As much as competition within the anthropological profession and over museum policy preoccupied Putnam, it was resistance to the Hyde Expedition within the Southwest itself that would ultimately prove the most damaging. The initial flurry of concern over the expedition's intentions was dampened by the remoteness of Chaco Canyon and a corresponding lack of information about the excavations. Regional interests, however, had been alerted to the value of archaeological resources, and when circumstances changed the Hyde Expedition became vulnerable to attack.

Figure 2.4   Artifacts from Pueblo Bonito in the American
Museum of Natural History, ca. 1900. (Courtesy
American Museum of Natural History Library)

The most significant shift in local interest in southwestern antiquities in the late 1890s was the appearance of popular archaeological societies throughout the region. The first of these was in Colorado, where the Durango Archaeological and Historical Society was founded in 1893. This was followed by the Arizona Antiquarian Society in 1895, and by the Colorado Cliff Dwellings Association and the Santa Fe Archaeological Society in 1900.[59] Membership in the new organizations reflected new trends in public interest in the southwestern past. The Colorado Cliff Dwellings Association and the Santa Fe Archaeological Society were based in larger urban areas, and drew their members predominantly from the business class, who rarely had direct commercial interest in antiquities but were interested in any scientific or cultural activity that showcased the resources and people of the region.[60]

Both the Colorado and Santa Fe organizations were in large part the creations of single individuals, who possessed significant organizational capacity and the personal magnetism to galvanize public opinion in the support of southwestern archaeology. The founder of the Colorado Cliff Dwellings Association was Virginia McClurg, who had first visited Mesa Verde in 1892 in her capacity as a journalist and thereafter lectured widely on the preservation of southwestern ruins. McClurg developed a strong base in local women's organizations, gaining the support of the Colorado Federation of Women's Clubs in 1897.[61] With statewide popular support and a mission to save Mesa Verde from exploitation, McClurg's association was already a potent force in Southwest archaeology by its 1900 debut.

The Santa Fe Archaeological Society was led by Edgar Lee Hewett. An educator by training, Hewett was recruited from the faculty of the Colorado State Normal School to become president of the New Mexico Normal University at Las Vegas. Hewett had been conducting informal archaeological investigations throughout the region since the mid-1890s, and the new position provided a more visible platform from which to promote the work. Shortly after his appointment he inaugurated a program of lectures on the antiquities of New Mexico through the university extension department. Hewett's advocacy of Southwest archaeology found fertile ground among the territorial elite. The core group around which the Santa Fe Archaeological Society formed shortly thereafter included L. Bradford Prince; John McFie, a justice of the territorial supreme court; and Frank Springer, a lawyer and rancher who was also a noted paleontologist.[62] The organization never enjoyed the grassroots popularity McClurg did, but the involvement of the political leadership of the New Mexico Territory gave it considerable influence.

Rather than treat antiquities as exploitable resources, as had relic hunters, Hewett, McClurg, and their associates argued that ruins and artifacts of the Southwest were cultural assets to be shared by local residents as a whole. The expanding Anglo-American population of the Southwest was preoccupied with issues of regional identity and the position of the Southwest within the Union. Resources such as mineral wealth, irrigable land, and a healthy climate were extolled as valuable assets of the southwestern states and territories. From the perspective of the local archaeological societies, antiquities were also unique resources, to be preserved and exploited for the benefit of Southwesterners. The concern for cultural identity that had received partial expression in Bradford Prince's idol collection in the 1880s flowered more completely in the more populous and more contested Southwest of the turn of the century.

The evolving sentiments of Southwesterners toward the value of archaeological resources were captured in an April 1900 issue of the *Santa Fe New Mexican*. A lead article criticized the rampant destruction of ancient ruins by outsiders: "already is the tourist being attracted from afar, and now that he had started on his deadly relic-hunting way the very walls of the cliff palaces are not safe for another year, while the possibility of scientific excavation will soon have passed forever away." A few pages later, however, an editorial argued that the promotion of tourism was "inevitable, and New Mexico cities and people should try their best to make a good impression."[63] Common to both arguments was the idea that south-western antiquities, whether as objects of scientific study or as touristic promo-tion, had to be exploited for the benefit of residents of the region, rather than for institutions and individuals elsewhere in the country.

After assailing relic hunters in general, the *New Mexican* next launched a direct attack on the Hyde Expedition itself. No mention was made of the institu-tional backing of the project, which was described as "a large freighting outfit which is busy freighting in supplies and freighting out relics."[64] The paper's opposition was part of a wider campaign against the Hyde Expedition coordinated by Hewett and his local allies. In May a special agent of the General Land Office, Max Pracht, was dispatched in response to a complaint filed by the Surveyor Gen-eral in Santa Fe about conditions in Chaco Canyon, itself based on the newspaper article and "a letter from Prof. Hewitt [*sic*]."[65]

Pracht's investigation, indicative of the Land Office's increasing interest in archaeological resources under its jurisdiction, was nonetheless cursory. After going to Durango, Colorado, and interviewing people familiar with the Hyde Expedition, Pracht reported that the excavations were being conducted by a scien-tific party from a reputable institution. More to the point, he also noted that no laws were in existence to prevent the work from taking place. After advising Land Office Commissioner Binger Hermann that direct communication with Putnam, in New York, would clarify the situation, Pracht wrapped up the investigation without visiting Chaco Canyon itself.[66]

For the members of the Hyde Expedition, the Pracht investigation was the first of several warnings of competition from a new quarter. Pepper attributed the rising controversy to "the fires of jealousy and spite" stirred by their enemies, but the conditions of research were clearly shifting. Frank Russell, Putnam's bicycling colleague, planned to spend the summer of 1900 doing archaeological research on the Hopi Reservation, but the request for permission to excavate was denied by the Office of Indian Affairs.[67] By the time the letter reached Putnam's desk, however, Russell was already digging in Arizona. "I am told the agent here is on my trail," he wrote, with "notices pasted at the stores, schools, etc. about the reservations." Russell managed to extricate himself, but the research effort was severely impacted.[68]

While Putnam mused over the implications of the Russell affair, Richard Wetherill took two steps to protect the Hyde Expedition from attracting federal scrutiny. Belatedly recognizing that the trading post venture had exposed them to criticism, he proposed to reinvigorate the scientific character of the project. Wetherill and Richard Dodge sent a plan to Talbot Hyde outlining future Chaco

Canyon research in which they proposed an elaborate record-keeping system, with standardized photography and note-taking procedures, as well as setting up a permanent baseline from which accurate maps could be made of the ruins. Dodge also recommended that a formal permit application be filed with the Department of the Interior.[69] There was no legal requirement for such a permit, but the application would have had the effect of regularizing the relationship between the Hyde Expedition and the federal government, and thereby would have afforded some level of protection for the expedition's activities.

Wetherill's second strategy to guarantee the survival of the Hyde Expedition was to gain direct control over Chaco Canyon itself. In the wake of the Pracht investigation Wetherill and Fred Hyde filed homestead claims on lands surrounding Pueblo Bonito and made plans to purchase property owned by the Santa Fe Railroad in the immediate vicinity.[70] If outright ownership of the ruins could be established, the expedition could proceed unmolested. A certain level of subterfuge was required, however, since homestead claims were intended to promote agricultural settlement rather than archaeological excavations. Attempts to acquire land and the restructuring of the research program were a coordinated effort by Wetherill and the Hydes to increase the security of their commercial and scientific activities. Putnam's implicit support for the homestead maneuver was ethically precarious, since while the Hyde Expedition was making an effort to evade governmental oversight of its activities he was busy promoting federal legislation for the protection of antiquities.[71]

The Pueblo Bonito affair was to evolve further in autumn 1900, because Hewett was not prepared to accept defeat. The party that accompanied him on his annual fieldwork that summer had included Territorial Secretary George Wallace and his wife.[72] Wallace, who had been considered for the post of governor of New Mexico in 1896, had the kind of political influence that would stimulate the Land Office into further action, and at Hewett's urging he dispatched a report of his own to Washington, detailing the accusations against the Hyde Expedition. In November the newly inaugurated Santa Fe Archaeological Society passed as its first act a resolution requesting that the Secretary of the Interior bring an immediate halt to "the spoilation of the cliff dweller ruins in the Chaco cañon which have been exploited for several years by a private corporation."[73]

The renewed pressure on federal authorities produced the desired response by the end of the year, when another special agent from the Land Office, S. J. Holsinger, was deputed to Chaco Canyon for a new investigation.[74] An aggressive promoter of federal oversight, Holsinger took a more activist stance than had Pracht. One of his first acts was to contact Bradford Prince, who on behalf of the Archaeological Society used his contacts throughout western New Mexico to obtain information about Chaco Canyon. The responses contained both factual and fanciful information about the Hyde Expedition, but they allowed Prince to construct a synthesis of the current situation at Pueblo Bonito. Prince's report continued the effort to paint the Hyde Expedition as a purely commercial operation: "Those in charge are accustomed to say that all the relics excavated go to a public museum in New York," he wrote, "but as a matter of fact they are believed to be sold wherever they will bring the most and I know of parties who have personally purchased rare articles from the establishment."[75]

Holsinger spent several days in Chaco Canyon in spring 1901, during which time he took statements from Richard Wetherill and Fred Hyde and examined the ruins on his own. Letters exchanged with Prince following the completion of the inspection make it clear that Holsinger distrusted the testimony he had received, and speculated that it would take further investigation to make a complete case.[76]

In his report to the Land Office, however, Holsinger reserved judgment on much of what he had seen, noting that the Hyde Expedition was "doing a great work for the Navajos." He also found no particular fault in the methods of the project, and relayed testimony that no artifacts were sold for commercial gain without comment. In the matter of the filing of the homestead claims, however, his skepticism was obvious, calling it a "curious coincidence" that both the original and the amended claims filed by Wetherill contained prehistoric ruins, that the land included in the amended claim had little agricultural potential, that the buildings on the property had been built by the company and not by Wetherill himself, and that there had been no attempt to improve Fred Hyde's own claim.[77]

Holsinger's surprise solution to the clash over archaeological resources neatly tied together the competing interests within the archaeological community. Sidestepping the issues of the legality of the excavations, the report proposed the creation of a "National Park of Prehistoric Ruins," by which means the antiquities of Chaco Canyon would "be perpetually preserved, not alone for the student of science but the everyday tourist, who will here not fail to find instruction as well as entertainment."[78] The creation of national parks was a theme of preservation interests in the West, who saw in them both some recognition of regional merit and the economic potential of tourism. The Santa Fe Archaeological Society, for instance, was already on record as promoting a national park for ruins on the Pajarito Plateau near Santa Fe, and would clearly respond favorably to such status being extended to Chaco Canyon.[79] Putnam's national advocacy for antiquities preservation was on record, and no one in the Hyde camp could publicly object to the concept. National Park status, which was slow in coming, would not of itself terminate the rights of archaeologists to investigate the ruins. It would, however, increase the level of federal government oversight, which in Holsinger's mind may have been conceived as a way of monitoring the activities and good intentions of all parties concerned. In the end, the restraining order placed on the Hyde Expedition prior to the beginning of Holsinger's investigation was never suspended, and became permanent in 1902.[80]

Perhaps the most ironic aspect of efforts to curtail the archaeological activities of the Hyde Expedition was how unnecessary they seemed to be, since the heart of the project, the Pueblo Bonito excavations, had been exhausted before the suspension took effect. Hyde failed to respond to Wetherill and Dodge's petition to reorganize the project. In New York, Pepper's report for 1901 implied that the decision to cease work had been an internal one, with the project's emphasis shifting to cataloguing, publishing, and exhibiting the earlier finds.[81] A similar statement appeared in the Museum's annual report for that year. Putnam, apparently with the conviction that the restraining order did not apply to him, brought Tozzer and Farabee to Chaco Canyon in the summer of 1901, but does not seem to have returned thereafter. The attention and resources of the Hydes were increasingly absorbed by the trading-post business, but they continued to supply financial support to the remnants of their team.

Hewett had played his cards skillfully. By manipulating the federal government into intervening at Chaco Canyon, he had minimized his personal involvement in the affair. By criticizing the Hyde Expedition's commercial activities rather than attacking its scientific staff, he was also able to avoid directly antagonizing Putnam, Pepper, and the others. This became increasingly important to him over the next few years, as his career as an archaeologist developed. In a circular on Southwest antiquities he wrote for the Land Office in 1904, Hewett described the "splendid collection" of artifacts from Chaco Canyon in the American Museum, and anticipated "a full report of this excellent piece of work."[82] The fact that he had worked diligently to undermine the project and its aims went unsaid.

The most telling symbol of the end of the Bonito excavations, and of the first phase of the American Museum's southwestern program, came at what was still called "Putnam" on August 2, 1902. Hewett, his wife Cora, and a small group of students and faculty from the New Mexico Normal School arrived by wagon. The party remained for less than a week, while Hewett "spent what time he had in excavating, with native help, and making extensive measurements and maps of the old ruins." One evening a dance was held at the Wetherill house like those witnessed by Tozzer the previous year.[83] This time, however, Hewett's students were the dancers, rather than Putnam's. It is reasonable to suspect that the journey was more of an inspection tour than a strictly scientific mission. The western archaeologists, having scored a victory over Chaco Canyon, were examining the prize.

Patrons and Collections

With the end of the Hyde Expedition's fieldwork at Pueblo Bonito priority shifted from the excavations, which had symbolized the control of archaeological resources, to the collections, which were important archaeological "capital" of another kind. The thousands of artifacts from Pueblo Bonito and Grand Gulch represented both scholarship and prestige, and were the target of competition just as the fieldwork had been. And it was questions about the future of those collections and their appropriate use that made Talbot Hyde, the beleaguered project's patron, once again the center of attention.

The most dramatic change to occur at the American Museum in the aftermath of Hewett's victory at Chaco Canyon was the resignation of Frederic Putnam from the Department of Anthropology. The success of Putnam's programs at the American Museum had in large part depended on his cordial relationship with the Museum's president. In 1897 Jesup had gone so far as to personally sponsor Putnam for membership in the Century Association, a prestigious midtown Manhattan club devoted to "culture."[84] The relationship had deteriorated, however, as Boas's influence grew, and Jesup came to believe that a department chair who was absent for most of the month was not in the best interests of the museum. During a meeting between the two men Jesup asked Putnam to devote more of his time to the Museum's business, at which point Putnam announced his resignation, effective December 1903.[85]

Putnam and Boas had also grown apart, a schism that resulted from their different visions of the organization of professional anthropology. Since both men had ambitions to establish anthropology on a national scale, their different perspectives were an inevitable source of conflict. Boas's aggressive construction of a course of student training built around Columbia University and the American Museum ran counter to the more traditional, eclectic program maintained by Putnam and his colleagues at Harvard. The specific root of their disagreement was a clash over the organization of a new Department of Anthropology at the University of California, but the real problem was generational.[86] Putnam returned to Cambridge, and spent time in California, but his productive years were nearing an end.

The overall impact on the department of Putnam's departure was muted, but it was a significant blow to the operation of the Hyde Expedition. Over the ten years since the World's Columbian Exposition, Putnam and Talbot Hyde had developed a close relationship. Through his generous financial contributions Hyde had made it possible for Putnam to promote his research programs, which in turn gave Hyde's own endeavors a sheen of scientific legitimacy. The professionally trained scholars of the new generation were less willing to accommodate the participation of interested laymen in anthropological work. Without Putnam there was effectively no scientific supervision of the continuing activities of the Hyde Expedition, and under the quickly changing circumstances at the Museum no one was available or interested to fill the gap.

Putnam's retirement also coincided with the final collapse of the Hyde Expedition as a trading enterprise. Tozzer had witnessed the high point of Wetherill's operation at Pueblo Bonito; the economic cost of such aggressive expansion was too high to be borne over the long term. Fred Hyde exhausted his own financial resources and the patience of his relatives, leaving his brother to extricate the family from the business. Talbot turned the management of the Hyde Expedition over to Arizona curio dealer J. W. Benham in December 1901, but his hope that the new arrangement would save the business rang hollow. "The whole country out there thinks the HEE business is going to smash, if it has not already gone up," he wrote Putnam, "but we will give them a surprise and hold it down."[87] Benham took over the more profitable aspects of the trading post business, such as the New York storefront, leaving Hyde to pay off creditors. When the dust settled in March 1902 the Hyde Expedition had been incorporated under New Mexico state law by Hyde, Benham, and other associates.[88]

Richard Wetherill was completely cut out of the new business, and thus the long-standing relationship between him and Talbot Hyde came to an end. Ultimately Wetherill's cultivation of both scientists and patrons failed to provide an opportunity that would allow him to enter the community of scholars. In a letter written to Hyde in 1903 he expressed hopes that he would "have time to dig up more earth and see what other people are doing," but economic necessity intervened. The fact that the letter made its way from Hyde to Benham, who used it to stir up further trouble with the land office, illustrated that Wetherill's network of patronage had largely collapsed.[89]

The entry of museum archaeologists into the Southwest field did not eliminate the relic-hunting business, but it did push it further toward the margins of respectability. The ongoing professionalization of archaeology also limited opportunities for those westerners who were not members of eastern scholarly circles. As Pepper's situation indicated, the criterion was not yet formal education, but access to the emergent networks of patrons, administrators, and scientists. The rise of a specifically western constituency for archaeology paradoxically also had a negative impact on relic hunters like Wetherill, since their primary clientele was in the East. Increasing regulation of federal land was popular with westerners because it theoretically protected cultural resources from exploitation by eastern museums and their minions. Hemmed in between Pepper, Hewett, and Holsinger, Wetherill had no place to turn, and disappeared from the archaeological scene.

In New York, the fate of the Hyde Expedition collections in the post-Putnam years was contested among three groups: those sharing Hyde's public-oriented and educational goals, Boasian professionals emphasizing the advancement of knowledge, and others who saw possession of the artifacts exclusively in terms of the prestige they conferred. After Putnam's departure Hyde increasingly saw himself as an anthropologist and spent considerable time at the museum promoting various educational schemes as well as throwing his support behind popular archaeological journals such as *Monumental Records*.[90] He formed a close relationship with Hermon Carey Bumpus, a New England biologist who was an outspoken supporter of museum education, and who when President Jesup's health began to deteriorate in 1902 was appointed "director" and placed in effective charge of day-to-day management of the museum. Bumpus had an interest in anthropology, and saw Hyde as congenial to his ambitions for new museum programs.[91]

Boas alternated between condemning Hyde and other proactive patrons for interfering with professional research and actively soliciting their support for his own projects. Privately, he described the Hyde Expedition as a failure, "an enterprise started upon with great vigor, but ending with disappointment."[92] He was also vexed by the autonomy of the "Division of the Southwest" within his department, circumstances created by Hyde's financial support. Boas and Bumpus became enemies almost immediately, further polarizing relationships within the museum.

The middle ground between these clashing personalities and agendas was occupied by George Pepper. He continued to catalogue the Pueblo Bonito collections, and became more deeply involved with professional associations. He was also a principal consultant for the Indian Hall at the new Hotel Astor: "expert anthropologists have acknowledged that one cannot hope to find a better place than the Indian Hall at the Hotel Astor," noted one brochure.[93] In his spare time Pepper worked for the Hyde Expedition store. He thus joined the company of anthropologists, such as George Dorsey at the Field Columbian Museum, who moved easily between science and commerce but were seen as a threat to the professionalization of the discipline by Boas and his students.[94]

The smoldering debate over the direction of the Department of Anthropology was fanned in 1904, when George Gustave Heye walked into Pepper's office and introduced himself. A thirty-year-old collector of Indian artifacts and heir to an oil fortune, Heye was immediately pegged by Pepper as a good source of future funding. Heye quickly gained the confidence of those in the museum who were out of step with Boas, particularly Hyde, whom he jovially called "Hosteen Hyde" in the Navajo fashion.[95] There were, however, profound differences between them. Hyde was a patron, but Heye was a collector. When Pepper enlisted Heye's support for excavations in Mexico in autumn 1904 Heye did so only with the assurance that he would have first choice of any discoveries.[96] For Heye acquisition was paramount, and he had neither scruples nor any loyalty to the American Museum. His involvement with Hyde and his colleagues suggests that he saw them as a means to an end, a way to enlarge his collection of Native American artifacts.

With the addition of Heye, the movement to reform the Department of Anthropology and bring it in line with the museum's educational mission gained steam. "Heye, Hyde, Pepper, and Bumpus had a four hour conference yesterday afternoon," Hyde wrote Putnam, adding that "by spring . . . duplicate sets of material illustrating the study of the North American Indians . . . will be available to the public."[97] Boas did not underestimate the threat posed by the cabal, and proposed to reorganize the department to safeguard his program. Under the new plan he was to be elevated to a position analogous to that held by Putnam, which would give him direct control of the entire staff.[98] Without such enhanced authority and in the face of the machinations of Hyde and Bumpus, Boas proposed to withdraw from the museum and devote his time to graduate training at Columbia.

In the end neither of the reform plans were successful, which produced even greater chaos at the museum. The educational collections were never assembled, perhaps because Heye, who was supposed to assist Pepper with the project, never intended to follow through. Boas was promoted to full curator, but his relationship with Bumpus had deteriorated to such an extent that he was unable to take advantage of the new position. In May 1905 the two men clashed over the installation of a new exhibit, and within a month Boas had resigned.[99]

The deterioration of the Department of Anthropology into competing camps of patrons, educators, and scientists was by the time of Boas's departure in 1905 largely complete. Hyde's control over the Hyde Expedition collections gave him considerable latitude within an institution with which he had no formal affiliation. Although he had lost access to the ruin itself, Hyde was attempting to use the collections to further his personal aims. A young assistant curator, Clark

Wissler, was placed in charge of the department, but real authority rested with Bumpus. Bumpus encouraged Wissler to discuss the educational collections with Hyde, but nothing came of the query. President Jesup's response to the entire affair was a loss of confidence in the department as a whole, and funding was cut back sharply.[100]

The Hyde Expedition collections, which had originally been perceived as both a scientific and an educational asset, had by 1906 become important for their prestige value alone. As George Heye gained ascendancy over Hyde and Pepper, the hold of the American Museum on the remaining assets of the work in Grand Gulch and at Pueblo Bonito grew increasingly tenuous. Pepper took a leave of absence to participate in a Heye-sponsored project in Ecuador, and after returning to the Museum spent increasing amounts of his time assisting Heye with his personal collection.[101] Hyde believed that Heye's increasing influence would be beneficial for the ultimate completion of the Southwest work: "Every month now sees his [Heye's] interest getting stronger in the work," he wrote Putnam. "In fact, he is so bound up in it now that even should anything happen so that I could not continue to take care of Pepper, he would unquestionably do so, and if this were the only result of the effort and sacrifice which both Pepper and I have made, it is certainly well worth while."[102]

The factional stalemate paralyzing the department was finally broken on January 22, 1908, with the death of Morris Ketchum Jesup. Jesup's actions as president had been motivated by what he perceived to be the educational needs of the museum, and in the process of serving those needs he had promoted scientific investigation to new heights. His death, preceded by the departure of Putnam and Boas, was the last step in the dismantling of the original web of patronage and policy on which the Department of Anthropology had been built. Jesup's successor, Henry Fairfield Osborn, was a scientist who had been with the museum for eighteen years and had brought the Department of Vertebrate Paleontology to national prominence. He also demonstrated an appreciation for the "public dimensions" of paleontology, and stimulated an active exhibit program. Osborn came into office with his own array of policies, one of which was that anthropology would no longer receive favorable treatment.[103]

Uncertainty over Osborn's intentions provided the opportunity George Heye needed to take control of the Hyde collections. He had been building a close relationship with George Byron Gordon, director of the University Museum in Philadelphia, funding expeditions and gaining new specimens for himself in the process.[104] Sensing that Gordon would prove more cooperative than Osborn, Heye agreed to deposit his own collections in the University Museum in exchange for a position of influence on the museum's board, and indicated that the artifacts from Grand Gulch and Pueblo Bonito would be included. Whether Hyde himself was consulted is unclear. He had recently undergone a personal crisis, involving both business and family matters, which had made him all the more reliant on what he called his "science interests."[105] But Pepper was part of the plan, and when he announced in December 1908 that he would resign to take a new post at the University of Pennsylvania it seems to have caught the administration of the American Museum completely by surprise.[106]

Conscious that an important asset was at risk, Osborn directed his staff to research the history of the Hyde collections, only to come up with the disturbing fact that they had never been formally donated to the American Museum and that there were thus no legal means of preventing a transfer.[107] Osborn turned to Hyde, who by this point was in full collaboration with Heye and Pepper. After an unsatisfactory discussion on "the future of Anthropology in the American Museum," Hyde sent a letter making his intentions clear. Arguing that the department had prevented him from developing an educational program, he had "decided to place [his] material in the University Museum and thereby assist the teachers and students of the University in their anthropological study work."[108] Unwilling to break completely with the expedition's roots, Hyde agreed to leave some of the artifacts in New York, although the bulk of the collections, along with associated records, would be transferred. Negotiations with Bumpus produced a list of the relevant material. Heye, who gloatingly informed Gordon that they had gained "*everything* we wanted," had the collections packed and moved south in the summer of 1909.[109]

It is ironic that what Hyde had been led to believe would be a new beginning for his educational plans destroyed much of the scientific value of the collections and proved to be the first step in his own exile from anthropology. Once the Hyde Expedition artifacts left New York, Hyde's own status dwindled to that of a pawn in George Heye's grander schemes. He was given a position on both the Board of Managers of the University Museum and a museum committee on education, but his residence in New York meant that he could exert no real influence on policy. His hope to prepare a textbook on Native Americans for schoolchildren was equally frustrated.[110] Isolated and no longer assured of Pepper's loyalty, Hyde found himself with little to show for his long and generous patronage.

For the next six years Heye intrigued with and against Gordon in an effort to expand his own influence, offering at times to return the collections to the American Museum and at others to ensure their permanent donation to the University Museum.[111] Osborn was entirely willing to negotiate, perceiving the danger that Heye might otherwise establish his own institution and challenge the American

Museum's anthropological preeminence in New York. These fears were shown to be justified when, after interminable maneuvering, in 1916 Heye abruptly withdrew the collections from Philadelphia to return to New York and build his own museum. Gordon's chagrin at finding himself in the same position Osborn had occupied eight years earlier can only be imagined.

The new institution was called the Museum of the American Indian, and Talbot Hyde had no place in it. In 1914 he had experienced a financial crisis and had sold his anthropological library. Heye, sensing weakness and having by long association ensured the complete loyalty of Pepper, then persuaded Talbot Hyde to sell him the Southwest collections as well, for a total of $1,200.[112] This was less than half what Hyde had paid Richard Wetherill for one of the Grand Gulch collections alone, and it is not difficult to imagine Heye pressing a hard bargain.

The incorporation of the major part of the collections into Heye's museum marked the end of the Hyde Expedition, and the loss to science was grievous. The separation of the records from the specimens was particularly damaging, made worse by a re-inventorying procedure at the Museum of the American Indian that removed the original numbers from the pieces in their possession.[113] Of the extraordinary finds from Pueblo Bonito that had been displayed at the American Museum, only a disorganized clutter of artifacts remained. Talbot Hyde drifted back into the museum in 1918 and was recruited by Osborn to try to make sense out of the remnant, but failed at this as he had many years before. Only through extreme persistence was Wissler able to goad Pepper into completing a monograph on the excavations, but it consisted of transcribed field notes with little context or analysis.[114]

Intended to begin a new tradition in Southwest archaeology, the Hyde Expedition's legacy was instead one of disappointment and loss. Even as a failure, however, the project had important historical significance. In their original form, the Hydes' plans for Southwest work had resembled only an expanded version of the artifact-oriented collecting trips that had been the rule throughout much of the 1880s and 1890s. By arranging for the involvement of the American Museum, however, they had not only expanded the scientific importance of the project, but had become central figures in a struggle for the control of archaeological resources. The tension between East and West, a manifestation of disparate cultural and economic conditions, found expression in the exploitation of prehistoric ruins, as it had in various forms of economic and political action. The removal of western antiquities to the American Museum of Natural History had its reflection in the fleecing of Hyde business interests by their western competition. Commerce was clearly a two-edged sword, and while promoting tourism as one economic solution to their ambitions or conniving in relic-hunting by local residents, westerners were able to use accusations of commercialism to oust eastern scientific interests and to assert their own tentative control over regional antiquities.

When not competing among themselves for access to archaeological sites, members of the anthropological community were embroiled in contests over the future direction of their own discipline. Building from an institutional base that was explicitly educational in nature, Franz Boas was bent on the promotion of a professional anthropology devoted to the pursuit of a scientific ideal. This transformation was shared with other social sciences of the period, and led to an extraordinary efflorescence of scholarship. In the process, however, the educational power of anthropology, as perceived by Morris Jesup and Talbot Hyde, was diminished. The public fascination with the antiquities of the Southwest had fueled the ambitions of both scholars and entrepreneurs, and it was in some sense disenchantment with the inattention of anthropologists to public interests that left patrons and institutions grappling for control of collections after they had been removed from the ground.

In the summer of 1910, while Pepper and Heye were arranging the Pueblo Bonito collections on the shelves in Philadelphia and Talbot Hyde was vainly trying to cobble together an educational program, Richard Wetherill was murdered in Chaco Canyon. The strains associated with the trading post had complicated his relationship with the local Navajos, one of whom shot him during an altercation. Chaco Canyon had, technically speaking, been a national monument since 1907, but its remoteness and the complexities of local land ownership had allowed Wetherill to continue to do business at Pueblo Bonito until he was killed.

A few years before he had faced another team of government surveyors, bent on reopening the government case against him. As told to the *Santa Fe New Mexican* after Wetherill's death, the surveyors "anticipated meeting a very disagreeable and rough man, living 60 miles from civilization," and had therefore been prepared for a fight. Instead, they found Wetherill a friendly and hospitable host, who accepted their mission with good grace and toured them through a house filled with Navajo rugs and antiquities. He sent them home with gifts from his collection, which the surveyor who told the story to the reporter still had on his shelf. "Instead of finding a semi-savage," he recalled,

> we found Wetherill exceedingly well informed on current events. . . .
>
> "[He] was known among the Indians as 'An-as-as-sa,' which means 'a digger of ruins.'"[115]

3

The "Western Idea"

Regional Agendas and Southwest Archaeology

In spring 1902, a few months prior to Edgar Lee Hewett's triumphal excursion to Chaco Canyon, his patron and friend Frank Springer traveled north from his home in Las Vegas, New Mexico, to deliver the commencement address at the Colorado State Normal School. The speech touched upon many subjects, one of which was the role of archaeology in the western states and territories. New Mexico's most unique resources, he pronounced, were the antiquities that,

> covered by the debris of uncounted ages, in number and extent to startle the investigator, crown the hills and dot the plains of that land of sky and sunshine. They invite the hand of exploration and science to uncover their mysteries and interpret their

meaning. What was the fate of those ruined civilizations; why they perished, are questions that the living present is now asking the dead past. For that fair and ancient land, touched at last by the spirit which has made the great West what it is, has awakened to a new life. Inquiry and investigation have joined hands with industry and commerce to wrest from it its secrets and its wealth.[1]

Springer's speech opened a new era for local participation in Southwest archaeology. The entrepreneurial zeal of Bradford Prince and other early collectors, the exhibition of southwestern artifacts in the state pavilions at the Columbian Exposition, and the local outcry over the archaeological expeditions sent out by eastern institutions paved the way for Anglo-American Southwesterners to explore the region's past for themselves. Influenced by the utilitarian pragmatism that had given rise to the relic-hunting economy, the members of the local archaeological societies also saw antiquities as a central component of an emerging southwestern identity. Adopting the rhetoric of "cultural nationalism," extolling the primacy of local resources and traditions, Springer and his colleagues promoted an archaeology that was substantially different from the scientific model taking hold in the museums and universities of the East. Supported by popular subscription as well as by individual donors, inviting public participation instead of professional exclusivity, what can be called the "western idea" provided a rationale for Southwest archaeology that was seen by observers as a credible alternative to other models for the conduct of American archaeology.

The Origins of the "Western Idea"

By the turn of the century, the focus of American society in the Southwest had shifted from the ranch and farmstead toward the town and city. The earlier generation of immigrants, who had entered a comparatively open range and moved as economics and other circumstances demanded, was giving way to new arrivals who came by train and found their employment in places like Albuquerque, Phoenix, and Colorado Springs. Between 1880 and 1900 the population of New Mexico nearly doubled, and the outlook of many of these residents more closely resembled that of Bradford Prince than that of Richard Wetherill.[2] A need to reproduce the attributes of "American civilization" they had left behind in other parts of the country had always been expressed by Americans in the Southwest, but the new circumstances made such demands more pressing. At the same time, however, there was a growing sense that the distinctive character of the Southwest also had value. The curio collections of Prince and others of his class reflected regional pride as well as scientific curiosity and commerical interest.[3]

The "Western Idea"

One of the expressions of the desire both to remake the Southwest and to establish its distinctive character was the creation of cultural institutions. Colleges and universities, for instance, were largely absent from the region until the 1890s, when the rising demands of the population resulted in the construction of educational facilities throughout New Mexico and Arizona.[4] Centers of intellectual life as well as pedagogy, colleges emphasized the importance of cultural achievement in a setting previously dominated by commercial interests. Traveling lecturers appearing at western venues found audiences eager for enlightenment and interested in demonstrating the achievements and landmarks of the local scene. Museums were also of great interest, since, as demonstrated decades earlier in the East, they functioned both as showplaces for local accomplishments and as vehicles for education. Since ancient artifacts were one source of western uniqueness, archaeology was closely identified with western museums from the outset. The *Santa Fe New Mexican* lobbied on behalf of a "museum of American antiquities" as early as 1900, a position shared by communities throughout the West.[5]

The establishment of museums, however, required complex relationships of patronage. Funding for institutions in the West was limited, and unlike the obvious importance of colleges the benefit of museums was less tangible. Little of the money made by the extractive industries of the West remained in the region, and the philanthropies that underwrote the museum movement elsewhere were largely absent. Proponents of museums in the Southwest frequently relied upon popular subscription. Making their pitch to the public on a platform of civic betterment, boosters also hoped to influence reluctant state and territorial legislatures to provide funding for the new institutions.

The creation of museums and related institutions, like the issue of regional identity, was also bound up in relationships between the local and national levels. Western boosters turned to national organizations as sources of financial support and used the prestige that accompanied such associations to further local causes. In turn the more established institutions, typically based on the eastern seaboard, saw western interest as a way to consolidate their own agendas and to establish a presence that was truly "national." Despite disparate goals and rationales, such alliances were often seen as mutually beneficial. Local pride and national sanction were not necessarily exclusive, as the example of the nationwide network of Carnegie libraries demonstrated.[6]

In 1903 the western desire for cultural betterment and the eastern interest in expanding circles of influence came together over archaeology and institutions through the initiative of the Archaeological Institute of America. In the twenty-four years since its founding, the members of the Institute had kept to the agenda

67

of humanistic, Old World archaeology established by its founder, Charles Eliot Norton, following his dictum that the archaeology of North America had nothing to contribute toward "the progress of civilization."[7] Since the completion of Adolph Bandelier's Southwest work the Institute had left the field to the Bureau of American Ethnology and other, "scientific" organizations. As their commitments abroad grew larger, however, Norton's successors realized that financial support exceeding that available in Boston would be required and that a national presence would promote greater legitimacy. In 1884 the Institute's bylaws were amended to allow for the creation of local affiliates, which, through their dues and contributions, would support the initiatives of the larger organization.[8] The reforms proved successful at first, but following a decline in membership a further elaboration of the affiliated society system was implemented in late 1890s targeting membership in the western states.

The Institute's leadership was aware of the interest of the western public in archaeology, and hoped to use this appeal to build a broader base of support. "It is not to be admitted that our West, full of energy and wealth, will fail to do her part," read one plea for expanded membership.[9] Appropriate activities for the new affiliates included the sponsorship of local research and providing venues for Institute lecturers, but these were expected to be secondary to the general goal of promoting classical archaeology. That local priorities might differ from those of the national organization was a concern, but one members of the Institute thought manageable, in part due to the superior cultural value of classical heritage they assumed was widely acknowledged.

The architect of the campaign to create western affiliates was Secretary Francis Willey Kelsey. Kelsey, raised in New York state, had joined the faculty of the University of Michigan in 1889 and applied himself to promoting classical scholarship in the Midwest. His numerous contacts with university professors and interested citizens beyond New England and the eastern seaboard convinced Kelsey that aggressive recruitment of affiliates would strengthen the Institute and increase its national presence. With the successful establishment of local societies in Detroit, St. Louis, and other cities of the central United States Kelsey's eyes turned further westward. In late 1902 and early 1903 he and Institute President John Williams White contacted Harvard and Michigan alumni in Colorado and on the West Coast to drum up support for a lecture series, which was held in November and December 1903.[10] The talks themselves were sponsored by local colleges, with considerable effort made to ensure that prominent members of the community would be in attendance. Afterwards, in more private discussions, Kelsey recruited interested parties to establish a local affiliate of the Institute. His success illustrates westerners' desire for cultural institutions. Upon his return

Kelsey reported that affiliated societies had been established in Kansas City, San Francisco, Los Angeles, Salt Lake City, and Denver, and that "the zeal and enthusiasm with which all have entered upon their work augur well for the future."[11]

It was in Los Angeles that Kelsey's efforts dovetailed most closely with western cultural nationalism, for the person he tapped to establish the affiliated society there was Charles Fletcher Lummis. A journalist who had attended Harvard, Lummis walked from Ohio to the West Coast on a publicity stunt in 1884 and spent the next two decades establishing himself as an authority on Southwest culture and a booster for the region on the national stage. From a platform provided first by the *Los Angeles Times* and later by the southern California magazine *Land of Sunshine* (subsequently renamed *Out West*), which he edited after 1893, Lummis founded a number of organizations and crusaded for causes related to western identity. The Landmarks Club, which promoted the preservation of the Spanish missions of southern California, was only one of these projects. Flamboyant and eccentric, Lummis was noted for his corduroy suit and strong opinions.[12]

Lummis argued that their shared Hispanic history linked California, Arizona, and New Mexico into a greater Southwest and that the cultural heritage of that region was a source of identity Anglo-American Southwesterners should treat as their own. He also considered the Native American past of the region to be the "birthright" of its modern inhabitants, and through his friendship with Adolph Bandelier had developed a strong interest in archaeology.[13] As early as the mid-1890s Lummis had campaigned for a public museum in Los Angeles. "Whatever makes for the benefit, intellectual or material, of Southern California," he wrote, "is *ex officio* important to us; and . . . a museum would be a benefit on both aspects."[14] The effort moved slowly, however, and despite his organizing skills Lummis had been unable to make significant progress.

The meeting between Lummis and Kelsey thus served the purposes of both men, and bore fruit almost immediately, since the new Los Angeles affiliate, which Lummis called the "Southwest Society," was a dramatic success. Kelsey saw California's burgeoning population as an important base of support for the Institute's wider initiatives, while the affiliation provided Lummis with the prestige of a national tie to further promote his ambitions for western scholarship and institutions. He poured his organizational energy into the new project, and by early 1904 reported lecture attendance of more than five hundred people. Presided over by prominent businessman J. S. Slauson, the first board of the society included the editor of the *Los Angeles Times,* the president of the University of Southern California, and prominent members of the Los Angeles business community. As secretary, Lummis recruited new members through a sophisticated program of mimeographs and mass mailings rather than the personal canvassing more customary at that time. Under his guidance the Southwest Society relied upon "the ingenuity, the continuity and the modern facilities which the progressive business man employs for money-making."[15] Within a few years the Southwest Society was the largest affiliate of the Institute.

It soon became apparent, however, that the Southwest Society would not serve as a passive source of revenue for the overseas projects of the Institute. Lummis had little interest in classical archaeology, and did not think it a particularly appropriate activity for contemporary residents of the West. Instead, he argued, resources should be directed toward the preservation of regional heritage, which was more tangible to the residents of California and the Southwest and also a more "appropriate" subject for study. The Southwest Society also took up Lummis's campaign for a new Los Angeles Museum, and acquired the Palmer-Campbell collection of southern California antiquities for display in a rented public gallery. The Southwest Society's initial program of research—what Lummis called "catching our archaeology alive"—was recording traditional Californian folk songs.[16] Both the museum and the folk song project attracted significant attention in Los Angeles, as he had intended, and by promoting local interests the new organization garnered substantial community support. As Lummis described it to Thomas Dale Seymour, a Yale professor who had become president of the Institute in 1904: "I find that even the most liberal and progressive of our members look a little cross-eyed at spending their money for a remote archaeological work, yet these same people (and many, many more) would most cheerfully 'put up' for the same kind of work which should glorify California— and I mean not merely in the boom sense, but in the higher sense."[17]

An archaeology based in the community, structured along "modern business principles," and designed to build local pride and institutions was what Lummis called the "Western idea."[18] The affiliation with the Institute brought prestige, but also provided a foil he used to whip up a sense of competition with eastern interests. "I am mighty anxious," Lummis wrote one prospective member, "to build up here a membership and a fund which shall jar the Boston dignitaries who think Southern California is populated only by boomers and bandits."[19]

Neither the building of museums nor the promotion of local research were priorities of the Institute as a whole, and while the promise of enhanced revenues encouraged Seymour and his colleagues they were uneasy over the implication of Lummis's activities for the future of the organization. An American committee existed within the Institute, but it was largely a personal project of Charles P. Bowditch, a wealthy Bostonian. Bowditch had a passion for the ancient Maya, and provided a fellowship for Central American archaeology that was administered through the Institute. The first fellow was Alfred Tozzer, who after his return from Chaco Canyon in 1901 conducted ethnographic research in the Petén rain forest of Mexico and Guatemala under Bowditch sponsorship.[20] The other members of the American committee, Frederic Putnam and Franz Boas, advised Bowditch and advocated American research, but played a small role in the councils of the Institute.

The increasing number of local affiliates, however, and the interest of their members in American work, would inevitably enhance the influence of the American Committee within the organization, and draw energy away from the program of Old World archaeology. The clash between the moral imperative of classical studies and the local demand for tangible relevance gradually divided the Institute into factions. The attitude of the more traditional leaders of the Institute toward the Southwest Society and the cause it represented was summed up by a witness to a lecture on the folk song project Lummis gave in Cleveland in late 1904. He described the talk as "not only not archaeological in any sense of the term, but also distinctly unscholarly, undignified, and altogether improper for the occasion." Kelsey and his associates in the Institute continued, however, to support the affiliate policy in general and Lummis in particular, arguing that Lummis's efforts would in time enhance the Institute's position and that he should be "given a free hand."[21]

Like Hewett's campaign to stop the Hyde Expedition's Pueblo Bonito excavations, Lummis's interests in archaeology were as much about control as they were about scholarship. The aura of scientific legitimacy afforded by archaeological expeditions, new collections for the museum's exhibits, and a regular flow of publicity would maintain the momentum of the Southwest Society and solidify its popular support. With or without the sanction of the national organization, the continued success of Lummis's program required active local involvement in local research. By establishing a presence in Southwest archaeology, Lummis would also stake a claim to the antiquities of the region for local interests.

After headlines about the folk song project began to fade, the Southwest Society inaugurated a program of archaeological field research under the direction of its curator, Frank Palmer. Palmer was a California antiquarian who stayed on to tend his collections after they had been purchased by the society. A close ally of Lummis, he had no archaeological training or expertise. In keeping with Palmer's personal interests, excavations were begun at an archaeological site near Redondo Beach, California, in summer 1905. Despite the local appeal, however, California antiquities did not satisfy Lummis's ambitions to make the Society and its new museum the hub of archaeological activity in the Southwest. After a brief season Palmer was next dispatched to Snowflake, Arizona, on the first of two "Arizona

Expeditions." The scope of the projects was relatively modest; in 1905 Palmer examined prehistoric sites and excavated in promising locations, assisted by his son and a local field assistant, T. J. Worthington. Efforts were largely directed toward obtaining high-quality artifacts, although some architectural features were cleared. In all, Palmer reported examining eighty different ruins in a ten-week period.[22]

Despite Hewett's successful derailing of the Chaco Canyon excavations, the study of antiquities in the Southwest after the turn of the century remained fiercely competitive. Jesse Fewkes had directed a series of excavations in eastern Arizona on behalf of the Bureau beginning in 1895, and as had happened in Colorado a decade earlier scholarly activity stimulated a wave of relic-hunting. By 1901, when Walter Hough of the U.S. National Museum began work in the same area, an elaborate network of collectors and suppliers of artifacts was in place, involving both Anglo-American and Hispanic settlers as well as Navajos. Sites Fewkes had reported intact only a few years earlier had been thoroughly pillaged. "No ruin is so obscure or inaccessible," Hough wrote, "that some sheepherder or prospector has not put in some of his tedious hours digging in it."[23] Private museums as well as curio dealers and federal institutions were involved in the trade. The Field Columbian Museum obtained a major collection of antiquities from J. F. Wattron, of Holbrook, Arizona, in 1901, while the Brooklyn Museum purchased artifacts in the region shortly afterward. "These most historic treasures . . . belong here and not in the tenderfeet country," Lummis complained to Seymour.[24]

By inaugurating a program of field research, Lummis and his organization were asserting the rights of "Southwesterners," broadly defined, to participate in the study and acquisition of southwestern antiquities. Lummis's opportunity to represent southwestern interests was in large part due to the failure of the more local archaeological societies to capitalize on their early successes. After building the Santa Fe Archaeological Society into an organization that could promote the study of local antiquities, with sufficient social visibility and political influence to attract funding, Hewett had lost his position at the New Mexico Normal School in a political fight.[25] This left him without an institutional base just at the point when his victory at Chaco Canyon promised new opportunities for archaeological research. Hewett subsequently abandoned university administration and began to build a career as a professional archaeologist, a process that compelled him to leave the Southwest. Over the years he had gained the acquaintance of many national figures in archaeology, and he sought to use these connections to create a place for himself, but after failing to obtain a research assistantship in the Carnegie Institution he went to Europe for graduate study at the University of Geneva in 1904. Without an organizer like Hewett the Santa Fe Archaeological Society quickly became inactive.[26] Similar fates befell the affiliated society of the Institute in Utah, and the Colorado organization put together by Kelsey had little direction.

By late 1904, then, much of the momentum on behalf of regionally based archaeological work had been lost, creating a vacuum that Lummis and his Southwest Society were prepared to fill. Ironically, the principal rival of the First Arizona Expedition in autumn 1905 was a modest effort sponsored by the Institute's other West Coast affiliate, based in San Francisco. Its leader was the anthropologist Alfred Kroeber, one of Franz Boas's first Ph.D. students at Columbia, who had been placed in charge of ethnology in the new department of anthropology at the University of California, Berkeley. Frederic Putnam was nominally head of the program but was absent in Boston for much of the year, leaving the young and ambitious Kroeber as the principal academic anthropologist in the West.[27] The San Francisco affiliate was founded during the same 1903 Kelsey tour that had established the Southwest Society, and the two groups immediately clashed over jurisdiction and membership. Like Lummis, Kroeber saw the Institute as a means to get around limited university resources and promote regional archaeological research. When a former student at the University, Joseph Peterson, was hired as a teacher in Snowflake, Arizona, Kroeber seized the opportunity to obtain a collection of artifacts for his museum at a relatively low cost.

The competition between Kroeber and Lummis, between poorly funded professionals and regional interests, superficially resembled the debates of the previous decade, but in 1905 southwestern cultural nationalists were in a stronger position. The funding base of the Southwest Society was strong, as was Lummis's determination to use archaeology in support of western identity. Kroeber's department, in contrast, was almost entirely reliant on the patronage of Phoebe Hearst, which relationship grew increasingly precarious as the decade wore on. In promoting purely scientific goals Kroeber was unable to tap public interest in western achievement, particularly since his own ambitions, like those of his mentor Franz Boas, were linked to the professionalization of anthropology. Moreover, he lacked Lummis's organizational acumen and populist touch, and the San Francisco Society suffered from low membership and limited interest.[28] The exchanges between Kroeber and Peterson resembled those between Putnam and Viets, with a willing fieldworker sending small collections to a patron who was hard pressed for the funds to keep the project moving. "I have not been able to find anything more about Dr. Palmer's intentions," wrote Peterson, in one of several reports on his rival's activities, but his efforts were destined for obscurity even while Lummis was bringing news of the First Arizona Expedition before the western public in *Out West*.[29]

Like other investigators of the period Lummis was exposed to conflicting federal policies concerning southwestern antiquities, but typically he managed to turn the difficulty to his advantage. A *pro forma* request for permission to examine sites on the White Mountain Apache Reservation was denied by the Acting Commissioner of Indian Affairs, who also suggested that "all such remaining fields of archaeological value should be reserved for Governmental exploitation." The regional societies generally perceived federalization as a way to increase the national visibility of Southwest antiquities but rejected attempts to restrict their own research agendas, and were quick to invoke the prestige of the parent organization in such cases. "The enclosed will show how the Institute has been buncoed, gold-bricked and generally played with," Lummis wrote Seymour, passing along the rejection note.[30] Rather than deal with the federal bureaucracy himself Lummis appealed to W. H. Holmes, who had been made head of the Bureau following Powell's death in 1902. Despite his advocacy of government science in general and of the prerogatives of the Smithsonian in particular, Holmes backed the Southwest Society. "The field of American archaeology is a vast one," he wrote, "and the larger the number of properly qualified institutions that engage in the work, the better for history and science." The permit request was reconsidered, and after establishing that the Southwest Society would submit to "oversight" from the Bureau, authority for the excavations on Indian land was granted on October 3.[31]

In later years Lummis described the wrangle over the research permit as a watershed in the promotion of Southwest archaeology, a victory of western tenacity over bureaucratic interference.[32] More accurately, it demonstrated the web of relationships that was forming in the community of Southwest archaeologists and that would increasingly structure the competition in the aftermath of the failed efforts of previous years. The arrangement between the Bureau and the Southwest Society, which amounted to an exchange of data and specimens, was more than satisfactory to Lummis, who gained another prestigious alliance for his organization. Holmes, who supported the American projects of the Archaeological Institute of America throughout his career, may have seen Lummis and his colleagues as useful foils against the academic anthropologists, particularly Boas, whom he despised.[33] Relations between western cultural nationalists and Smithsonian scientists were unpredictable, and even while relying on the support of Holmes local southwestern organizations were antagonized by the activities of Jesse Fewkes, who was consolidating a Bureau monopoly on the archaeology of northeastern Arizona that would last for another twenty years. Nonetheless some broad areas of common interest were established, and in the councils of the Institute and elsewhere representatives of the Smithsonian increasingly sided with western interests, often in opposition to those promoting purely professional programs for American archaeology from inside universities and museums.

Although scholars felt betrayed by the results of the First Arizona Expedition— "all he was after was specimens," wrote a disappointed Putnam—its application of the "western idea" marked a watershed for the relationship between archaeology and southwestern identity.[34] From the perspective of the Southwest society, *participation* in exploration was the important point, rather than the advancement of any particular scholarly agenda. The artifacts added to the shelves of the nascent Southwest Museum were tangible sources of local prestige no matter how rudimentary Palmer's notes on their discovery nor how vague his interpretations of their meaning. The goal of cultural betterment was advanced. Local interest in southwestern antiquities was also enhanced, which aided Lummis in promoting these resources as historical assets for the region's new residents. What Anglo-American Southwesterners needed, he argued, was "a sense of home, a sense of place, a sense of the history of the American West."[35] Through development of western institutions and exploration of the western past for the benefit of the local population, this goal could be achieved. With the patronage of the community, and with allies in both the American Institute of Archaeology and the Bureau of American Ethnology, Lummis anticipated years of productive involvement in Southwest archaeology.

Even in its auspicious beginning, however, Lummis's program for Southwest archaeology betrayed signs of a contentious future. Without a unifying focus or theme, archaeology as manifest in the "western idea" was exclusively an extension of local ambitions. As such, its impact on a national scale would inevitably be limited. This was, of course, of little concern to Lummis, but as he relied on the prestige of the Institute his methods inevitably came under scrutiny. Under the Institute's umbrella a broad-based program of Southwest research might have been achievable, but Lummis was not prepared to accept partners. Hostility between the Southwest Society and the Institute's San Francisco affiliate, even stripped of its professional/amateur debate, indicated that local agendas would dominate even in situations when cooperative action might be more effective. At the heart of Lummis's promotional campaign for the Society and its museum was the idea that Los Angeles was destined to become the cultural capital of the Southwest, to the exclusion of its rivals. This, as Lummis's detractors had so quickly pointed out, had little to do with archaeology. Yet Lummis was only one part of a movement behind southwestern archaeology within the Institute, and as the first decade of the century wore on other proponents came to the fore who took the "western idea" and built from it a far more credible public alternative to professional archaeology.

Hewett, Preservation, and the Western Coalition

One matter on which the disparate voices in American archaeology after the turn of the century found agreement was the need to preserve antiquities. The cause was particularly important in the West, where accelerating Anglo-American settlement posed a serious threat to the region's ruins. On the national level interest in preservation was related to the cultural nationalism that stimulated the creation of national scenic parks as well as to the antimodernist backlash that grew among the elite classes in response to encroaching industrialization. Independent lobbying by members of the eastern elite in 1889 had resulted in the first effective action to preserve western antiquities, when Congress authorized the president to purchase the Casa Grande ruin and earmarked funds for its repair.[36] Western motives for preservation were complex but arose from the same impulses for cultural betterment that promoted museums and local research. Preservation of the ruins of Mesa Verde was the principal goal of Virginia McClurg's Colorado Cliff Dwellings Association, which had even negotiated directly with the Ute Indian tribe to acquire the portion of their reservation on which some of the antiquities were located. "The movement on behalf of the preservation of the prehistoric ruins in New Mexico has not died out, nor is it sleeping," editorialized the *Santa Fe New Mexican* as it requested congressional action on the matter.[37]

Federal protection, in fact, not only prevented individuals from profiting from the exploitation of antiquities at the expense of the community but also affirmed the importance of the resources themselves, enhancing local prestige.[38] By 1900, popular and scholarly interest in Southwest antiquities had increased to a point where more comprehensive legislation seemed possible, and national organizations such as the American Institute of Archaeology joined the legislative fight. At its annual meeting in December 1903 the Institute created a "Committee on the Preservation of the Ruins of American Antiquity," which in a few months included most prominent American archaeologists. President Seymour argued that the national membership base of the Institute made it particularly qualified "for ascertaining what is best and what is practicable" in the preservation movement.[39] Kelsey played an active role on the committee, testifying before congress in 1904 that awakening public interest mandated greater efforts to preserve American antiquities. His remarks, couched in nationalistic terms, echoed those made by members of the Institute's western affiliates.[40] For the time being the preservation movement was thwarted by hostile interests, but in the process the Institute made common cause with the U.S. National Museum, the Bureau of American Ethnology, and other "scientific" groups with which it had previously maintained only distant relationships. It also shored up its relationship with the affiliates by involving itself in an issue that affected them more directly, since Kelsey and other members of the leadership had almost no direct experience with southwestern ruins themselves.

After a series of failed legislative efforts the movement heated up in the winter of 1905–6, a time that also saw the reemergence of Edgar Lee Hewett as an influential player in Southwest archaeology. Hewett returned from Geneva in late 1904 anxious to reestablish himself in the archaeological community, and found the preservation movement to be the ideal vehicle. He went first to Washington, where from an unsalaried post at the Bureau provided by Holmes he worked on a manuscript based on his earlier southwestern work and planned for a new field season in the region.[41] There was little long-term potential for Hewett at the Bureau, however, due to the presence of Jesse Fewkes. In any event despite his recent graduate training Hewett's true expertise remained in political networking and negotiation, and while in Washington he quickly joined the lobbying campaign for antiquities legislation. He had been active in efforts to preserve archaeological resources since at least 1900, when he had written President McKinley on the subject, and his administrative and pedagogical skills made him exceptional among his colleagues.[42] Hewett had also just completed his report for the General Land Office on the status of southwestern antiquities, so his name was known to many of the individuals within the government who had an interest in the new legislation. In particular the votes of western congressmen were critical, and Hewett's regional connections opened doors closed to other archaeologists. His close relationships with Holmes, Kelsey, and other national figures date from this period, and as the year went on Hewett's voice gained influence in professional councils.

Hewett was aware that his public constituency in western cities and his personal experience with the region's archaeological resources remained unique strengths, and while Palmer was preparing for the First Arizona Expedition in the summer of 1905 he was conducting southwestern excavations of his own. The work focused on northern New Mexico's Pajarito Plateau, a formidable landscape of high, flat mesas covered with piñon and ponderosa pine. The region had been an important population center for Ancestral Pueblo people, and included the

Figure 3.1   Cavate ruins on the Pajarito Plateau near
Puyé in New Mexico. (Courtesy Denver
Public Library, Western History Collection)

important ruined pueblos of Puyé, Otowi, Tsirege, and Yapashi as well as the cave
dwellings of the Rito de los Frijoles. Its rugged character largely prevented the
systematic relic-hunting that had prevailed elsewhere, yet the Pajarito was only a
day's ride from Santa Fe and had thus been a focus of scholarly and public curiosity from an early date. Residents of the Pueblo of Cochiti had led Adolph Bandelier through the region in 1880, and many of the first generation of Southwest
archaeologists had followed.[43] By 1900, however, Hewett had largely made the
Pajarito his personal fief. His long-term goals continued to include more spectacular southwestern sites such as those of Chaco Canyon, yet Hewett's familiarity with the Pajarito ruins and, importantly, their importance and proximity to his
Santa Fe allies meant that the archaeology of the plateau remained at the center
of his agenda for the subsequent decade.

Hewett excavated sites throughout the summer of 1905 and peppered
Holmes with letters promoting larger projects.[44] At the same time he renewed
contact with many of the acquaintances who had been his avid supporters two
years before. The enhanced role of the Archaeological Institute of America

through its affiliates was a new factor in the region, one with which Hewett's encounters with Kelsey had clearly familiarized him. When it became evident that further Bureau funding would not be forthcoming, Hewett turned to this new source of support, and by late 1905 was appointed delegate for the Colorado Society of the Institute at its annual meeting.[45]

Hewett's meteoric rise within the Institute was assisted by his usefulness to the various factions struggling for dominance within American archaeology. To Kelsey he represented an aggressive ally in attracting the interest of the public and galvanizing political support for popular programs. For government archaeologists Hewett was a useful counter to academic rivals within the archaeological profession. As they supported Lummis in his efforts to obtain a research permit for the Southwest Society, Holmes and Fewkes were also promoting Hewett for the Bowditch fellowship, which had become vacant on Alfred Tozzer's elevation to the Harvard faculty. In the absence of a qualified student candidate Hewett's nomination moved ahead, despite the misgivings of Bowditch, who preferred a more malleable candidate, and Boas, who thought his training was deficient.[46] Despite these misgivings, Hewett received the fellowship in January 1906, completing a year that saw his rise from uncertainty to a solid position in the archaeological establishment.

Bowditch and Boas were justified in their concern, for while the fellowship was intended to promote research and training, Hewett used it to establish a permanent niche for himself and to shift the American program of the Institute toward a more popular constituency. For much of the year he served as mobile liaison for both Kelsey and Holmes, lobbying Congress, conducting surveys for the government, and lecturing before public audiences. As he traveled, Hewett reinforced his position as the spokesman for the western societies at the national level. In Colorado he participated in a survey establishing boundaries for the proposed Mesa Verde National Park.[47] In New Mexico he found the Santa Fe Archaeological Society revived and lobbying for the creation of a national park on the Pajarito Plateau, while the Utah Society was also becoming involved in the preservation movement.[48] Byron Cummings, a professor of classics at the University of Utah, had been elected secretary of the organization and adopted a more activist policy than his predecessors. Like Hewett, Cummings had come west in the early 1890s to take up a career in education. Although a summer course in archaeology at the University of Chicago was the extent of his formal training, he saw southwestern antiquities as an important cultural resource. "I felt it was a duty of the western institutions to make a closer study of this chapter of American history," he later recalled. Stimulated to action by Hewett's lecture tour the Utah Society mounted a campaign of their own on behalf of antiquities legislation. "A society has just been organized here that has for its object the study of these ancient monuments," announced a letter to the Utah congressional delegation. "We want these preserved in their natural place and the material found in the ruins kept for the benefit of the state and nation for historic and scientific study."[49]

Hewett's final western mission was a visit to Los Angeles, where preparations for the Southwest Society's Second Arizona Expedition had begun. Rumors that the scientific aspects of the 1905 work had been substandard reached Kelsey's ears, and he was concerned that the scholarly reputation of the Institute would suffer. Arriving in California in mid-May, Hewett assessed Palmer's abilities as more along the lines of a curator or collector than a scientist.[50] "I should say it is doubtful if he can attain eminence," he wrote to Kelsey, suggesting instead that the best way to ensure good results was for himself to accompany the team into the field in a supervisory capacity. Lummis had also decided to accompany the party, and by the end of the month the three men were in Arizona. Rather than return to the Snowflake area they instead excavated sites at Cañon de Chelly, probably at Hewett's suggestion.[51]

This encounter united the two strongest proponents of southwestern archaeology under the auspices of the Institute, and Lummis and Hewett immediately recognized each other as kindred spirits. "In this age of scrubs of all sorts," wrote Lummis, after Hewett had departed, "it does me good to meet a human being." Hewett responded with similar warmth.[52] He sized up Lummis and his base in the Southwest Society as having greater potential for his own future plans than the other western organizations, while in Hewett Lummis found the results-oriented fieldworker he had thus far failed to identify in California. Palmer, as Hewett had discerned, lacked the combination of showmanship and scientific acumen necessary to maintain momentum for the construction of the Southwest Museum while popular interest was high.[53] No formal understanding was reached at Cañon de Chelly, but close collaboration between the two awaited only the proper opportunity.

The cause of preservation and Hewett's prestige among his western constituency received another boost in June 1906 when Congress passed the Lacey Act, establishing protection for archaeological sites on federal land and providing legal authority for the president to establish national monuments at sites of scientific or cultural importance. The final bill was largely based on Hewett's draft, and he was widely considered to have been a major force in its passage. Another victory came on June 30, when Mesa Verde was made a national park.[54] The passage of antiquities legislation achieved a level of protection for ruins that had been desired by the western societies, as well as national recognition of their own aspirations. Hewett's ambitions expanded noticeably in the process. "Estoy muy contento," he wrote Holmes, from his camp on the Rio Chico in northern Mexico, having finally yielded to Bowditch and heading south to take up work in Central America.[55]

Another beneficiary of the new antiquities legislation was the Institute's American committee, which gained influence within the organization as a whole. Bowditch, Putnam, Boas, and their allies used the new momentum to promote the American field, further professionalize the discipline, and consolidate the hold of the universities and major museums on the conduct of archaeology. In the rise of Hewett, however, they faced a rival who was constructing a personal network largely beyond their influence. Hewett's western experience and background in pedagogy also made him sympathetic to new rationales for archaeology that were anathema to the others. Poised to capitalize on its new prestige, the committee instead found itself sliding into an argument over the proper conduct of American archaeology that would grow more vociferous over the coming years. The commitment of the Institute to American archaeology, however, was by 1906 an established fact.

A fourth impact of the Lacey Act, and one that took its proponents by surprise, was the new level of federal involvement in Southwest archaeology. Whereas researchers had been faced with an unpredictable mosaic of policies in earlier years, the new law established a clearer role for governmental oversight that was to prove onerous to many who had aggressively lobbied on its behalf. The first to discover the implications of this shift was Alfred Kroeber, whose request for a permit covering Peterson's work at Snowflake in the summer of 1906 was tabled indefinitely pending the issuance of new regulations.[56] For the time being Peterson was advised to stay off the public domain, but clearly a realignment of forces was under way. One beneficiary was the Smithsonian Institution, which as the home of the archaeologists in government service was to have a decisive voice in the permitting process.

The landscape of Southwest archaeology after 1906 had thus been substantially redefined. The elevation of the preservation cause to the level of national policy was a significant victory for all parties, but one that would impact the conduct of archaeology to an unforeseen extent. The competition between traditional interest groups in eastern museums and universities and western organizations took on new intensity. The cultural nationalism of Lummis's "western idea" in combination with Hewett's unceasing activism had brought the local southwestern societies to the brink of a new era. In such an environment alternative rationales for archaeology would gain new adherents where few had existed previously, fueling the struggle between professional and public interests. For the moment all sides basked in success, but the realignment of forces under way would become only too evident before many weeks had passed.

As he traveled south in the summer of 1906 Hewett left behind a budding network of avocational groups interested in the promotion of southwestern archaeology under his leadership and backed by the general authority of the Institute. He had already displaced Frank Palmer in Lummis's plans, and the summer of 1906 also saw Byron Cummings leading the first archaeological reconnaissance of the Utah Society.[57] Audiences in Colorado and Santa Fe, flush with the success of the preservation movement, were receptive to new endeavors.

Lummis's great success in Los Angeles had demonstrated the potential of local organizations in the promotion of southwestern archaeology, but the scope of the Southwest Society was too narrow for Hewett's national ambitions. In his travels he had begun to formulate a model for the conduct of research based on the western enthusiasm for archaeology on a regional, rather than a local, level. The success of the strategy would depend on his ability to build a coalition from the disparate organizations gathered under the umbrella of the Institute, and he had gone over the ground carefully. A lecture in Denver, he wrote Kelsey, had been "sufficiently popular in character for everybody who would be likely to attend," while also establishing "a foundation for solid, scientific local work in the future on special problems."[58]

In order to knit the western societies into a working coalition, however, Hewett would have to overcome the inherent structural liabilities of public organizations, in particular a shortage of funds and rampant factionalism. Patronage of the sort needed to underwrite large projects remained elusive in the southwestern states and territories. Popular subscription was one solution to this dilemma, as Lummis had shown, but divisiveness within the organizations was endemic. The struggle between Lummis and Kroeber was as much about which society represented California as about the difference between public and professional aspirations. Rivalry had threatened to divide the constituency for the preservation of Mesa Verde, since Virginia McClurg perceived the establishment of the Institute's affiliate in Colorado as a threat to the Colorado Cliff Dwellings Association. When Lucy Peabody, McClurg's legislative chair, resigned over a dispute in early 1906, she decamped to the Institute, and the split was widened by personal animosity.[59] Factionalism was also a factor in Salt Lake City, where prior to Cummings's involvement conflict between the Mormon and non-Mormon members of the community had kept the local affiliate from flourishing.[60]

Hewett's solution to these difficulties was to develop a broad research theme, to be implemented in various parts of the country by the local affiliates, under the general supervision of the Institute in the person of a new director of American archaeology. The actual fieldwork was to be coordinated by the director himself, with the affiliates supplying financial support. Local research priorities could also be accommodated, since the state of archaeological knowledge in most of the Southwest was sufficiently rudimentary that any exploration would produce useful results. In this way local resources could be devoted to promoting local archaeology while understanding of the American past could be advanced on a national scale. In outline, such a plan was a logical synthesis of scholarly and public priorities. It was also anathema to many in the professional community, who saw greater public involvement in archaeology as contrary to their efforts to promote graduate training and professional standards. Public outreach was accommodated within museum settings, but did not extend to actual participation in archaeology, nor to the setting of priorities for archaeological research. Hewett's ideas for a fieldwork coalition were innovative to some but threatening to others.

Reasonably assured of the support of the western societies, Hewett next required the sanction of the Institute to put the coalition plan in motion, calling upon an influential new ally: Alice Cunningham Fletcher. Another of the self-trained scholars of Putnam's generation, Fletcher had been at the forefront of American anthropology for thirty years, having at various times been associated with the Bureau, the Peabody Museum, and the American Association for the Advancement of Science. She had risen from the same milieu as Virginia McClurg, and intuitively understood the value of grassroots organizing. As one of the few tenacious women who had established themselves in the largely male scientific community, Fletcher was a powerful moral force and proponent of American work. "Since the founding of the Institute," she wrote Kelsey, "I have waited and kept my membership, never losing faith that the day would come when the Archaeological Institute of America would be a true name."[61]

Hewett and Fletcher met in Mexico in the summer of 1906, and she was quickly convinced that his plan for the conduct of American work under the auspices of the Institute would succeed. At Fletcher's suggestion, the goal of the work was to be the compilation of a "culture area" map of the United States, illustrating the distribution of various historic and prehistoric peoples.[62] Hewett would manage the project with the assistance of a staff derived from a proposed "School of American Archaeology." Such a school, an American equivalent to the Institute's schools in Rome and Athens, would provide both training for students and a logistical base for the American operations. Since Institute funding for the school would be limited, the creative, coalition-based support system Hewett was developing for archaeology in the West provided a model for a new institution organized along unique lines.

The plan, discussed and approved at the Institute's 1906–7 winter meetings, was more a blueprint than a contract, and it was clear that considerable maneuvering would be required before the School of American Archaeology became a reality. Direct opposition to the scheme was muted, since the idea of a culture area map was sound and despite growing professional distaste for Hewett there were no other credible candidates to lead the effort. Kelsey's support was unwavering, and the hand of the new Director of American Archaeology was further strengthened when Lummis was named to the American Committee the same winter. In the meantime Hewett canvassed his supporters throughout the West for funding to support the fieldwork.[63] Equivalent amounts were solicited from each society, which would entitle them to an equal share of the specimens.

In developing an educational program for the school Hewett drew upon his fifteen years' experience in western colleges. He was a firm believer in what later would be called "experiential learning," and his inclusion of fieldwork in the curriculum of the New Mexico Normal School had been a point of controversy with the more traditional members of the board. At least at the outset, however, he concurred with Boas and other members of the committee that graduate training should be the highest priority. Until then the universities that provided academic training for student anthropologists and archaeologists had been unable to establish a consistent program of field education. Some, like Putnam, took advanced students into the field but failed to institutionalize the activity; others produced graduates who were largely self-trained in fieldwork. It was generally agreed that a more systematic approach was desirable, but the form this approach would take was unclear. Standardization of method was central to the professionalization of archaeology, and a program such as that assembled by Hewett promised to solve this dilemma.

The training of archaeologists also played a pragmatic role in Hewett's fieldwork plan, since it connected him to the universities that would supply the students who would become the nucleus of the staff he required to operate the program. Hewett had always used the involvement of students in his fieldwork as a component of the larger political agenda. One of the participants in the Chaco Canyon trip of 1902, for example, had been Ruth Raynolds, whose father Joshua Raynolds was a prominent New Mexico banker and politician and whose name Hewett often invoked with political authorities.[64] Since the greatest resistance to Hewett came from academic circles, his involvement in student training provided a way to neutralize that opposition.

Hewett sent to a number of universities letters announcing opportunities for "a limited number of advanced students" who would be taught field methods and would "participate in the fieldwork of the expeditions as volunteer assistants."[65] At Harvard the notice appeared in the *Crimson,* where it attracted the attention of two young men who would go on to become giants in American archaeology: Alfred Vincent Kidder and Sylvanus Griswold Morley. Putnam and Tozzer set aside their misgivings over Hewett's professionalism to the extent that they felt their students could benefit from the experience. "How I wish I were with you again," Putnam wrote, "investigating the old cliff houses." Hewett also encouraged Byron Cummings to recruit students from the University of Utah to fill out the team for the summer's work, and by late May the various components of the project were in readiness.[66]

The field school that followed in the summer of 1907 is prominent in archaeological folklore and scholarship but was only one aspect of the larger effort.[67] Hewett needed to demonstrate that the plan he and Fletcher had put together could work, and that the goodwill of the regional societies could be translated into action and into financial support for archaeology. If the coalition model was to be successful, professional education and western cultural nationalism would combine to advance the goals of scholarship and to make Hewett's position in the Institute unassailable.

The first phase of the fieldwork, sponsored by the Colorado Society, took place in the McElmo drainage in the southwest corner of the state. Since the Mesa Verde region remained central to local archaeological interest, Hewett seems to have convinced the organization to fund work in areas that were close by but comparatively little known. The Harvard party, consisting of Kidder, Morley, and John Gould Fletcher, traveled to a ranch west of the town of Cortez where they began an archaeological survey of the region. The assignment came with minimal instruction; Hewett met them and provided a few pointers, but shortly moved on to assist Cummings's party in Utah. This education-by-immersion became Hewett's trademark, and he argued that living up to the challenge encouraged creativity and self-reliance. The field team bickered and struggled with logistics, with Fletcher in particular finding fault with the arrangement. "Kidder . . . told him to go to hell," Morley noted in his diary for July 13. Nevertheless, the work was finished by the time Hewett returned.[68]

The Utah expedition was in the meantime recording ruins near the town of Bluff, using the $1,000 contributed by society president Col. E. A. Wall to stake its own claim to the southwestern past.[69] Cummings had been aggressively building up the Utah Society, convincing the presidents of both the University of Utah and the Latter Day Saints University to serve as officers. Popular interest in the organization was sustained through a series of "parlor talks" intended to "develop a spirit that shall demand a state archaeological museum and proper protection of the ruins found in our borders." The printed schedule for the 1906–7 series listed lectures on "The Cliff Dwellers of Nine Mile Canyon," "A Utah Museum of Art and Archaeology," and "The Value of Christian Archaeology."[70] Cummings stoked local interest, and prepared to implement a scientific program for the society along the lines indicated by Hewett and Fletcher, beginning with a circular to be sent to teachers and other interested parties throughout the state inquiring about archaeological resources near their communities.[71]

The summer projects of the Utah and Colorado societies were intended to continue the process of basic documentation of southwestern antiquities and establish the educational program on a sound basis. Three students from the University of Utah participated in the work, including Cummings's nephew Neil Judd, who would also rise to prominence in southwestern archaeology. Hewett remained with the group for two weeks before returning to Colorado and the Harvard students. "A right glad sight withall," wrote Morley. When the McElmo project was completed at the end of July Hewett took them to Mesa Verde, where the enmity between the Colorado Society and the Colorado Cliff Dwellings Association had revived over selection of a superintendent for the new national park.[72] Over the course of two weeks Hewett conducted seminars on Southwest archaeology, supervised student excavations in Spruce Tree House, and monitored the wrangling of Peabody and McClurg from a safe distance. By the time the candidate opposed by McClurg, Major Hans Randolph, was appointed to the position in August 1907, Hewett had moved his students on to New Mexico. "The lady does not know when she has been whipped," wrote a victorious Peabody.[73]

The final stage of the 1907 season took place in Hewett's traditional domain on the Pajarito Plateau. Throughout the early summer he had remained in contact with Judge McFie, of the Santa Fe Society, and with Lummis, to finalize arrangements for the project. Lummis had obtained $400 for the work from Southwest Society board member Mary Foy, and similar funding was solicited from Santa Fe boosters.[74] Putting earlier plans aside Hewett proposed to excavate the ruins of Puyé, a mesa-top pueblo on the Santa Clara Indian reservation near the northern end of the Pajarito Plateau.

The Puyé excavations were intended to be the centerpiece of the summer's work, promoting the achievements of the fieldwork coalition while providing a trove of artifacts for its sponsors. "My idea," wrote Hewett, "would be to put on a big force, clear out as much of it as possible this year. Make a 'show-ruin' of it . . . have your Society write the Santa Fe Archaeological Society, Board of Trade and the head men of the Institute in the west to visit the ruins and witness the excavations in progress. Run an excursion up from Santa Fe early in the morning and back same evening. Have a lot of Indians with their teams at the station to carry the visitors out to the work."[75]

The use of Puyé as a demonstration project was in accord with the interests of the Santa Fe Society, then in the midst of a promotional campaign touting archaeological tourism in New Mexico. Articles, display cards, and circulars had been sent out, and a traveling exhibit featuring photographs of scenic ruins to be placed in railway stations and post offices was in preparation. The Society, through an ad hoc "committee on cliff dwelling tours," had also been studying the practical aspects of getting travelers to the Pajarito ruins.[76] Considerable debate surrounded Puyé, since it alone of the major Pajarito sites was on Indian land and was thus likely not to be included in national park proposals covering the area. The high visibility of the project promised to generate the attention needed to reopen the issue and possibly lead to adjustment of the reservation boundaries. "I am inclined to think," Hewett wrote to McFie, that local involvement in the Puyé excavations "would have a desirable influence in bringing about what you all so much desire with reference to archaeology."[77]

Lummis saw the rationale behind Hewett's proposal to make Puyé a "show-ruin," but as in the two Arizona expeditions satisfying the demands of his own organization required specimens. "The clearing out and clearing up of the ruin is not immediately and distinctly to our general plan," he wrote. "Presumably the things we want are in the burials." The work was intended to demonstrate the Southwest Society's "general and continued ability to fill the museum," and unless exhibition-quality artifacts were obtained, there was risk that support in Los Angeles would flag. The absorption of the Santa Fe Society by the Southwest Society, which both men thought likely, was also incentive, and Hewett held out the promise of late-season work farther south on the Pajarito at sites that promised more artifacts.[78] All parties to the arrangement were convinced that Hewett was acting to further their own interests, and with the arrival of the field crew from Colorado the components of the project were in place.

The excavations at Puyé began on August 19. The ruin was located on a long, narrow mesa extending from the Jémez mountains, in a densely forested landscape broken at intervals by white cliffs of volcanic tuff. Puyé itself consisted of four large blocks of rooms oriented around a central plaza (fig. 3.2). It had been visited by anthropologists as early as 1886, when Adolph Bandelier sketched the site and collected pottery.[79] Hewett had dug there in his early years, and in 1900 the Reverend S. B. Cole had attracted the displeasure of local newspapers for excavating burials at the site. According to Hewett, Cole's work had been ineffectual, and he started his own team at work in the residential area called the

Figure 3.2   Edgar Lee Hewett at the ruins of Amoxiumqua in New Mexico. (Courtesy Photo Archives, Fray Angélico Chávez History Library, Palace of the Governors, Santa Fe; neg. no. 42033)

"south house."[80] As at Chaco Canyon a decade earlier, the hard labor was done by Indians, with fourteen on the payroll. Hewett cultivated relationships with the people of the Tewa pueblos, particularly San Ildefonso and Santa Clara. Santiago Naranjo, who served as governor of Santa Clara, was one frequent participant in Hewett's projects, and periodically called upon him to intercede with local and federal officials on the behalf of the pueblo.[81] With Kidder, Morley, Fletcher, and a student from Columbia University named Daniel Denison Streeter as supervisors, work proceeded rapidly. The archaeologists shared a tent camp in the valley below with an extended party that included Donizetta Wood, who represented the Santa Fe Archaeological Society, and Constance Goddard Du Bois, an ethnologist who was to do fieldwork in the vicinity.[82]

Despite the fact that the project represented needed income, concern over the handling of antiquities was evident among both the laborers themselves and the authorities at Santa Clara Pueblo. Puyé was an important ancestral site to the Santa Clara people, a claim first documented by Bandelier.[83] The expansion of the reservation to include Puyé had been a victory for the community, which the designs of the archaeologists threatened to overturn. On the fourth day of excavations a delegation from the pueblo visited the ruin to, in Morley's words, "protest against our digging on their land," but Hewett managed to dissuade them from taking further action.[84]

Excavations in the ruins were also disturbing to the local Tewa people because of cultural prohibitions concerning the dead. Folktales recorded by anthropologist Elsie Clews Parsons in the 1920s referred to people dying after digging up burials at Puyé. "The foot of a digger was caught by one of the dead, who said, 'Don't take me from this ground.' The digger got scared, he jumped out and said, 'I don't know who is talking to me underground.' He got sick and died."[85] Despite this underlying unease about the project and what it represented, cash wages proved sufficient enticement to maintain a workforce. Hewett was able to keep the Puyé excavations open, but his manipulation of the Tewa made his defense of Indian rights ambiguous.

Hewett also continued to rearrange the conditions under which the project was conducted. The funding from the Santa Fe Archaeological Society fell through, although Hewett portrayed this development as his own choice; "let's hog the whole thing for the Southwest Society this time," he wrote Lummis, "and get generous later on when we can better afford it."[86] In any event, the exposure of the Puyé ruins as a tourist attraction was the principal goal of the Santa Fe Society, and as yet they had no facilities in town to store or display artifact collections.

The final results of the Puyé work were mixed. Nearly the entire south house was cleared, producing "not less than 3000 museum specimens" to be shipped to Los Angeles, including "pottery, stone and bone implements, flutes," and what Hewett called a "fine ceremonial set." In scientific terms the Puyé work was to produce, by Morley's hand, the first substantive report of an excavation of an ancestral Tewa pueblo. For their contribution the Southwest Society published Morley's opus in their new publication series and received the entire collection of specimens.[87] Plans for a grand excursion faded, however, as did the promise to work elsewhere on the Pajarito. Despite Hewett's insistence that their efforts to encourage "individual visitation" had been successful, the frantic summer schedule had prevented him from maximizing the publicity value of the work as he had intended.

At summer's end Hewett had established the Institute as one of the principal arbiters of Southwest archaeology, a position equaled only by the Bureau. He had demonstrated an ability to negotiate with a number of parties simultaneously to accomplish a common goal; the Colorado and Utah projects had been successful, and more fieldwork was promised. The field school had also worked well, and Hewett was to find much use for Kidder and Morley in subsequent years. On a personal level Hewett had supplanted Palmer as the field agent for the Southwest Society and looked to turn that connection to his advantage. In his end-of-season report to Kelsey his sense of satisfaction was palpable.[88]

Ultimately, however, friction between the local organizations was also not as easy to suppress as Hewett had hoped. The constant maneuvering to hold the coalition together resulted in ill feeling at season's end, a pattern that was to be as much a Hewett trademark as his frenetic travel schedule. The members of the Santa Fe Archaeological Society failed to express much interest in linking themselves to the Institute, either through incorporation into the Southwest Society or through direct affiliation with the national organization, although they did discuss the issue.[89] In correspondence with Hewett over the affair Lummis made it clear that his principal interest in absorbing the Santa Fe group was to reserve the best archaeological finds from the region for his own museum. "We could also contribute to them some of our own exchange articles from this region," he wrote, "as compensation for taking the cream from New Mexico."[90] Such condescension may have been sensed by McFie and his associates, for the matter was quietly dropped. Rivalry between the local societies, which had first been glimpsed between the Southwest Society and the San Francisco Society in 1905, was to be a recurrent feature of the Southwest work despite Hewett's attempts to coordinate effort.

Despite new artifacts and research materials, the impact of the Puyé work on the Southwest Society was largely negative, an outcome that reflected both the internal politics of the organization and dissatisfaction with Lummis's grand plan. Palmer, who only the previous winter had expressed gratitude for Hewett's assistance in Arizona, now realized that his own position was threatened. His response, according to Lummis, was to announce that "not to save the life of the whole Executive Committee would he mend one piece of these broken potteries sent by Hewett."[91] Dissatisfaction with the quality of the Puyé materials was expressed by others on the board of the Southwest Society, including Mary Foy, who had contributed the funds for the excavations and subsequently allied herself with Palmer. Over the next two years the Los Angeles organization was increasingly polarized between Lummis and Palmer, with the founder of the society forced to respond to charges that the Puyé funds had been mismanaged. Despite the fact that he had impressed upon Hewett the importance of artifacts for display, Lummis had to use Hewett's own arguments for the scientific and touristic importance of the project in his own defense.

> In the first place, the work was done in the proper way—not gophering for Museum relics and leaving a tousled graveyard behind; but incovering [sic] the

noble ruin and leaving every door, window, and fireplace visible in 120 rooms. There it stands a prehistoric American "city" for future generations to see—and hundreds of travelers are now visiting this monument to the work of the Southwest Society on that great plateau in New Mexico while the beautiful and curious artifacts from these old homes are on view in our Museum exhibit.[92]

In the complaints of the board of the Southwest Society over Puyé can also be detected a concern that the project itself was not in accord with the ambitions of southern Californians. Lummis's vision of Los Angeles as the capital of a greater Southwest, bringing together areas with shared Hispanic and Native American heritage, did not prove as popular with his constituents as he had hoped. The cultural identity of the West Coast was evolving in a different direction, and Lummis's success in "catching our archaeology alive" did not readily translate to support for excavating antiquities in a place hundreds of miles away which few Californians had ever seen. Ironically, the lack of interest in "classical" archaeology Lummis had pointed out to Seymour was echoed by limited curiosity over anything not immediately relevant to everyday experience. For the backers of the Southwest Society, the museum was the important thing, not what went in it, and as the decade wore on Lummis had little time to pursue any other angles. He eventually defeated his opponents and forced Palmer and Foy to resign, but the fieldwork program of the Southwest Society was put on hold. Despite his personal desires and Hewett's continued lobbying, it would be years before Lummis was again able to convince his board to fund major excavations in the Southwest.

Despite the fact that the "western idea" had originated with Lummis, then, it was Hewett who took the concept to the next level. The fieldwork coalition represented a compromise between local interests and national priorities, a model Lummis's intense partisanship would not have allowed to succeed. With the 1907 season behind him, Hewett took the logical next step: turning the School of American Archaeology, which existed only as a field program and a plank in the American Committee's platform, into a reality.

The School of American Archaeology

The debate over the School of American Archaeology began among professional archaeologists within the councils of the Institute but quickly spread to boosters and other residents of the civic centers of the Southwest. To the scholarly community, the issues concerning the location, administration, and program of the school were those of control. The training of students and the coordination of research would have a direct impact on American archaeology and were a source of contention between the humanities-oriented scholars of the Institute, anthropologists in the universities and private museums of the East, and the government scientists of the Smithsonian. To westerners, the school represented the promise of institutions with national sponsorship, boosting prestige and promoting local participation in scientific exploration. Competitive forces, each with a distinct agenda, thus shaped the discussion and through it the structure of Southwest archaeology as the end of the first decade of the century approached.

Even though the various factions within the Institute were in accord on the need for a School of American Archaeology, conflict quickly emerged over its location. The possibility of such a school was one matter Hewett had discussed with the local societies during his fellowship year, and it is clear that he had always perceived the institution as a complement to his western programs.[93] The professional archaeologists within the American Committee, however, had other plans. As early negotiations over the school progressed through 1906 Bowditch became the leading advocate for a site in Mexico City, from which his program of Central American research could be pursued. Bowditch contacted the Carnegie Foundation for a grant to study the Mexico City site but quickly ran into opposition from Kelsey, who saw in the maneuver a threat to the decision-making structure of the Institute. Arguing that the conflict was due to "the anomaly of having an amateur at the head of an important scientific committee of a scientific organization," Kelsey came out against Bowditch and the Mexico site. After a series of meetings and memos it was agreed to postpone any action on the School until the end of 1907.[94]

In the meantime the initiative shifted to the western societies, which began individual lobbying campaigns to bring the school to their communities. Santa Fe, Los Angeles, and various Colorado cities had been mentioned as possible sites, both because of the high local interest in archaeology and because Hewett used the promise of the school to shore up his support among the affiliates as he passed through. The school thus became another topic of contention between the organizations. Lummis in particular saw the establishment of any such institution in the Southwest outside Los Angeles as a threat to the jurisdiction of the Southwest Society, and warned that if the Institute placed its school elsewhere they would build one of their own.[95] Political influence was brought to bear where possible, and a proposal from the Santa Fe Archaeological Society to place the school in New Mexico was followed by a personal plea to Kelsey from the governor of New Mexico, Herbert J. Hagerman, a member of the Society and the son of a University of Michigan alumnus. Touting the proximity of Santa Fe to the archaeologically significant districts of the Southwest as well as the historic character of the city, the proposal also offered the enticement of a headquarters in the Palace of the Governors, the former seat of civil authority in the state and a prominent public building. "From assurances which have been given," stated the proposal, "there is no doubt that the Territory would be willing to give this building as a free gift to the Archaeological Institute on condition that a School of American Archaeology be maintained in it." For his part, Governor Hagerman noted the local public's interest in archaeology and that placing the school outside the United States, as he understood had been "suggested," would be an unfortunate choice.[96]

Rather than expedite the selection process, however, the generous offer of the Palace seems to have awakened the Institute to the possibility of obtaining concessions from potential bidders. Direct financial support from the Institute would be modest in any event, and substantial local patronage would be required to make the school a success. Kelsey also told Hewett that obtaining further "incentives" would assist them in defeating the Bowditch plan, which had become more formidable with the addition of Franz Boas to those in favor of the Mexico City site.[97] It was ironic that the professionally oriented Boas, who shared an appreciation for the importance of Latin American research, was prepared to make common cause with Bowditch despite the latter's amateur status, while the more publicly oriented Kelsey took the opposite view. In any event Boas's advocacy of Mexico City sharpened the divide between the academic anthropologists on the committee and those, including Fletcher and Lummis, who backed Hewett. Putnam, who wrote to Kelsey of his regret that the Pueblo Bonito excavations of six years before hadn't been transformed into such a school, remained on the fence, but as it became clear that the debate really concerned control of the Institute's American agenda attitudes hardened all around.[98]

The New Mexico territorial legislature's passage of legislation turning the Palace over to the Institute only emboldened Hewett to ask for more. "It is now time for you to butt in," he wrote Lummis, while requesting that McFie look into the possibility of additional financial support.[99] Rumors circulated that a $500,000 endowment would be made available if the school was located in Colorado, while an offer came from the president of the fledgling University of New Mexico in Albuquerque to house the school there.[100] With increasing discord within the American committee and Hewett distracted by another round of lobbying over the regulations intended to enforce the Lacey Act, the matter slid into abeyance.

The event that showed the strength of the western societies and doomed the Mexico plan came at the end of 1907, when the Institute was thrown into disarray by the sudden death of President Seymour. Despite the opposition of the New

England academics who had controlled the Institute since its founding, Kelsey was able to rally western support amid the confusion and have himself elected as Seymour's successor. "The vote was exactly a tie," Hewett wrote Lummis, "when the bunch of proxies from the Southwest dropped in the hat and it was all up . . . Your misspent life is redeemed."[101] Kelsey, who had chafed under the previous regime and at one point during the wrangle with Bowditch had threatened to resign, would put the weight of the presidency behind the affiliate system he had built up.[102]

The westerners were quick to grasp that the change in leadership meant increased support for their goals. In a general letter to his membership, Lummis wrote that "the work of the Southwest Society in the last few years had its fruition in an entire change of policy of this foremost scientific body in America."[103] The ascendance of Kelsey finalized the alliance between Hewett and the humanities-oriented scholars of the Institute and effectively eliminated the influence of the university anthropologists within the organization. With the leadership of the Institute now dominated by supporters of a Southwest site for the School, Bowditch and Boas quietly shelved the Mexico plan, and while they remained on the committee, neither man was assigned a place on the school's new managing committee when it was created.

In February 1908 Hewett toured the western cities yet again, reassembling the fieldwork coalition, stumping for the School and continuing his quest for an endowment. For the first time, he also suggested that a museum would be an important part of the arrangement. This appealed to the Santa Fe lobby, since the modest facilities of the New Mexico Historical Society were too small to exhibit or store the large quantities of antiquities that were expected once community involvement in archaeology increased.[104] It was also an indication that Hewett was learning from Lummis, using the appeal of museums and related institutions to bolster his local constituency. With the national battle largely won, he returned to the cultural nationalist rhetoric that had been used so effectively by his allies and had played such a major part in the Chaco Canyon campaign. "The time has come for the West to build up its own museums and educational institutions," he wrote Virginia McClurg the following year. "It is fitting that they should look toward the higher culture of their own people."[105]

Summer 1908 marked the high point of Hewett's coalition of regional archaeological societies and Institute affiliates. The Colorado Society again contributed for the McElmo work, even issuing a brochure for the benefit of its members who wished to visit the area.[106] Additional sponsors included the Colorado Historical Society and the State University of Colorado. Work in Utah continued, with A. V. Kidder serving as nominal director but with most of the responsibility in Cummings's hands. The Santa Fe Society, with assurances that a share of the artifacts would remain in the planned museum, supported excavations at the Rito de los Frijoles in association with the Peabody Museum. With the collapse of Southwest Society support Hewett had prevailed upon Alfred Tozzer himself to participate in a party that included fellow Harvard anthropologist Roland B. Dixon in addition to Kidder and Morley. "There are no Fletchers this year," Tozzer reported to Putnam, as they searched for artifacts and burials in ruins on the canyon floor.[107]

In the fall, with artifacts from the Frijoles excavations in Santa Fe and exhibit space under preparation, Hewett made yet another tour of inspection, this time in the company of Alice Fletcher. Fletcher was received with great fanfare, with the *Santa Fe New Mexican* describing her as a scientist and author, "a woman of marked and recognized executive ability." Most important, however, was her avowed support for American work, said to date from "the days when the leaders of classical culture in this country insisted that there was no archaeology outside of the classic realms of the Old World."[108]

Fêted by the Santa Fe Archaeological Society and assured by its leaders of imminent legislative action on behalf of the proposed museum, Fletcher and Hewett left Santa Fe with the fate of the School largely decided. A few weeks later the American Committee met in Boston and, over the continuing objections of Boas and Bowditch, accepted the offer to place the School in the Palace of the Governors in Santa Fe.[109]

At the end of the 1908 season Hewett submitted a report to the Council of the Institute that was his manifesto for a new way of conducting Southwest archaeology.[110] He had spent the five years since leaving the Normal School creating a niche for himself in the increasingly professional scholarly world of American archaeology, and had pursued many angles. In the "western idea" of Charles Lummis and the Southwest Society, however, Hewett found a model for archaeology that would, he believed, advance education, further regional agendas, and provide sufficient scope for his own ambitions.

Hewett's report discussed the scientific accomplishments of his coalition, but his primary emphasis was on organization. Rejecting the professional argument for concentration of scholarship in a few universities and training programs, he argued that it was "the establishment of relations with the educational and scientific forces of the states" that would do the most for the promotion of archaeological research. Using what he called the "healthy activity" of the western societies under his organization as an example, Hewett advocated a decentralized system of scholarship in which national bodies such as the Institute played the role of coordinator. Such a network would promote the establishment of museums and other educational institutions throughout the country. "The question of the wise use of museum material," Hewett wrote, "so as to make it serve the greatest good of the greatest number, is one that demands to be considered."

Emphasizing regional issues and education in archaeology would require reordering of priorities. As an example, Hewett described his recent campaign at the Rito de los Frijoles, during which time he supervised the reconstruction of one of the prehistoric dwellings lining the canyon walls for the edification of visitors. Typical artifacts of the period were to be displayed inside, with the entire exhibition intended to illustrate for the tourist the context for the material that had been excavated there and would be eventually displayed in the museum in Santa Fe. "The educational value of our American ruins to the whole people can be vastly increased by the use of this idea," Hewett wrote. "It is the beginning of the field museum in our country."

Hewett's conclusion, that "there can be no question as to the wisdom of this policy," was a gauntlet thrown down to the professional community. With western dominance of the Institute, a western setting for the School of American Archaeology, and a research program catering to the needs and ambitions of local western archaeological societies, Hewett was poised to refocus American archaeology as a whole. To his audiences in the Southwest, the people who traveled by mule across the mesas and crept down cliffside trails to have picnics at the Rito de los Frijoles and prospect among the ruins, Hewett's ambitions reflected their own priorities. In contrast, the response of his rivals in the academic community to this manifesto would illustrate contrasting goals, the tension between the two demonstrating that for archaeologists the Southwest would continue to be contested ground.

4

Archaeology as Anthropology

The Huntington Southwest Survey

The end of the first decade of the twentieth century was perceived by many in the developing community of professional American archaeology as a time of crisis. One anthropologist, returning from a Washington meeting in 1912, reported that "Fewkes, Holmes, and others were lamenting the decline of archaeology in America in contrast to the very great advance in ethnology."[1] The achievements of the preceding years, which had established archaeology as a part of the national scientific agenda, were increasingly forgotten as the generation of scholars who had made those discoveries grew older. In contrast, ethnology had been invigorated, principally due to the efforts of Franz Boas and his students, and was expanding in influence. In Boas's vision of anthropology as the coordinated study of humanity archaeology was the weak link, and he considered only a few American archaeologists capable of productive scholarship.[2] As his students finished their studies at Columbia and took up university posts, archaeologists in the old power centers of Washington and Cambridge perceived the waning of their influence and the increasing disregard for their accomplishments.

This sense of lost ground was in part a result of the process of professionalization and in part a result of the older generation's failure to establish a rationale for archaeology in the face of intellectual and social change. As the first decade of the century drew to a close Frederic Putnam, Jesse Fewkes, and W. H. Holmes remained the pivotal figures in American archaeology but were themselves products of a preprofessional age. Despite the fact that the Bureau of American Ethnology and the U. S. National Museum continued to be centers of scholarly activity, the government science model on which they were based was thirty years old and dated to a time before the expansion of the American university system and the rising demand for a formal training regime within anthropology.[3] Of the three, only Putnam devoted attention to training students, with mixed results. With a background that favored experiential learning and high personal motivation he was ill prepared to supervise a rigorous academic regime such as the one Boas had designed at Columbia. John Reed Swanton, who had participated in the Hyde Expedition while a student at Harvard, described graduate study there in 1900 as eclectic and disorganized. Swanton's doctoral examination consisted largely of random and unrelated questions from Putnam and Charles Bowditch, a process faculty member Frank Russell called "foolish."[4] Only after Roland Dixon and Alfred Tozzer rose to positions of authority on the Harvard faculty was a more formal educational regime established. In the meantime students of Boas were pursuing ambitious research agendas of their own from within newly established university posts, as was the case with Alfred Kroeber at Berkeley.

Inadequate training programs affected archaeology's position within the structure of the profession. But the absence of a clear rationale for the study of American antiquity posed an equally serious problem. At a time when ethnologists were turning their attention to issues of the organization of human culture, archaeologists' preoccupation with pottery and burials was increasingly viewed by their colleagues as antiquarian pedantry. The rhetoric of cultural nationalism and the community-based scholarship being promoted by Edgar Lee Hewett and Charles Lummis also had little appeal to scholars in eastern institutions, except as a political foil to use against rivals closer to home. What archaeologists in universities and at public museums faced was the challenge of building a rationale for archaeological scholarship that would be a component of the larger agenda of anthropology and a "scientific" alternative to the populist, humanistic approach being promoted through the School of American Archaeology.

Just as the Southwest had been the scene of new, professional initiatives in the 1890s, so it offered an opportunity for the development of a new rationale for American archaeology in the 1910s. Fittingly, this effort rose from the ashes of the Hyde Exploring Expedition and was directed from the chair once occupied by Putnam at the American Museum of Natural History in New York. As Hewett was consolidating his gains in Santa Fe and promoting his agenda on the national stage, his former rivals in New York were developing a research strategy designed to reestablish archaeology within the scholarly discipline of anthropology. Like the "western idea," what was later termed the "chronological revolution" had its origins in specific social contexts and was shaped by relations of patronage, professional ambitions, and institutional competition. Although its impact on American archaeology was profound, it had particular significance for the Southwest, the site of its most notable successes and the principal stage on which the strategy was put into motion. The effects of decisions made in New York were manifest in dusty ruins in New Mexico, leaving a legacy of continuing relevance to Southwest archaeology in the modern era.

Clark Wissler and Anthropology at the American Museum

The event that propelled the American Museum of Natural History back into the field of Southwest archaeology was, ironically, the final collapse of the Hyde Exploring Expedition in 1909. The hiatus in Southwest research that followed the end of fieldwork at Chaco Canyon in 1901 illustrated the weakness of the old patronage system, since the influence of Talbot Hyde and George Pepper effectively prevented the department of anthropology from undertaking any new southwestern initiatives while they remained associated with the museum.[5] This had been a source of considerable frustration for Boas and for his successor Clark Wissler, since during the same time period their rivals, particularly George Dorsey at the Field Columbian Museum, were mounting their own Southwest projects. "While the Messrs. Hyde have provided abundantly for archaeological investigation in New Mexico," Dorsey flattered his patron, Chicago industrialist Stanley McCormick, "I am sure their support has not been so generous as yours."[6]

Through the lean years following Boas's departure Wissler had learned patience and the political skills necessary to juggle the research and educational missions of the American Museum. Wissler's personal background, ironically, was similar to that of Hewett. Both men had been born and raised in small midwestern farming communities (Wissler in Indiana, Hewett in Illinois), and had begun their careers in education. Wissler taught school for five years, studying at Purdue in the summers and then at Indiana University. Unlike Hewett, who saw graduate education largely as a means to an end, Wissler took his advanced studies seriously, and after a short stint teaching at Ohio State he went to Columbia University to study with psychologist James McKeen Cattell. There he met Boas, from whom he took several courses during his final year of doctoral study in 1901. Never a member of Boas's inner circle, Wissler nonetheless took a strong interest in anthropology, and when a more favored student backed out of a research expedition in the summer of 1902 Wissler was sent to the Dakotas to study Sioux decorative art on behalf of the American Museum.[7] Wissler remained associated with the institution for more than forty years, and his fierce loyalty and competitive instincts played a critical role in the development of the agenda for anthropology at the museum.

Wissler's vision for a museum-based anthropology integrated field research, collections acquisition, and exhibition. Rather than emphasize detailed, long-term studies of particular culture groups, as advocated by Boas, Wissler promoted cross-cultural research through the study of culture "traits."[8] Analysis of traits allowed for a focus on material objects: "We are giving our attention . . ." he wrote, "chiefly to the material culture and the arts—partly because they have been neglected and partly because they are nearer the province of a museum."[9] Acquisition of collections was thus a high priority. Wissler's own background made him sympathetic to the educational function of museums, and he anticipated an aggressive exhibition program in addition to collections-based research. He also had a talent for addressing the concerns of the different constituencies to which he was beholden. Early in his career Wissler cultivated the friendship of museum director Hermon Carey Bumpus, whose education-oriented policies had ultimately forced Boas to resign. Wissler's exhibit plans appealed to Bumpus, whose support for anthropology thus countered the indifference of museum president Henry Fairfield Osborn. Wissler was able to promote the professional goals of anthropology by conducting research conjointly with collecting expeditions. Although this was a traditional strategy of anthropological research and in outline resembled Putnam's program of the previous decade, Wissler's close coordination with the museum's administration greatly reduced the antagonism that had previously existed between scholarship and public programs.

With the obstacle of the Hyde cabal removed and even before Pepper's resignation was finalized Wissler began organizing a new Southwest expedition, which required assembling a professional staff, developing a research plan, and obtaining patronage. His close relationship with Bumpus meant that new staff positions were quickly made available. In hiring new personnel Wissler looked to members of his own professional cadre, people with sufficient university training to address the intellectual issues of anthropology and with their own links to the developing professional structure of the discipline. Before the end of January 1909, Wissler had recruited Herbert J. Spinden, a Harvard doctoral student who had recently conducted North American fieldwork for the American Museum; and Pliny Earle Goddard, an established scholar at the University of California.[10] The professional training of both men set them apart from previous staff appointments, and they were linked by training or experience to the three teaching centers of Columbia, Harvard, and Berkeley. Within this professional framework the members of the Museum's revived Southwest program formed the nucleus of a department whose thoroughly revamped structure represented a significant departure from previous years, and were well positioned to make the planned program of research a success.

A second obstacle to Wissler's ambitions was the disastrous decline in museum funding for anthropological research, which required him to seek support from outside sources.[11] Hyde and Pepper's departure had removed an impediment to the professional development of the department but also cut off access to the network of funding that had supported Southwest work in the past. Wissler's solution to this was to cultivate another patron, one with potentially far greater resources than Talbot Hyde had ever offered: Archer Milton Huntington.

Huntington was the adopted son of the founder of the Central Pacific Railroad, Collis P. Huntington.[12] He was born in 1870 and, while trained to follow his father in business, ultimately devoted his life to philanthropic pursuits. In an interesting parallel to Talbot Hyde, Archer Huntington also made a long and influential journey in 1892—not to Colorado's cliff dweller ruins, as Hyde had, but to Spain. A lifelong interest in Hispanic civilization was the result, and one of his major projects was the founding of the Hispanic Society of America in 1905. By that time Huntington was a productive and active promoter of science and culture in New York City, serving as the president of the American Geographical Society as well as the American Numismatic Society.[13]

Museum president Osborn began making overtures to Huntington early in 1909 in an effort to place people congenial to his interests on the Board of Trustees. Despite his disinclination to favor anthropology, Osborn realized that cultural concerns were more important to Huntington than strictly scientific matters. Wissler, for his part, was alert for an opportunity to attract Huntington patronage for the Southwest research program, since the Huntington family had supported California fieldwork organized by Franz Boas several years earlier.[14] When Huntington agreed to join the board and expressed a willingness to fund museum projects, Osborn and Wissler's objectives coincided. Osborn contacted the new patron, intimated that the Southwest plan was a prelude to a larger Latin American initiative, and captured Huntington's interest. By March 1909 Bumpus was able to write to Wissler with congratulations "upon the prospect which the kind and intelligent cooperation of Mr. Huntington in this department of your work holds forth." Three months later Wissler received a $5,000 check, and what was ultimately called the "Huntington Southwest Survey" came into being.[15]

Assured of financial support, Wissler designed the expedition to fulfill both scientific and educational priorities. Goddard, whose primary expertise was linguistics, was dispatched to study Athapaskan languages in the Southwest. Spinden's more broadly defined duties were "to work among the living tribes of the Southwest and to care for the archaeological collections from the same region," and he began his work in the Rio Grande pueblos in September 1909.[16] Both men were expected to acquire artifacts as part of their research, a course of action that emphasized the material culture orientation of the project and appealed to the trustees. "The collections received are most satisfactory demonstrations of the wisdom of this undertaking," read an early report on the work, which also looked forward to building an exhibit area for the new southwestern collections that would be both "architecturally attractive and of exceptional educational importance."[17]

The successful launch of the Huntington Southwest Survey reintegrated archaeology and anthropology in the research expeditions of the American Museum. In the tradition established by James Stevenson, Adolph Bandelier, and Frank Hamilton Cushing, Wissler's initiative was designed to collect linguistic, ethnographic, and archaeological information on the native peoples of the Southwest.[18] Putnam's had always been biased in favor of archaeology, and the intellectual hostility that had grown up between his students and the Boasians at the American Museum concerned whether archaeology or ethnology was at the core of the discipline. Wissler, an ethnologist who had been interested in archaeology since exploring an "ancient Indian village" near his childhood home, saw the two as complementary.[19] Wissler also avoided the pitfalls of patronage that had dogged the Hyde Expedition, since Huntington played no direct role in fieldwork or collecting. Within the museum the funds were administered by a "Committee on the Primitive Peoples of the Southwest" that had only Huntington and another trustee as members, providing Wissler with a freer hand than his predecessors had been permitted.[20]

Although Wissler's efforts reinvigorated the American Museum's Southwest program, they did not represent a significant departure from tradition, and it was only after visiting the Southwest himself that Wissler grasped the character of the region and its importance for particular anthropological issues. With Goddard and Spinden in the field, Wissler himself went west in autumn 1909, both to inspect the progress of the work and to conduct ethnographic research of his own. In the several months he was absent from New York, Wissler corresponded extensively with Bumpus, passing along research plans, ideas for exhibits, and observations on southwestern life. He also familiarized himself with the competition among Southwest anthropologists and their respective institutions. Relations between scholars and curio dealers remained close, and the purchase of collections from such prominent merchants as the Fred Harvey Company's Indian Department became one focus of this rivalry.[21] The wealth of George Heye made his emissaries particularly formidable, and despite the backing of Huntington, Wissler felt that many archaeological and ethnographic artifacts were being snapped up ahead of him.[22]

The rise of the regional societies was another new factor in the Southwest. In Los Angeles Wissler visited Lummis and Hector Aliot (Frank Palmer's successor as curator of the Southwest Museum) and was invited to review their plans for the new museum building. Lummis made his philosophy clear: "He wanted to see a museum for the boys and girls of Los Angeles County, not for scientists of any kind and certainly not for any fool anthropologist who happened to stray into it," Wissler wrote Bumpus.[23] Despite the professional community's opposition to the cultural nationalism of the Southwest Society and similar organizations, issues concerning museums and education were common to both camps, and Wissler made a serious evaluation of Lummis's activities and the impact they would have on future research in the region.

In the course of his travels, Wissler gained a thorough understanding of the dynamics of anthropological scholarship in the West, made the personal acquaintance of some of the major players, and developed new ideas for ways southwestern data could be brought to bear on the central questions of American anthropology. With a regular flow of artifacts expanding the museum's collections and information pouring in from Goddard and Spinden, his next goal was to enhance the Survey's professional goals by adding a more sophisticated element to the project—what later generations would call a "problem orientation." Moving beyond satisfying patrons and building collections for inductive research, Wissler saw the Southwest as providing an opportunity not present elsewhere in North America, a chance to resolve some of the questions of population and chronology that had vexed American anthropology from the beginning. Wissler's new initiative, which he began working on the moment he returned to New York in spring 1910, was to have a dramatic impact both on Southwest archaeology and on the intellectual development of the discipline as a whole.

Archaeology, Chronology, and the Southwest

Establishing a chronology for the human occupation of the Americas had preoccupied scholars since well before anthropology began to emerge as a profession. The rise of Darwinian theory in the mid-nineteenth century and the subsequent search for an "American Paleolithic" provoked a debate over archaeological evidence and interpretation that continued to rage sixty years later.[24] As Wissler and other ethnologists after the turn of the century studied the distribution of cultural traits among Native American peoples, it became obvious that changes in the spatial distribution of these features over time would have to be understood before they could be explained. Chronology was thus a critical factor but controlling for it in an age when a standard set of methods and strategies had yet to be developed remained an uncertain proposition.

After 1910 ethnologists interested in the distribution of cultural traits began to call for a new rationale for archaeology, one that would provide the chronological information needed to complete their studies.[25] This involved reconceptualizing the scientific value of American antiquities. "Archaeology is not . . ." Wissler wrote Bumpus, "a thing of itself; it is only a method of investigating cultures by the spade and the scoop. I am sorry to say that in America some, who ought to know better, think the whole thing is digging up pots and gloating."[26] Although Putnam and his contemporaries had been aware of the temporal significance of their work, their theoretical frameworks and unsystematic approach to archaeological resources had not allowed them to make a substantial contribution to the subject. Some archaeologists working in North America, such as Max Uhle, had taken an interest in chronology, but circumstances had prevented their work from being widely influential.[27] Ironically, it was pressure from ethnologists, rather than from within the archaeological community itself, that stirred interest in chronological applications.

What Wissler had found in the Southwest was the opportunity to conduct archaeological research focusing on the chronological issue, and he proposed to incorporate this focus in the research agenda of the Huntington Survey. Somewhere in North America, he had told Bumpus, anthropologists needed to find "a long base line from the present to great antiquity by which to be guided, and to serve as a gyroscope." In the ruined pueblos of the Rio Grande, with their similarity to modern native communities and their association with abandoned churches of the early historic period, Wissler believed he had found such a baseline. Despite the debunking of mound-builder myths and other "lost tribe" theories, in much of the country the connection between historic Native Americans and archaeological sites remained controversial; such associations, Wissler believed, were much clearer in the Southwest. With the appropriate methods and the careful selection of sites for excavation, he argued, the Huntington Survey would be in a position to conduct "a timely and epoch-making bit of research" on the chronological question that would be a valuable contribution to both science and institutional prestige.[28]

The principal problem Wissler faced in implementing an archaeological strategy for the Huntington Survey was a shortage of staff. Spinden, despite his original charge, spent more time conducting ethnological research in the pueblos than pursuing archaeology, and in any event had what Wissler referred to as a "tendency to yield to discouragement" that may have made him unsuitable for the new scheme. The only other archaeologist in the museum, Harlan Smith, was a survivor of the Putnam regime whose research interests were largely confined to the Northwest Coast and Great Plains.[29] Wissler had also lost ground with the museum administration when his friend and supporter Hermon Bumpus resigned under a cloud in the summer of 1910. To replace Bumpus as director Osborn hired the biologist Frederick A. Lucas, who was not expected to be as friendly to anthropology as his predecessor had been.[30] Wissler returned to patient politics and sought out common ground. Since both Osborn and Lucas had interests in human evolution and thus in the European Paleolithic, he proposed that the museum hire an archaeologist who had expertise in that area and who could assist Osborn in planning research and associated exhibitions. This individual would also, in Wissler's calculation, participate in the Huntington Survey and thus conduct the desired chronological studies.

Wissler's attempt to get an Old World prehistorian for the Department of Anthropology was clearly a subterfuge, but the expectations raised over the new post were to prove critical both to the Museum's projects and to Southwest archaeology. Osborn was intrigued by the idea, and late in 1910 the search began in earnest. Between Wissler and Osborn, the new archaeologist would have two entrenched superiors whose expectations would be formidable and who would subject him to competing demands. In a day when anthropology graduate programs remained small and finding even a single qualified candidate challenging, locating an individual with the breadth of experience and appropriate skills required by the American Museum was a difficult task.[31] In their search, Wissler

and Goddard made full use of the professional network, and in a short time settled upon one candidate they thought capable of the job: Nels C. Nelson.

Nels Christian Nelson was born on a farm near Fredericia, Denmark, and emi-
grated to America in 1892 to work on the farm of an aunt living in Minnesota.[32]
There he learned English, attended school, and aspired to the ministry. Instead
of enrolling in a nearby college, however, Nelson traveled to California, where he
worked various jobs and spent time at Stanford before switching to the University
of California. On completion of his undergraduate work in 1907 Nelson opted to
pursue graduate study in anthropology rather than attend a Unitarian seminary
as originally planned, describing the scope of his new interest to be "as wide as
human nature itself." A later observer remarked on Nelson's pragmatic, empirical
orientation. "Nels was always scientific, in his approach to everything. Obviously
there was something in his character that was there from the beginning."[33]

In the course of his studies at Berkeley, Nelson was influenced by Alfred
Kroeber and, perhaps more influentially, John Campbell Merriam, a national
authority on vertebrate paleontology and historical geology. Nelson eventually
worked for Kroeber as an assistant curator and instructor at the university
museum but it was Merriam who, by inviting him along on a 1906 reconnaissance of shell mounds in northern California, introduced him to archaeology.
Merriam had also been the backer of Max Uhle's earlier excavations in the shell
mounds, and his geologist's concern for stratigraphic relationships is arguably
the root of many of the methodological innovations linked with both men.[34]

At Merriam's instigation Nelson spent most of his summers locating and
excavating shell mounds along San Francisco Bay and associated waterways.
During the winter he taught courses for Kroeber and worked in the museum.[35]
After four years at Berkeley he had acquired considerable field and museum experience, making him a prime candidate for a higher position elsewhere. A tight
web of professional ties linked the University of California with the American
Museum, and in early 1911 Merriam was contacted about Nelson's fitness for the
planned position.[36] Despite Nelson's lack of personal familiarity with prehistoric
Europe, Goddard and Wissler convinced Osborn that he was the appropriate candidate. When Harlan Smith resigned to take a job in Canada the way became
clear, and Nelson was hired before the end of the year.[37]

Wissler immediately moved to put Nelson in the field in the Southwest and
to begin the chronological project. To keep from antagonizing Kroeber, however,
Nelson did not leave California until the end of the academic year, spending the
interim months familiarizing himself with the anthropological literature on the

Southwest and exchanging letters with his new employers. Wissler proposed "to excavate some of the sites abandoned about the time of the Spanish occupation and correlating the results of these with Dr. Spinden's work on the living peoples to establish, if possible, a base line or level; then to excavate some of the assumed older sites."[38] The critical issue was thus where to excavate, a decision constrained partially by the nature of the data, and partially by political considerations. Concentration on the link between historic and prehistoric periods meant that the work would be restricted to the Rio Grande region, where Spinden's efforts had been concentrated. The Rio Grande valley, however, was relatively distant from the area of the Museum's previous archaeological work at Chaco Canyon, and being more heavily populated presented issues of access different from those faced by the earlier generation.

The Rio Grande region was also the archaeological domain of the School of American Archaeology, and in planning work there Wissler was placing his new anthropological rationale for archaeology in direct juxtaposition with the populist archaeology of Edgar Lee Hewett. Wissler wanted neither to cross Hewett nor to alert other professional competitors, whom he thought might "seize upon the problem themselves," so he cautiously solicited advice from trusted colleagues.[39] After floating a number of possibilities Wissler focused on the Galisteo Basin, a comparatively unstudied area south of Santa Fe rich in archaeological potential but close enough to the city to simplify logistics. Several villages had existed in the Galisteo at the time of the first Spanish entradas, but warfare and disease had resulted in the virtual abandonment of the basin within a hundred years. Both Spinden and Goddard had visited the area and reported vast pueblo ruins with the remains of masonry and adobe missions nearby. The Galisteo Basin offered great potential for the linkage of the ethnographic present with the prehistoric past, and had the advantage of being unclaimed by Hewett or any other archaeological interests.[40]

With the general plan in place, Nelson's first responsibility was to familiarize himself with the Southwest in person, and he arrived in the region in late May 1912. He was accompanied by his new wife, Ethelyn, who had been Alfred Kroeber's secretary, and the two traveled slowly up the Rio Grande from El Paso to Albuquerque, examining sites and collecting information. The people they met in the small valley towns and ranches along the way had considerable knowledge about antiquities and long experience with archaeologists. Nelson's journal relates a discussion with a Major Van Patten, of the town of Las Cruces, an "old scout guide, soldier, etc." who allowed that he had known both Bandelier and Cushing. "Van P. holds the Apache to be Chinese and the Navahoes to be Norwegian. He also claims the prehist. Amer. worked iron. . . . He speaks 5 Indian languages & is 'Chief' of the 'Federation' that fought Montezuma and later revolted against the Spaniards. . . . Actual information is difficult to get from him because he is prejudiced against Eastern Institutions."[41] Despite such dubious guides the Nelsons managed to visit many large and small ruins along the Rio Grande before meeting Wissler in Santa Fe in midsummer, and arrived considerably more familiar with the task ahead than when they had set out.

Nelson was the representative of the Huntington Survey in the field, but the intellectual and political authority for the expedition rested with Wissler, and his appearance in Santa Fe was intended to make that point to local interests. In any event Hewett was in Europe, and when he returned on July 16 Wissler found him to be "amicably disposed" toward the American Museum's intentions.[42] Hewett had always preferred a veneer of cooperation with even his principal institutional rivals, and since his own field research continued to focus on the Pajarito Plateau to the northwest, there would be little overlap of their spheres of interest. Throughout the summer relations between the American Museum and the School of American Archaeology would be polite but remote, the political relationship matching the intellectual distance between the different paradigms represented by the two institutions.

When the time came to put the research strategy into action, however, it became evident that neither Nelson nor Wissler knew what to expect, nor what methods would be useful in deriving chronological information from archaeological remains. They had decided to begin work at Pueblo San Cristóbal, one of the most prominent of the Galisteo Basin sites, with standing remnants of an early Spanish mission preserved adjacent to a substantial pueblo occupied in both historic and prehistoric times (fig. 4.1). The site was owned by a prominent politician, Senator B. F. Pankey, who favored the work and would provide logistical support. San Cristóbal was a vast ruin, and Nelson's experience with shell mounds had not prepared him for the complexities of stone and mud architecture. He later confided to Kroeber that he had hoped "to be turned loose on some simple isolated ruin, without any big problems to it." But with only the most general instructions to follow, Nelson was expected to call upon his archaeological expertise to develop the method that would produce the desired chronological results.[43]

Nelson's work at San Cristóbal quickly demonstrated the complexity of turning an abstract concern with site chronology into practical results. The site was located in a shallow valley backed against a series of low, forested ridges along the east rim of the open basin. More than a dozen cactus-studded and apparently multistoried roomblocks arranged around plazas were visible on both sides of a small stream, as was a tall, masonry remnant of the seventeenth-century mis-

Figure 4.1   Excavations at Pueblo San Cristóbal, ca. 1912.
(Photograph by Nels Nelson; courtesy American Museum of Natural History Library)

sion. For a camp the Nelsons set up a tent in the lee of a hill, using an adjacent rock shelter as a kitchen. Supplies (including water, since the creek was bad) were brought by wagon from the village of Galisteo. In the beginning Nelson used a bicycle to get back and forth. Nearby ranches provided a pool of unskilled labor, and by the end of July ten men were on the crew. Despite the fact that surface indications proved no clear guide to the arrangement of buried architecture the work progressed with remarkable speed, with an average of ten rooms a day being cleared. "I have looked for the simplest buildings," Nelson wrote Goddard, "or those that seemed to offer the fewest difficulties." Mrs. Nelson assisted in the correspondence and record-keeping, on some occasions supervising the crew when her husband was called elsewhere.[44]

Unlike the popularly oriented fieldwork being conducted by Hewett on the Pajarito Plateau the same summer, Nelson and Wissler preferred to conduct their research out of the public eye. Nelson's aversion to publicity was personal, but Wissler's intent to keep a low profile was in keeping with his conception of professional scholarship. The "public face" of the Huntington Survey was in the controlled environment of the American Museum's exhibit halls. The Galisteo Basin, in contrast, was the domain of research, where the distractions of local interest were to be avoided. The relative anonymity of the project also suited local archaeological interests, whose endeavors were underwritten by a loyal public. Wissler's research orientation was in this case perfectly compatible with Hewett's concern with dominating the regional spotlight. Its proximity to Santa Fe, however, meant that visitors regularly made their way to the site, and as a politician Senator Pankey saw the value of what Nelson called "taffy and advertisement."[45] Any deeper interaction with the public was discouraged.

Nelson's wrangling with the issue of chronology was expressed in his initial summaries of the San Cristóbal work, relayed to Wissler after six weeks of excavation. By that time 262 rooms had been excavated, many associated features cleared, and a trench put through the main refuse heap. Rather than focus on descriptions of rooms and their contents, as Pepper and Wetherill had at Pueblo Bonito, Nelson concerned himself primarily with the overall history of the site. Several building phases were evident, leading him to infer great antiquity for the ruin as a whole and a "decline" associated with the historic occupation.[46]

A more detailed accounting for these changes, however, was elusive. The complexity of immense ruins such as San Cristóbal made identifying fine-grained temporal variation difficult. Nelson was gradually discovering that traditional methods meshed poorly with the problem orientation of Wissler's project, and that a new approach to the southwestern archaeological record would be required to better address chronological questions.

In addition to his prodigious efforts at San Cristóbal, Nelson made excavations at seven other major ruins in the vicinity and visited still more. He also paid attention to the smallest category of archaeological information, the potsherds scattered by the thousands across the landscape. Interest in prehistoric pottery was spreading among southwestern archaeologists, with A. V. Kidder's ongoing dissertation research in particular focused on changes in ceramic style.[47] Nelson noticed variation in the types of pottery found on different sites but at first was uncertain as to its significance. Such a large body of data contained considerable chronological variation, and Nelson hoped to use it to identify the temporal patterns he was seeking.

The 1912 season of the Huntington Survey set a new standard for archaeological research and established the pattern for the American Museum's Southwest work for the next decade. By the time the Nelsons finally departed for New York in December, they had amassed a quantity of archaeological data greater than that produced by all previous projects in the Rio Grande combined. Compared to the more detailed but dilatory work of the Hyde Expedition at Chaco Canyon and Hewett's poorly documented excavations throughout the region, Nelson's methodical fieldwork represented a bold new approach. Although the chronological problem remained intractable, the general success of the season ensured that work would continue.

With different patrons, different attitudes toward the relationship between professionals and the public, and different rationales for archaeological research, the gulf between the Huntington Survey and the School of American Archaeology was wide. The concept of local control of archaeological resources that had brought about the collapse of the Pueblo Bonito excavations in 1900 was far from monolithic, and Wissler had negotiated the political terrain with sufficient skill to bring the American Museum back to Southwest archaeology after a hiatus of twelve years. The demands of the new problem-oriented professional research and the negotiations between Hewett and Wissler resulted in a *modus vivendi* that dominated archaeological research in the Southwest for decades. Eastern museums sponsored field teams that operated parallel to, but distinct from, archaeologists from the regional institutions. Interaction with the public was relatively limited. While excavations were extensive, the artifacts recovered were subjected to minimal analysis targeted at the professional community. Even the collection of exhibition-quality artifacts received less emphasis than they had a few years earlier. Nelson's goal was scientific research, and so long as the patron remained willing to support the effort, the Museum administration was prepared to acquiesce.

The success of Nelson's first season also transformed the organization of the larger project of which it was a part, ironically blunting hopes for a truly integrated anthropological project. Although originally planned as the centerpiece of the Huntington Survey, the integration of archaeological and ethnological information to compare historic and prehistoric pueblo "traits" in the Rio Grande region was never accomplished. While Spinden's collections made good exhibits, his research interests shifted to the Maya area and the study of Pueblo art and technology was never completed. Goddard's scholarship also proved relatively unproductive; he devoted much of his time to administrative matters. The museum had a number of ongoing research efforts, and for the time being Wissler was unable to find the funding or personnel to revive the ethnological component of the Huntington Survey. With archaeology producing the most tangible results, Wissler was willing to let it take precedence to ensure that Huntington funding was maintained.

Issues of personnel and patronage thus pushed Nelson's share of the Southwest project to center stage. Rather than pulling anthropology and archaeology together, however, the ultimate effect would be to drive them further apart. In another irony, it was not to be the vast quantity of data from the Galisteo work that suggested to Nelson the means to tackle the chronology problem, but the circumstances of his employment. President Osborn had not forgotten the arrangement that had brought Nelson to New York, and was shortly to assign him to an archaeological mission that would take him far from the Southwest. It was only there, exposed to new data and new ideas, that Nelson was to put together the ingredients that would lead to the "chronological revolution" in Southwest archaeology.

Cracking the "Southwest Problem"

While Nels Nelson was raising clouds of dust in the Galisteo Basin during the summer months of 1912, Henry F. Osborn was touring southern Europe and setting the agenda for an educational initiative that would involve his new archaeologist. Osborn was accompanied by George Grant MacCurdy of Yale, one of the few Americans familiar with European prehistory, and the two men toured cave sites in France and Spain in the company of some of Europe's premier archaeologists. In the northern Spanish province of Santander they visited Castillo Cave, then being excavated for the new Institute for Human Paleontology by Hugo Obermaier and the Abbé Breuil. The deep deposits at Castillo represented most of the cultural periods of the European Paleolithic, and Osborn saw them as important and tangible evidence for changes in human culture over time.[48]

Obermaier agreed to allow the American Museum to construct a model of the stratigraphy at Castillo Cave for a new exhibit on evolution. The project required detailed measurements, and Osborn turned at once to Nelson. Thus after only a few months in New York organizing the Galisteo Basin collections the new museum archaeologist found himself sailing to Europe at the end of April 1913.[49] It was a unique opportunity, since even at that time interaction between European and American scholars was infrequent.

Nelson spent two months working at Castillo, and what he learned there enhanced his appreciation of the potential of stratigraphic excavations for the establishment of relative chronologies.[50] It was generally accepted that stratigraphic layers in archaeological sites conformed to different temporal periods. In North America, however, sites that exhibited clear stratigraphy were rare, a phenomenon that had generated much debate about the antiquity of the human occupation of the Western Hemisphere. Max Uhle had reported stratigraphic relationships in the California shell mounds, but although Nelson observed layering during his work on the same sites, he was not entirely convinced that they represented cultural changes.[51] The European caves and rock shelters, however, were considered to provide the classic examples of stratigraphic deposits. With the "Southwest problem" on his mind, Nelson had a unique opportunity to see archaeological chronology worked out under ideal conditions.[52]

If he expected the relationship between stratigraphy and chronology at Castillo to be clear-cut, however, Nelson was in for a disappointment. "The whole thing looks more like a rock quarry than anything else," he wrote Wissler. "Blasting is continually necessary." The differences between the cultural strata were also hard to see, "not well enough differentiated," he continued, "as to color and composition."[53] Nelson nonetheless gamely measured the deposits and collected information for Osborn's exhibit, critically discussing the project and its implications with the other members of the excavation team, and over the course of the summer derived a different lesson from the excavations. After a tour of Paleolithic sites in France and England, Nelson was headed home by mid-September.

The idea Nelson carried home from Castillo was that the relationship between stratigraphy and artifact style held the key to establishing chronology. Despite the fact that the various strata were indistinguishable to the eye, the style of the artifacts within them was clearly different. Although the complex architectural remains of the pueblos of the Galisteo Basin provided very little in the way of stratigraphy, they did contain ceramics of distinctive style that differed from site to site. If this diversity could somehow be linked to an excavated sequence, it would then be possible to place the different types in chronological order. The regional distribution of particular ceramic types, then, held the clues to changing "traits" in prehistoric and historic southwestern society.[54]

The chance to apply the lessons of Castillo in the Galisteo Basin, however, did not come immediately, even though Wissler worked hard to maintain the momentum behind the Huntington Survey. Huntington had contributed another $5,000, and Nelson was sent west almost immediately upon his return. The 1913 season, however, was essentially intended to demonstrate the museum's commitment to the project and to wrap up details left unfinished the previous summer. Familiar with the routine, Nelson visited the sites of the Galisteo Basin once more, equipped with plane table and alidade, mapping until winter weather made further work impossible.[55]

It was not until the end of the 1914 season that the final piece of the chronological method fell into place. For most of the summer Nelson expanded upon his sample of regional sites, excavating in the pueblos of San Pedro Viejo and Tunque on the flanks of the Sandia mountains southwest of the Galisteo Basin (fig. 4.2). In November, however, he returned to Pueblo San Cristóbal and made a final excavation in the thick trash deposit adjacent to the ruin. "Nearly all of last week," he wrote, "was spent on the Pankey ranch, where with my own hands, I tried out a 3½ x 6½ ft. section to 10 ft. deep—of the largest refuse heap. The

Figure 4.2   Ethelyn Nelson excavating at Tunque, ca. 1914.
(Photograph by Nels Nelson; courtesy Division
of Anthropology Archives, American Museum
of Natural History)

results are data (of a nature suitable for graphic illustration) showing three suc-
cessive stages of pottery making."[56] There was no visible evidence of stratigraphic
layering in the deposit, but since he assumed that the refuse had built up over
time he guessed that the style of the artifacts found within it should reflect
change. Nelson excavated the deposit in arbitrary, one-foot levels, and then compared the artifacts found in the units to each other. In this way he was able to
place the different pottery types in chronological order—the deepest being the
earliest—which would allow him to develop an understanding of how sites in

the region related to each other over time on the basis of what artifacts they contained.

Word of the innovation spread quickly and boosted the prestige both of the Huntington Survey and of anthropology at the American Museum. A solution to the "Southwest problem," it was also a means to perpetuate the museum's involvement in the rich southwestern field. Nelson's emphasis on "graphic illustration" meant that he was aware of the significance of this discovery from the outset, the final piece of a carefully assembled argument that could be presented to a professional audience. In papers and an article combining the San Cristóbal stratigraphy with regional data collected during that and previous field seasons, Nelson was able to suggest a sequence of occupation for several sites on the basis of firm evidence. Kidder called Nelson's stratigraphic method "the most valuable discovery yet made in the Southwest and one which will be of tremendous importance."[57]

From Wissler's perspective, the new results vindicated three years of patient investigation, and he immediately moved to expand the project. "This is the first time a definite chronological sequence has been established for any part of the Southwest," he wrote Huntington, requesting funding for two more years of fieldwork.[58] The prestige of the discovery brought with it important intellectual capital that Wissler was prepared to use. In rapid succession, he formed an alliance with the University of Colorado for new archaeological work and laid plans for two new projects to reinvigorate the ethnological component of the Huntington Survey—one at Hopi, the other at Zuñi. Wissler also contacted A. E. Douglass, of the University of Arizona, about dating tree rings from wood found in archaeological contexts—correspondence that played a key role in the development of dendrochronology. As the Huntington Survey expanded, so the American Museum solidified its reputation as the center of professional anthropological research in the American Southwest.[59]

While Wissler saw the expansion of the Huntington Survey as a way to address important anthropological issues and enhance the influence of his institution, it had a severe impact on Nelson's own work. Applying the new chronological strategy would require excavations and collection of surface data at sites throughout the region. The sheer quantity of information involved would take many years to collect and more to process. Nelson's patient empiricism had borne fruit, and he expected that continued effort in the same vein would be the most productive form of scholarship. Wissler, however, needed someone to keep tabs on the different expedition teams, and he delegated this job to Nelson as the museum's senior representative in the field. Despite the perception that Nelson would somehow "manage" the various projects, authority remained firmly in

Wissler's hands; as a result Nelson not only found his time in the Southwest increasingly devoted to traveling between the different research sites but realized that he was not even in a position to make decisions regarding what he found. He spent the first part of the 1915 season making hurried excavations at Galisteo sites he had not studied before, in particular the major ruin of San Marcos, which in many respects resembled San Cristóbal in size and importance. But he was also obliged to travel to Colorado, where the young archaeologist Earl Morris, the University of Colorado's representative, was busy working on ruins along the La Plata; and then to hasten to Zuñi to check up on the work there.[60]

Despite its touted "problem orientation," in fact, from 1915 onward the Huntington Survey was driven more by competition and institutional priorities than by the demands of scholarship. Patronage in particular was at issue, since Huntington's contributions remained static even as the southwestern projects under the survey's banner proliferated. Wissler sought unceasingly for more museum funding but was rebuffed by Osborn, who saw the new efforts as deviating from the museum's own priorities. The rationale of the research was also increasingly difficult to maintain, since at first there was no chronological component to any of the work except for Nelson's. By keeping parties in the field and maintaining a high professional presence, Wissler sought to either force Osborn's hand or attract new funding. In the process, the core of the program became increasingly difficult to define.

Chronological archaeology continued to advance in 1915, but surprisingly the major contribution was made by Alfred Kroeber. Kroeber was on a sabbatical from the University of California that year, and asked for the opportunity to join one of the American Museum's expeditions. Wissler had need of Kroeber's expertise, and assigned the Zuñi project to him. Prior to the beginning of the season Nelson had spent a month in California writing up old shell mound reports and discussing the progress of his research with his former teacher. After he arrived at Zuñi Kroeber devoted himself to kinship studies as requested, but also spent time visiting archaeological sites near the village. He observed the same variation in pottery styles that Nelson had described for the Rio Grande, and was moved to tackle the chronological issue himself. Kroeber worked quickly, and before summer's end completed and mailed a manuscript on the subject to New York. "I believe you will think I have built high on a narrow foundation," Kroeber wrote. "I have. But outside of Nelson no one has yet really tackled the archaeological problem of the Southwest—unless my memory fails me badly—and I want at least to crack the ice."[61]

Kroeber's study, published as *Zuñi Potsherds,* used the statistical frequencies of different types of ceramics found at different sites to establish a relative chronological sequence.[62] The strategy, known as frequency seriation, developed logically from Nelson's method, but was not based on excavated data. Instead, a ceramic type was identified as either earliest or latest in the sequence on the basis of external information; sites with the highest frequency of that ceramic type were then considered to represent one end of the scale, and other sites were placed in chronological order based upon the frequency of sherds of that and other types found there. Using this method Kroeber placed several sites in the vicinity of Zuñi in what appeared to be a rational sequence.

Wissler's response to Kroeber's report indicated that he saw it more as a threat to the newly established preeminence of the American Museum in chronological work than as an advance in science. Since Kroeber's long-term allegiances were to the University of California rather than the American Museum, he was as much a potential rival as a collaborator. "He has gone into the subject a little deeper than I anticipated," Wissler wrote Nelson, "and perhaps has skinned most of the cream off of this milk." To Kroeber, Wissler expressed tepid gratitude while observing that only with excavation could the results be considered more than preliminary.[63] He immediately began planning for new work at Zuñi, reasserting direct control.

Wissler's sense of urgency at the end of the 1915 season was warranted, since after a period in which the American Museum had much of the region to itself, new projects and old rivals were beginning to proliferate. In 1915 A. V. Kidder had begun excavations at Pecos Pueblo on behalf of the Phillips Academy in Andover, Massachusetts. Nelson arrived at Zuñi that summer too late to catch Kroeber but instead found George Heye, who with anthropologist Frederick Webb Hodge was planning major excavations at the nearby site of Hawikuh.[64] Rivalry with Heye was especially keen due to his ambition to launch a competing institution in New York. "I understand that the supporters of Mr. Heye maintain that we should take the Old World for our field and give the New to them," Wissler wrote to Osborn. "But there is every reason why we should not do so."[65] Subsequent sparring between Hodge and Wissler over who had priority at Zuñi suggests that control of the archaeological resources of the area in the interests of professional and institutional politics were often more critical than scientific motivations. Nelson, wearying of the hectic pace, reluctantly agreed to take on work at Zuñi. "It has become a rather monotonous grind," he wrote Wissler. "Still, for the sake of ideal completeness, I should be only too glad to return for one season more."[66]

Expanding the Huntington Survey in the face of heightened competition required still greater levels of funding, and Wissler was prepared to modify the research orientation of the effort to attract new patronage. His decision was to begin yet another new excavation, but one that would serve as a marquee attraction to generate headlines and keep the museum's work in public view. The Galisteo Basin work, while rich in information, had produced few exhibit-quality artifacts, and Wissler believed that something more spectacular was required. This shift in direction, ironically, more closely resembled the collections orientation of the Hyde Expedition than anything the Huntington Survey had done thus far. To make the parallel more complete, to find an appropriate subject Wissler's attention turned toward northwestern New Mexico, and the still spectacular ruins of Chaco Canyon and its environs. At the end of 1915, Wissler was thinking about a new site with great promise, Aztec Ruin, and an old museum interest, Pueblo Bonito.[67]

Aztec Ruin and the Return to Pueblo Bonito

Aztec Ruin was a massive masonry edifice located near the San Juan River in northwest New Mexico. The area had been an attractive location for Anglo-American settlement, and the site had been the favored relic-hunting ground of local residents for a generation. Despite these ongoing depredations and periodic raids on the mound for construction material, its sheer size suggested that it had high potential for important finds. Earl Morris had grown up nearby, and it was probably at his urging that Wissler suggested Aztec Ruin as the site of the American Museum's new excavations.[68]

Artifacts were the important consideration at Aztec, since Wissler hoped that it would be a sufficient anchor to attract a new patron and that some of the new funding would be applied to the more strictly scientific aspects of the Survey. Unlike Zuñi and Galisteo, Aztec had no known connection to historic pueblo populations and was less useful for chronological purposes. Instead, Wissler described the site as "more promising even than the famous Bonito," a comparison that played upon Pueblo Bonito's reputation as a source of spectacular discoveries.[69] This message attracted the personal interest of Osborn, who dodged requests to contribute from the Jesup bequest but attracted a patron of even mightier reach than Huntington—Museum Trustee J. P. Morgan. Morgan was persuaded to contribute $2,000 toward the Aztec excavations, and although the balance was to come from existing departmental funds Wissler clearly expected that temporary belt-tightening would pay off in the long run.[70]

Earl Morris was chosen to lead the Aztec project. Negotiations over excavation rights to the site were completed on April 1, when owner H. D. Abrams agreed to the plan. His own conditions, reflecting traditional concerns, were that the walls of the ruin be stabilized and that a collection of duplicate specimens be left on the premises. The American Museum was given a five-year lease and the project commenced on August 1, 1916.[71]

As the Aztec work began, Wissler turned his attention to a final piece of unfinished archaeological business: Chaco Canyon. Despite the fact that Pepper's report remained incomplete and the collections were in disarray, the Hyde Expedition was still remembered by some as an important milestone in the history of anthropology at the American Museum. At a time when excavation rights were being negotiated on all sides, Wissler clearly felt that it was time to demonstrate the priority of his institution's claim to Pueblo Bonito.

Nelson had visited Chaco Canyon in 1915, marking the first return of a museum representative to the scene of its first Southwest triumphs in more than a decade. After the death of Richard Wetherill and the departure of his family the group of dilapidated buildings once known as "Putnam" had been sold to a rancher named Miera, and despite the fact that the vicinity had been made a National Monument in 1907 there was little evidence of federal stewardship. From Nelson's perspective Pueblo Bonito had been "practically cleaned out" by Pepper and Wetherill, and the exposed stone walls were tottering dangerously (fig. 4.3). The other ruins in the vicinity showed more promise, however, and Nelson spent several days taking photographs and making basic sketches. With most of Pepper's notes in Philadelphia, even the most basic documentation for the early work was lacking.[72]

Nelson came away from Chaco Canyon with the idea that stratigraphic techniques might be profitably employed in the refuse dumps of Bonito and some of the other ruins. Wissler encouraged the idea, hoping that new work might salvage the initial investment, which was still seen as a failure. "Since we have an abortive piece of work on our hands," he wrote, "I would like to do something to right the case." Wissler also sensed that modest excavations might solidify the Museum's claim, and in March 1916 a permit for archaeological work in Chaco Canyon was received.[73]

The anticipated competition emerged only a month later in the person of Edgar Lee Hewett, who in collaboration with W. H. Holmes and Charles F. Currelly of the Royal Ontario Museum requested a permit for his own project at Chaco Canyon. The irony that Hewett's interest in Chaco Canyon had revived at the same time as that of his old antagonists there appears to have gone unnoticed at the time. The issues, however, were not the same as they had been sixteen years earlier. The Hewett team was seeking a congressional appropriation to stabilize Pueblo Bonito and other ruins in the vicinity and repair the crumbling walls left behind by the earlier project. In order to secure the agreement of all parties to

Figure 4.3 Pueblo Bonito, 1915. (Photograph by Nels
Nelson; courtesy American Museum of
Natural History Library)

his own Chaco plan Hewett and his allies went so far as to contact Talbot Hyde
to obtain permission to work on the land he still claimed in the vicinity of Pueblo
Bonito.[74]

What just a few years earlier had been an environment in which the American Museum had worked relatively unmolested had become a crowded field of
competing archaeologists and institutions. The restoration of Pueblo Bonito was
technically the responsibility of the American Museum, but without the incli-
nation or funding to carry it out, Wissler was perfectly willing to pass on the
responsibility. He agreed to modify his own permit request and restrict his sur-

vey's efforts to the Bonito refuse mound.[75] In the end Hewett failed to obtain the desired appropriation, and the stabilization project was postponed. Heye's Zuñi project was also postponed, and for a brief interval the competitive pressure let up. Heye's withdrawal of his collections from Philadelphia in early 1916 and the establishment of the Museum of the American Indian, however, signalled that the respite would be only temporary.

In another sign of the transformation of Southwest archaeology since the days of the Hyde Expedition, Nelson was to spend less time at excavating at Chaco Canyon than his predecessors had required to set up camp. Between June 30 and July 3, 1916, he examined Pueblo Bonito and began excavating in the trash mound Wetherill had briefly examined in 1896. Morris and an assistant arrived from Aztec to help, and two trenches were completed on July 3. It was immediately apparent, however, that the chronological method applied so successfully in the Rio Grande would be problematic in the very different Chaco ruins. Nelson was disappointed with the results, noting in his journal that the mound appeared to have been constructed of building debris, "hence it has accumulated relatively rapidly, in consequence of which the potsherds found do not show any great change from bottom to top of the heap." Without the ability to conduct comparative excavations in other sites, the stratigraphic project showed signs of being a failure.[76]

Despite his disappointment at his results from Pueblo Bonito, Nelson found the archaeology of the canyon compelling. In view of the plans of the "Washington people" to excavate the other ruins, Nelson remarked, "the Museum might come to feel itself under moral obligation to do something with Bonito and . . . the knowledge that there is some pay dirt in it yet might be of value in this connection."[77] He may also have seen work at Chaco Canyon as a way to maintain his position within the Huntington Survey. The Aztec excavations proceeded smoothly, and earlier in the summer Nelson had worked in the Zuñi region with a new member of the team, Columbia graduate student Leslie Spier. Nelson had little interest in Aztec, feeling that a focus on a single site had little significance in the overall plan of the survey, and Spier rapidly took hold at Zuñi. Following what Osborn later referred to as the "Bonito Trail" may have been his way of avoiding a purely supervisory role. Nelson spent the rest of the summer exploring the country between Chaco Canyon and the Rio Grande, investigating the relationships between the prehistoric peoples of those two regions.[78]

The summer of 1916 was the high-water mark of the Huntington Survey, an interval when the precarious balance between research and prestige was most successfully maintained. Some of the credit was extended to Nelson: "I think you are certainly to be congratulated on the way the work in the Southwest has turned out," Goddard wrote him. But Wissler remained the architect of the program.[79] The two-pronged approach he had developed over the years, pressuring the museum administration for greater funding while assuring his patrons of the value of the work they supported, was continued. In view of the increasingly competitive quality of Southwest archaeology, Wissler's exhortations drew a clear link between the prestige of the American Museum and its ability to support science. To Huntington, he emphasized the sweeping successes of the Huntington Survey. Wissler described Nelson's work as providing a key to the spatial distribution of recent Pueblo culture and linking it to Chacoan ancestors, articulating with Kroeber's ethnographic work at Zuñi as well as Robert Lowie's work at Hopi, and Goddard's among the Apache.

The impact of the Huntington Survey on Southwest archaeology was, in fact, increasingly evident. Among Nelson, Kidder, and some of the other younger archaeologists working in the Southwest, there had developed a sense of camaraderie and common purpose that began to manifest itself both in a collective emphasis on the new chronological approach and in criticism of the older generation of researchers. A. V. Kidder and Sylvanus Morley, who had struck a successful balance between Tozzer on the one hand and Hewett on the other, were early promoters of the new strategy. Steeped from a young age in the study of Southwest prehistory, they realized that an emphasis on chronology would ultimately provide the means to tackle large-scale problems of population movement and the organization of societies. In this way an archaeology of relevance to anthropology could be established.

The members of the younger generation also increasingly saw the senior archaeologists who oversaw the Southwest work as obstacles. Antipathy toward Hewett was widespread but largely unspoken, perhaps since his grip on northern New Mexico remained unshakable. Opposition to Jesse Fewkes, who as an employee of the Bureau of American Ethnology was perceived as having exclusive access to Mesa Verde and important areas of northeastern Arizona, was voiced more frequently. In late fall 1916 Franz Boas asked Nelson to give a paper on the issue of Southwest chronology at the annual meetings of the American Anthropological Association, apparently to provide Fewkes a chance to respond to criticism from his younger colleagues. "Dr. Fewkes has no ground for complaint," wrote Nelson. "He has had the SW for a lifetime and ought to be satisfied."[80] Fewkes, who only a few years before had complained about stagnation in American archaeology, was discovering that new ideas were accompanied by a restless spirit that had little patience for his own generation.

Even as concepts built on his own insights gained influence, Nelson found himself steadily losing ground in his own institution. As early as 1914 he had begun to feel that his personal ambitions would suffer in the face of his responsibilities to Wissler and Osborn. "The spirit and management of this institution doesn't encourage accomplishment," he wrote Kroeber.[81] In their different ways Spier and Morris each exhibited a strength of purpose that Nelson, stretched thin by his proliferating duties, no longer felt. His desire to trace the diaspora of the Chacoan peoples through the patient strategy employed to such effect in the Galisteo Basin was given short shrift. By 1916 Wissler, the theorist behind the chronological revolution, had led Southwest archaeology through a period of innovation and was prepared to consolidate his gains. As the skirmishes with Heye and Hewett had demonstrated, maintaining a presence in the Southwest required professional alliances, skillful negotiation, and a reasonable expectation of funding. Wissler seems to have been increasingly convinced that protecting his funding base was the highest priority, even at the cost of slighting earlier gains. Aztec was a holding action, and Osborn was adamant: "we must constantly keep in mind," he wrote, "that the American Museum of Natural History is primarily a museum and not a Research Institution. This was the purpose for which it was founded, and exploration and research are contributory to this end."[82]

Despite the constant resistance of his superiors, Wissler had over the eight years of the Huntington Southwest Survey revived the concept of "archaeology as anthropology." To the professional community, the chronological approach gave new meaning to an American archaeology that had been nearly dismissed as irrelevant a decade earlier. The success of the American Museum had reestablished both its own prestige in the Southwest field and the claims of other public institutions to work in the region. The rise of competing endeavors, such as those of George Heye, was in many ways an index of Wissler's success.

While attuned to the educational needs of his own museum, however, Wissler had largely ignored the local initiatives of Hewett and his associates. The tension between the two approaches remained unresolved. While the storage rooms of the American Museum were being stocked with the relics of Pueblo San Cristóbal, the protagonists of the Southwest societies had continued their separate course, with implications for an era when the American Museum could no longer be assured of dominance in the Southwest field.

5

Archaeology
as Heritage

The Pajarito
Summer Sessions

The announcement in late 1909 that the Palace of the Governors in Santa Fe would be the permanent headquarters of the School of American Archaeology was followed a few months later by legislation establishing the Museum of New Mexico in the same facility. After a long wait, the museum's public galleries opened in August 1910 to the applause of local citizens. "For the lovers of art," wrote the *Santa Fe New Mexican,* "of romance, or of the antique; for those who would plunge into the secrets of an ancient and mysterious people who once saw the same skies as now hang overhead and who once breathed the same air as now makes us buoyant, all roads will lead to the Old Palace tonight."[1]

With the completion of arrangements for the School and the museum, Edgar Lee

Hewett had finally established an institutional base from which he could promote his model for American archaeology. Patient nurturing of the western eagerness for cultural institutions and sovereignty had borne fruit. Under the Hewett plan, science would be firmly wedded to education, identity, and the promotion of local interests.

By embracing the "western idea," however, Hewett tapped a wellspring of interest in archaeology that he could neither entirely control nor completely understand. His own ambitions had always been national in scope, and as he tended his new power base in New Mexico Hewett fought to establish the relevance of his model in the national debate over the proper role of archaeology and its development as a professional discipline. The significance of the work of the School *within* the region, however, had less to do with archaeology itself and more to do with the aspirations of the southwestern public.

The rationale for archaeology that appealed to Hewett's supporters and attracted community backing for his projects concerned the issue of cultural identity in the Southwest. From the perspective of southwestern cultural nationalists, the region's antiquities could be made into a source of heritage for the new possessors of the land. Scientific research, while laudable in the abstract, was secondary in importance to the symbolic value of a storied past. The evolving concept of "archaeology as heritage," with its populist implications, was alien to the professionalizing interests of archaeologists in eastern institutions. As the two approaches diverged, it became increasingly difficult for even a consummate deal maker and negotiator like Edgar Lee Hewett to play both sides.

Archaeology and Moral Value

The Southwest in 1909 was a region on the verge of a political transformation. The continuing influx of immigrants from the East and Midwest had expanded the Anglo-American population, which was increasingly concerned about its role on the national stage. The movement for the construction of museums and similar institutions was one indication of the need to establish the suitability of the southwestern territories in the drive for statehood. Congressional reluctance to admit New Mexico and Arizona to the Union on equal terms was strong, however, based in part upon fears that the Hispanic and Indian residents of the region would resist cultural assimilation.[2] This conflict presented a challenge to the new residents of the Southwest, who desired the legitimacy conferred by statehood but for whom the widespread use of the Spanish language and influence of the Catholic church were everyday realities. Many members of this community thus sought to downplay the uniqueness of the southwestern environment, both environmentally and culturally. "The man from the east or the middle west who goes into New Mexico," advertised the Territorial Bureau of Immigration, "will not go into a land of strange people and strange conditions. He will find the same kind of people as have been his neighbors 'back home.'"[3]

For others, however, the distinctive characteristics of the Southwest provided an opportunity to create a new identity for the region's inhabitants that would allow them to override the objections of eastern politicians. These individuals, who included longtime boosters like Charles Lummis as well as the artists and writers who began to flock to the Southwest after the turn of the century, looked to the land and to its various inhabitants for inspiration. In California, where a similar search for identity had been in process since the 1850s, the Hispanic past, Mediterranean imagery, and even classical Greek ideals were manipulated to create images that would be distinctly Californian but would also preserve connections between these residents and their own cultural roots. This invention of tradition allowed Charles Lummis to claim that the Anglo-American southern Californian "was the cultural descendant of both Puritan and conquistador."[4] With their smaller immigrant population and more limited resources, the southwestern states and territories used a more select set of models in their own search for identity, with the unique properties of the landscape and climate receiving considerable attention.

Antiquities represented another fertile source of inspiration for Southwest identity. Twenty years of economic exploitation of southwestern ruins and the more recent establishment of scientific organizations and institutions had stimulated widespread interest in archaeology. As the ruins were revealed by excavations local knowledge about them increased, a process accelerated by improvements in roads and transportation. The romantic and humanistic symbolism of ruins was as evocative in the early twentieth century as it had been in the nineteenth, and the southwestern audience was eager to derive meaning from the antiquities scattered across the landscape. Even as New Mexico's dry air and sunny days were being touted as *natural* assets, the evidence of its ancient past was being presented to the public as a *cultural* asset. More than a subject of curiosity and investigation, these antiquities were increasingly construed as heritage, a legacy Anglo-American Southwesterners had inherited along with the land, and thus a central feature of their new identity.

As Hewett settled down in Santa Fe, a number of old allies came to his support and contributed to the development of the School. The influence of these individuals, who had little contact with the centers of professional anthropology in the East, was critical in the development of a western agenda for archaeology and in the construction of archaeology as heritage. Most prominent among them was Frank Springer, who had brought Hewett to the Normal University and had resigned from the Board of Regents to protest the removal of his protégé. Springer had been raised in Iowa, attended university there, and moved to New Mexico to become legal counsel to the Maxwell Land and Cattle Company. A prominent member of the Republican Party, he served in the territorial senate on two occasions and wielded considerable influence. In addition to his high political standing and personal wealth he also developed a national reputation as a scientist, specializing in the fossil crinoids he had collected in Iowa quarries during his youth. Introduced to archaeology in the late 1890s, Springer spent the years between 1898 and 1917 as an observer and strong supporter of the study of Southwest antiquities and a patron of the School of American Archaeology.[5]

Springer's perspective on archaeology was strongly colored by the utilitarian values of the West and infused with a patriotic sensibility. He understood the significance of the School and the Museum of New Mexico, both in providing a home for local science and in stimulating the pride and intellect of the population. While prestige might be represented by various types of institution, archaeology's particular importance was its ability to derive object lessons from the past.

In his 1902 address to the Colorado Normal School, Springer had identified the *process* of archaeology as an important component of an emerging Southwest identity. In later years he developed this idea further, arguing that the *results* of archaeological exploration had an even greater significance for the local audience. Regarding the portrait of ancient "man" emerging from the digs of Hewett and others, Springer was explicit. "For we may learn from him many things on which it is useful to reflect—reverence for the powers of the universe; the value of the spoken word when passed; respect for Age, obedience to Authority, and devotion to the State—which should make for better citizenship, for more unselfish patriotism, and for the greater security of our national ideals."[6]

In many ways Springer's thoughts on the moral value of archaeology echoed those of Lummis, who wrote that it was the "humanness" of the story emerging from the ruins of the Southwest that would have the greatest appeal to the public. Hewett picked up the refrain as well, remarking that the archaeological evidence of the ancient southwestern peoples amounted to "their own picture of themselves, their testimony as to how they met and tried to solve the problems that all humanity has confronted."[7]

In order for a southwestern past to be used as a source of moral lessons, however, it had to be held in high esteem. Despite efforts to cast them as peaceful, civilized agriculturalists, contemporary pueblo people were rarely characterized as the equals of the Anglo-American population.[8] The cultural nationalists who looked to the past for their models of identity, therefore, made a subtle effort to disassociate the ancient peoples from their modern descendants. This was done in three ways: by the assignment of extreme antiquity to Southwest ruins, by "classicizing" those remains and their makers, and by casting doubt on any direct relationship between the contemporary Indians and the ruins themselves.

Prior to the widespread implementation of tree-ring dating in the 1920s, archaeologists could not assign absolute dates to their discoveries. Even Nelson's chronological method, when developed, ranked sites by relative age rather than providing calendric dates. Despite the acknowledged similarities between the material culture of modern pueblos and that found in archaeological sites in the vicinity, it was common to assign dates of "hoary antiquity" to southwestern ruins. Scholars viewing Pueblo Bonito had no compunction in declaring that it had been built as much as 3,000 years before the Christian Era. This was not a fringe perspective, and even some of Hewett's protégés argued that the "Cliff Dwellers" had lived before the Ice Age.[9]

The effect of assigning great age to southwestern ruins was to make that past less immediate and thus more amenable to reconstitution. Lummis, Prince, and other writers used dramatic metaphors to describe the people who had lived on the Pajarito Plateau, calling their modest communities "cities" and "fortresses."[10] A Santa Fe poet, writing about old trails at the nearby ruin of Tsankawi, assigned them to a seemingly antediluvian epoch:

> Old-time trails across the rock
> Knee-deep nearly, sheerly worn
> Here converge and interlock
> Old when Babylon was born.[11]

But to western readers Babylon was not only ancient, but also a prominent cultural icon. Through the use of imagery from the European historical tradition, Hewett and the cultural nationalists built an image of the southwestern past that was the conceptual equal of the biblical and classical models with which their audience was familiar. In one brief article Hewett compared Santa Fe to Damascus, referred to a local hilltop as an acropolis, and concluded that "in truth, there is no reason why the Indians of the towns on the site of Santa Fe should not have been living their simple lives in the same days that the aboriginal Latins were basking in the sun of the Seven Hills, baking pottery by precisely the same methods as the Indians and, in the same way, folding up the bodies of their dead for burial along the Via Sacra."[12]

Metaphorical comparisons between Pueblo and Greco-Roman ruins had the effect of "classicizing" southwestern antiquity. The association of the School of American Archaeology with the Archaeological Institute of America also played a role in ennobling the ancient Southwest, since the study of Greek, Roman, and biblical heritage was the Institute's primary purpose. The traveling lecturers of the Institute dealt largely with classical subjects, but shared the stage with their American counterparts. Hewett, in this fashion, reversed the calculation originally made by Charles Eliot Norton in promoting American work. The Institute had tolerated American archaeology in order to build interest in its overseas projects, but the close association of classical and New World archaeology also made the New World past more respectable in the eyes of the public. Hewett skillfully built up comparisons between his work and that of his classical counterparts. "Classical archaeology has long had its constituency of scholars," he wrote, "consistently true to the ancient shrines, keeping alive the literature, art, and drama of the people who set standards for the modern world. . . . The Indian race has had few to maintain its sacred fires. The disposition has been to put them out rather than to save them."[13]

In many ways the association of the western cultural nationalists with the scholars of the Institute was a good fit. Classical archaeology was a humanistic endeavor, and its practitioners were accustomed to the concept of finding moral values in antiquity. Even though their southwestern counterparts were working with different subject matter, their strategy was the same. In contrast, the scientific designs of the professional anthropologists of the eastern museums and universities, emphasizing the documentation of "cultures," had since the decline of John Wesley Powell and the end of the active involvement of anthropologists in the Indian reform movement largely avoided moral issues. From this perspective American archaeology was an important area of study, but with little relevance for contemporary issues.

Enhancing the southwestern past also meant casting doubt on the historical relationship between modern Native Americans and their ancestors. In the early twentieth century westerners remained profoundly divided over the Indian peoples in the region, an ambivalence reflected in the pages of daily newspapers. The *Santa Fe New Mexican* described local antiquities as "evidence of the highest order of prehistoric culture" even while the editor was calling efforts to assign an Indian name to the new state "contemptible."[14]

Hewett's response to such ambivalence was to disassociate modern Native Americans from the archaeological past he was uncovering. He suggested, for instance, that evidence cast doubt on the relationship between the ancient inhabitants of the Pajarito Plateau and residents of the surviving pueblos in the area. Such an interpretation flew in the face of accepted scholarship. Both Adolph Bandelier and Charles Lummis had written tales about the ancient Pajarito based on the traditions and oral history of Cochiti Pueblo.[15] Hewett's early writings had described the association as "customary," an assumption he criticized even as he provided information in its support.[16] In 1909, however, he began to use the term "Pajaritan culture" to describe the ancient residents of the region, arguing from the evidence of different cranial shapes and ceramic designs that they differed from more recent occupants of the region. Even the direct claims of Pueblo peoples concerning their ancestry could be attributed, he argued, to uncertainty over property rights. Following his 1907 conference with the elders of Santa Clara Pueblo regarding the Puyé excavations, Hewett claimed that once he had assured them that they would retain ownership of the land the pueblo authorities admitted that they had moved into the region only in the time of the Spanish entrada.[17]

The distance thus established between ancient and modern was both temporal and lineal, creating space within which a noble past free from biased associations could be constructed. The professional response to Hewett's definition of the "Pajaritan culture" is uncertain, but his principal target was the public. When a prehistoric burial was dug up on the fringe of Santa Fe, Hewett had no compunction in identifying it as having belonged to the Pajaritan culture, which he then linked to other ruins previously destroyed within the city limits. By implication Santa Fe, the "new Damascus," had been founded on a site hallowed by noble ancients whose remains were therefore the proper study of the new occupants of the land.

The cultural nationalist perspective on southwestern antiquity is evident from late nineteenth- and early twentieth-century tourist literature from New Mexico. Promotional brochures and pamphlets typically assigned ruins and relics to a misty and forgotten time. "Some authorities date the advent of the Cliff Dwellers," wrote one author, "to any where [sic] from 3,000 to 10,000 years; other scientists claim a greater age for the ruins." Archaeological discoveries were "buried under the debris of time."[18] Terms such as "pyramids" and "cities of the dead," with their Old World associations, were common, as were more explicit analogies to ancient Egypt and Mesopotamia. The association of ruins with the Native American population was left open to question through the use of ambiguous terms such as "prehistoric man," allusions to a "vanished race," or descriptions of Indian peoples as the "civilization that followed" the more ancient society represented by the ruins.[19] "Let those who deem America without a past and think antiquity synonymous with the East go to New Mexico," reads one 1907 brochure, "and stand amid the ruins of the Seven Cities of Cibola. There in that land of mystery slumber the 'sheeted dead' of a thousand generations; there among the crumbling walls still stands the ghostly past awaiting a newer day."[20]

Hewett's ambitions to establish a new model for American archaeology and the strategies he adopted to enact that plan were not always compatible. In promoting the School of American Archaeology to the Santa Fe audience, he argued that the work unearthed heritage of moral value to the local community. He adopted this position to enhance his base of popular support, but allies such as Springer and Lummis were more personally concerned with western identity. Tying the new Anglo-Americans more closely to the land, they believed, was a key to prosperity and the establishment of the Southwest on a more equal footing with the eastern states. Archaeology, as well as landscape and history, would provide such a sense of place.

The cultural nationalist rationale, however, conflicted with the national aspirations of the School, its parent organization, and its leaders. The School had been established to train students in American archaeology and to promote research, not to support a narrow regional agenda. While Hewett continued to receive F. W. Kelsey's support, the discrepancies between what he was telling local audiences and what appeared in his reports to the national organization were an inevitable source of friction. Caught between the western agenda of Springer and Lummis, Kelsey's national ambitions, and the demands of the eastern professional archaeologists, Hewett was hard pressed to adopt a plan that would satisfy all requirements. In the aftermath of the founding of the School, it remained to be seen whether these national and regional, scholarly and educational agendas could be pulled together to form an American archaeology with a popular base and a humanistic purpose.

Field Education and the Summer of 1910

In 1908 and 1909 the School's promoters had focused on consolidating their coalition and finalizing arrangements to take over the Palace of the Governors. In 1910, however, with Hewett and his associates firmly established in Santa Fe, it was time to turn the promises of the previous five years into reality.

Control of the Palace had not come without a fight. The most influential local opponent was Bradford Prince, whose New Mexico Historical Society already maintained rooms in the Palace and who correctly perceived that the School would eventually require the entire space. Despite his role as one of the founders of the Santa Fe Archaeological Society Prince had always viewed Hewett as a competitor rather than an ally. Local associations notwithstanding, Hewett was not a part of the community of collectors and avocational archaeologists in the city, some of whom saw him and his national aspirations as a threat to their own ambitions. Prince had gone so far as to complain to Institute President Thomas Dale Seymour, and had stirred up controversy in the legislature during the successful effort to establish the museum.[21] There was also concern that the renovations of the Palace would disturb another memorial treasured by some of the local population: the room in which former territorial governor Lew Wallace had written *Ben Hur*.[22]

The lack of unanimity in local support for the Hewett program made the success of the Museum, as the public face of the School, all the more critical. What Hewett and his allies needed was an institution that would draw broad popular approval and overcome the criticism of Prince and his circle. Springer wrote Alice Fletcher that the museum was to be "more than a mere storehouse for the relics of the prehistoric races of the Southwest. It is to be, first of all, an educator, in which the student and the thoughtful visitor may find adequately presented the architecture, industries and life of these ancient populations."[23]

Artifacts from local sites, including material excavated under the sponsorship of the Archaeological Society, were to be the centerpiece of the new museum, placed in rooms honoring "Puyé" and the "Rito de Los Frijoles." Hewett also made an effort to contact other museums and to exchange new material for specimens obtained from the Pajarito Plateau in earlier years. One collection in particular, at the U.S. National Museum, was described as having "considerable sentimental value, because of its having been the result of [the] first local interest in this branch of science."[24] In keeping with the broader educational agenda outlined by Springer, however, the artifacts were to be arranged in such a way that their original context could be understood by the viewer. This meant that the archaeological materials would be augmented by models, plans, and artwork designed to convey a sense of their original state. Painting in particular would be used as an educational device, as Springer described for the planned "Puyé Room." "Upon the walls will be depicted, in an extensive series of large oil paintings, the surrounding landscape . . . the Cliff in its original state, together with suitable details of the structures restored, and the life and ceremonials of the people . . . the word 'decoration' is scarcely a proper term, for these paintings will take a definite and highly important place in the representation and description of these ancient populations and their works."[25]

The exhibits at the Palace were conceived as the first stage of a process to educate the viewer on the antiquities of the Southwest, the second stage being a visit to reconstructed sites on the Pajarito Plateau itself. Hewett considered the environmental and cultural context for archaeology more important that the details of artifacts, and the museum in the Palace, as well as the "field museums," made

Figure 5.1   The interior of the Museum of New Mexico during the 1910s. (Photograph by Jesse Nusbaum; courtesy Photo Archives, Fray Angélico Chávez History Library, Palace of the Governors, Santa Fe; neg. no. 46787)

this point to the visitor (fig. 5.1). This approach appealed to local pride as well, since it construed the scenic aspects of the landscape as both important attractions and scientific assets.

The intellectual strategy inspiring the museum plan was complemented by a pragmatic administrative structure that gave Hewett a free hand. The legislation authorizing the Museum had stipulated that its Board of Regents include members of the School's managing board, one "representative citizen of New Mexico," with the governor and the head of the Archaeological Society given ex officio status.[26] Springer and Lummis were named regents due to their positions on the board of the School, along with R. W. Corwin, a supporter of the Institute from Pueblo, Colorado. Territorial Secretary Nathan Jaffa represented the interests of the citizens, while McFie wielded considerable influence. These congenial arrangements provided ample political insulation. Hewett also created a "Ladies' Board," made up of the wives of the regents and other prominent Santa Fe residents. The Ladies' Board increased the visibility of the Museum as a cultural institution and expanded Hewett's circle of supporters to include men who were not otherwise interested in the Museum, but could be influenced through their wives.

The Museum's galleries were scheduled to open in August 1910, and a variety of events were staged to build excitement for the event. Archaeological articles appeared frequently in the *New Mexican,* which was edited by Paul Walter, an associate of Hewett's, and the work of the school received regular coverage. When the noted western artist Wesley Rollins visited Santa Fe in June, Hewett arranged an exhibit of the painter's work in the Palace. The Ladies' Board provided refreshments, and the public came in large numbers to view Rollins's work and to examine progress on the archaeological displays. A temporary exhibition featuring reproductions of ancient codices from Mexico and Central America was also scheduled for the summer.[27] At summer meetings of the Archaeological Society funds were appropriated to assist in the completion of one of the exhibit rooms, while the name of the organization was changed to "The Archaeological Society of New Mexico" to reflect its widening constituency.[28] By the time of the actual opening, on August 20, excitement had clearly been honed to a keen edge.

Accounts of the reception itself, while colored by Walter's partisan enthusiasm, suggest that the event lived up to its promise. In no western city outside of Los Angeles, announced the *New Mexican,* was there "such a lodestone to attract an assemblage of artists, scientists, political powers, and literary men, and women." The presence of the political leadership of the territory and many prominent visitors underscored the Museum's importance as a cultural asset befitting a "capital city."[29] The staff of the School, the assembled regents, and members of the Ladies' Board made an impressive showing, but it seems evident that all the overt political symbolism did not entirely obscure the message being conveyed by the exhibits themselves. The murals in the Puyé and Rito de los Frijoles rooms, painted by Carl Lotave, seem to have been particularly effective in demonstrating the utilitarian value of the archaeological study of the southwestern past. "Gazing intently at these illustrations of the story written in the cliffs," continued the *New Mexican* reporter, "one feels a growing respect for the cliff dwellers who lived so long ago and in their crude way grappled with the same problems of 'bread winning' and 'habitation' that have confronted the human race since the time of Adam's fall."[30]

In the successful establishment of the Museum of New Mexico, Hewett carried through on at least part of his ambition to mobilize local resources in the promotion of archaeological research and education. The opening of the public galleries coincided with congressional passage of the Statehood Enabling Act, strengthening the association between promoting cultural institutions and achieving political goals. Throughout the next several months, which featured a constitutional convention, the Museum stood at the center of New Mexico life. Many of the people who were to decide on funding for the Museum's future attended receptions in the halls of the Palace, and probably looked at the murals of Puyé even if they had not seen the ruins in person. As an example of the potential of archaeology to provide useful lessons for a southwestern audience, the Museum of New Mexico in its inaugural year was a significant success.

The second major activity of 1910 was the School's summer session. The fieldwork alliance, in which Hewett had expressed great confidence just two years before, had proven unwieldy. Funding had been more limited than he had hoped, but more particularly local societies were interested only in projects of immediate local relevance and were resistant to an overall coordination of effort. The Utah Society continued to support a research program and had considerable success working in the Tsegi Canyon district of northern Arizona, but while Hewett was grudgingly considered to direct the effort it was Byron Cummings, ostensibly only "field officer" of the project, who was the real authority.[31] Hewett had also inaugurated a program of fieldwork in Central America under the sponsorship of the St. Louis Society, but that was largely an independent endeavor as well. By 1910, with the local societies either becoming inactive or pursuing separate agendas, the Institute's program of American archaeology was increasingly focused on the research and educational activities of the School itself.

As setting for the 1910 fieldwork Hewett again turned to the Rito de los Frijoles. "What a beautiful spot, this Rito!" wrote Adolph Bandelier, who first visited the area in 1880 and returned several times during his Southwest explorations.[32] The visual drama of the canyon, which descended in a smooth curve from the mountains of the Jémez range to the Rio Grande, was enhanced by the hundreds of rooms that had been pecked into the sheer northern cliff by its ancient inhabitants. Masonry rubble from the buildings that had once lined the high walls extended for more than a mile, while buried kivas and the ruins of a communal pueblo Bandelier's Cochiti guides had called "Tyuonyi" were found amid groves of cottonwoods and ponderosa pine on the open canyon floor. The Rito itself was the only perennial stream in the vicinity, a resource for both the original inhabitants and the archaeologists who came to study the ruins. Over time the romantic vistas of the Rito attracted a considerable number of visitors from Santa Fe. Hewett's own introduction to the Rito probably occurred in the late 1890s, and he made repeated visits over the next thirty years. The 1908 excavations, sponsored jointly by the Peabody Museum and the Santa Fe Archaeological Society, had marked the first attempt to dig in the ruins of the Rito on a large scale, and the effort had been continued in 1909.

Pragmatic as well as aesthetic reasons made the Rito an appropriate loca-

tion for the expanded 1910 program. Hewett's efforts on behalf of the Archaeological Society had gotten a road built to within reasonable proximity of the
canyon, which facilitated transportation across the rugged plateau. In 1907 one of
Hewett's Santa Fe supporters, Judge Albert J. Abbott, had built a summer home
along the Rito, which he and his wife Ida B. Abbott called "the House of the Ten
Alders." The Abbotts, who had been alerted to the opportunity when their son
was serving as a forest ranger in the district, had planted orchards and gardens,
built a trail into the canyon, and served as caretakers and guides when it was
required.[33] Their modest establishment was available to tourists visiting the
ruins and provided a convenient commissary for archaeological parties. Despite
Hewett's previous attempts to establish nearby Puyé as a "show-ruin," the Rito
offered advantages for a larger-scale effort that were not present elsewhere.

The amenities of the Rito had been tested at the end of the 1908 season.
Hewett's staff and the Harvard representatives gathered when the excavations
were finished for what he called "a series of conferences . . . on the various problems of the American field." The meeting, with eighteen in attendance, can be
considered the earliest precursor of what was to become a regular practice in
Southwest archaeology—the end-of-season conference. A. V. Kidder, who formal-
ized the tradition in his annual Pecos Conferences after 1927, attended the Rito
meeting, and probably drew his inspiration from it.[34] A meeting of the Board of
Managers of the School had been held at Puyé in August 1909, but without the
amenities of the Rito that setting does not seem to have been viewed with favor
thereafter.[35]

In an article written for *Science* at the end of the 1910 campaign, Springer
outlined the intellectual program of the summer session and the future activities of the School in the Southwest. The work, he wrote, was an "investigation of
the character and probable origin of the native races of this continent." Cultural
interaction during the historic period meant that archaeological evidence would
be the most reliable source of information on indigenous traditions, but excavation and survey were to be supplemented by linguistic, geological, and botanical
studies. The incorporation of such diverse lines of evidence into what was otherwise an archaeological endeavor was one of the distinctive characteristics of the
program, and gave a foretaste of modern research strategies.

In Springer's view, however, the central purpose of the School's work was
utilitarian, bearing on what he called *psychology*. "For it is the human mind that
we are studying," he wrote, "and the ultimate aim of these correlated investigations is to find out how the mind of man has been influenced by his environment;
how his beliefs and life have been created, modified, continued, or destroyed by
his physical surroundings."[36] To Springer and his contemporaries the character

of the country influenced the character of the people, and archaeology would provide evidence on the challenges faced by Anglo-Americans as they adapted to the southwestern landscape. The absence of a genetic relationship between the ancient Pajaritans and the modern Santa Feans was thus rendered moot, since they walked the same hillsides and drank from the same streams.

In addition to the importance of the School's program for clarifying the relationship between environment and psychology Springer was also convinced that it would make an important contribution to American scientific education in general. In particular, he drew parallels between the summer session and the school for naturalists that had been founded by Louis Agassiz on Penikese Island in Massachusetts in 1873. The Anderson School of Natural History had been established to train teachers in an outdoor, coeducational setting, and although Agassiz's death brought it to a premature end, it was considered a major step in infusing science with the utilitarian experience of living with nature. Penikese had spawned a series of imitators on the Massachusetts Coast from the 1870s through the 1890s, all of which served a perceived educational need. Springer had met Agassiz as a young man, and had been persuaded by the encounter to keep up his scientific activities even while pursuing a legal career. Frederic Putnam and Jesse Fewkes had been trained by Agassiz, and while Putnam's experience there may have influenced his interest in archaeological field schools Fewkes was explicit that his support for the summer session resulted from its emulation of the Penikese experiment.[37]

The staff assembled for the summer session included several important figures in American anthropology. The permanent employees of the School included Sylvanus Morley, Jesse Nusbaum, Kenneth Chapman, and Percy Adams. Even the aging Adolph Bandelier had been put on the payroll, to compile documentary evidence on "events that took place when the native American races first came in contact with the Caucasian." He remained in New York, however, and did not return to the Southwest.[38] Linguistic research was conducted by John Peabody Harrington, who even in 1910 had a reputation for genius and eccentricity. Harrington had just returned from graduate work in Germany in 1908 when he met Hewett, who recognized his extraordinary abilities and found funding for some of his studies. Two years later Harrington was one of Hewett's most prominent assistants and had been dispatched to Seattle to present a series of lectures and build up interest in anthropology in the Northwest.[39] During his New Mexico fieldwork he became one of the few Anglo-Americans to achieve fluency in the Tewa language, useful both for research and in coordinating the excavation teams.

Another participant in the summer session was the Oxford-trained ethnologist Barbara Freire-Marreco. One of the first to pass the Diploma in Anthropology at Oxford, Freire-Marreco was encouraged by her mentors to seek field experience abroad. With a fellowship from Somerville College in hand she first contacted Fletcher, who in turn recommended her to Hewett. Freire-Marreco's impending arrival in Santa Fe was noted by the *New Mexican,* under the humorous headline "Will Oxford Co-eds Understand American[?]."[40] Hewett also recruited geologist Junius Henderson and botanist Wilfred Robbins, both from the University of Colorado, to conduct the planned natural science studies. The field team was rounded out by Neil Judd and Donald Beauregard, two of Cummings's students who were idle while their professor was studying in Berlin that summer. Judd had developed considerable expertise at excavation, and Beauregard's principal assignment was to write and distribute news accounts of the School's activities.[41]

Hewett was also eager to use the summer school to build new alliances between anthropological institutions. In January 1910 Frederick Ward Hodge had been named head of the Bureau of American Ethnology, succeeding W. H. Holmes. Hewett and Holmes had long been allies, but Holmes had resisted various requests to fund the School's fieldwork. Hope sprang anew with Hodge, who was a veteran Southwest archaeologist, having participated in the Hemenway Expedition in 1886. He was also the editor of *American Anthropologist,* another position of great influence within the archaeological community.[42] Immediately upon becoming "ethnologist in chief" Hodge received a proposal from Hewett outlining a plan of cooperation between the School and the Bureau that included sponsorship of archaeological research. Hodge, perhaps anxious to return to a field from which he had been absent for some time, agreed, and planned to visit the project himself. To further cement the bond, Hewett corresponded with Smithsonian Secretary Charles Walcott about an exchange of specimens between the two institutions, in addition arranging to send skeletal collections from Puyé to be analyzed by Aleš Hrdlička, who several years earlier had established himself at the U.S. National Museum.[43]

With his distinguished scientific team and a new alliance with the Bureau, Hewett lacked only one critical ingredient to fulfill the School's stated mission: students. His relationship with the Harvard faculty had been a casualty of the 1908 season, which had produced little in the way of specimens or data for the Peabody Museum. The subsequent resolution of the School issue, in which the Harvard faculty had lined up with Bowditch, had deepened the rift. Calling Hewett's actions "disgraceful," Roland Dixon refused to take further part in the School's activities, a response echoed with even greater fervor by Alfred Tozzer.[44] Boas had also been burned in the School fight; he would not encourage his students to participate in the School's summer session, while Kroeber's department at Berkeley was under financial duress.[45] The repercussions of Hewett's victory in the turf battles associated with the School thus threatened to undermine the educational program that had been the rationale for the creation of the School in the first place.

Ever resourceful, Hewett turned to his favorite constituency, the public. Through local newspapers and his contacts in archaeological societies throughout the country, he announced that the 1910 summer session would be open to ordinary citizens. In creating the opportunity for the public to become involved in the work of the School Hewett elaborated still further his model for archaeology. Creating southwestern heritage through the process of unearthing the past became an activity everyone could participate in (or at least observe).

Hewett thus brought the scientifc/educational and cultural nationalist rationales for archaeology together with the humanistic sense of curiosity and exploration that had always been strong with the public. The popular appeal of this integrative approach was demonstrated by the large number of people from various walks of life who arrived for the summer session.[46] Some were longstanding acquaintances, often officials in affiliated societies with which Hewett had been involved, such as F. W. Henry, an officer in the Colorado Society who attended with his wife. Several other Colorado residents participated, including Maude Woy, who as a teacher of history at the Walcott School in Denver provided Hewett with an opportunity to curry favor with the School's director, Anna Wolcott, a politically well-connected patron. Residents of Santa Fe, like Nathan Goldsmith and his mother, probably saw the summer session as a way to have a closer look at the antiquities on their doorstep and a pleasant way to pass a holiday. Artist Wesley Rollins sought inspiration in the Rito work for his own projects, one of which, called "The Historian," was described in the *New Mexican* as "the figure of an Indian standing on a ledge of rock, carving some hieroglyphics for future generations."[47] A Mr. and Mrs. Nairn, of Hartford, Connecticut, traveled the farthest to attend the summer session, staying for a week before moving on to other New Mexico sights.

The summer's fieldwork began before the summer session opened to the public. In keeping with his tradition of covering as much ground as possible Hewett had dispatched Morley, Judd, and Adams to the Ojo Caliente Valley north of Santa Fe in June to make test excavations in a series of large prehistoric sites.[48] They completed the work on June 29, by which time Freire-Marreco had also arrived, and by July 3 activity had shifted to the Rito. The camp itself consisted of tents placed among the cottonwoods, with a "study tent" housing a modest research library and an open clearing facing the stream for lectures and meetings. Some, such as Judd and Beauregard, preferred the shelter of the caves cut into the

Figure 5.2   Early excavations at Tyuonyi, ca. 1910. (Courtesy
Photo Archives, Fray Angélico Chávez History
Library, Palace of the Governors, Santa Fe; neg.
no. 130374)

canyon walls, setting out their bedrolls there away from the other campers. Food
was prepared and served at Ten Alders, which featured a dining room that could
serve thirty at a time.[49]

Excavations recommenced at the ruins of the communal pueblo of Tyuonyi
and in the "talus pueblos" along the canyon walls (fig. 5.2). The Tewa crew from
Santa Clara and San Ildefonso, a highly skilled work force with several years'
experience, again performed most of the actual excavation. Away from their villages these workers were more amenable to providing ethnological information,
and both Freire-Marreco and Harrington spent much of their time learning the
Tewa language and asking questions about Tewa society. Henderson and Robbins arrived in early August to begin their own studies, while Hodge came shortly
before the finish of the season.[50]

Complementing the fieldwork was a range of activities designed to appeal to
the nonprofessionals in attendance. Evening lectures were held with Hewett as
the principal speaker, although most of the younger staff of the School were prevailed upon at one time or another to make formal presentations on anthropological subjects. Morley discussed his work in Central America, for instance, while

Freire-Marreco spoke on the "judicial and the quasi-judicial procedure among uncivilized people." Visits were made to the talus pueblo that had been reconstructed a few years previously as an example of ancient life, and tall ladders were erected to make the interior of a rock shelter known as "Ceremonial Cave" accessible to students and other visitors.[51] Excursions were also made to sites outside the canyon as well as to Indian dances. At camp, Beauregard and Maude Woy collaborated on a "Rito de los Frijoles Gazette" that featured sketches of the participants and witty commentary on the events of the day.[52]

The camp's population swelled to more than fifty people in late August, when the annual meeting of the Regents of the Museum of New Mexico was held.[53] This tradition had begun the previous year at Puyé and was already an eagerly anticipated event. McFie, Nathan Jaffa, *New Mexican* editor Paul Walter, Frank Springer, and their families were joined by Charles Lummis, who had come from Los Angeles for the event with two of his children. The evening before the meeting featured a bonfire within the plaza of Tyuonyi. Workers from San Ildefonso performed an Eagle Dance, and Lummis sang folk songs.

The drama of the Pajarito landscape had a strong effect on the summer session's participants. To Freire-Marreco, the contrast between light and shadow, the sudden bursts of rain after the heat of the day, and the vivid colors of the forest were ultimately as compelling as the intellectual issues that had brought her to the canyon. In her journal she described walking through the woods in the aftermath of a thunderstorm, a scene in which "the cañon was full of the noise of roaring water and thunder . . . the jagged space of sky framed by the cliffs was fiery suffused rose color—but only for a few moments; quickly, quickly it faded into pink and grey, and then in a moment more it was sundown and dark evening. We hurried home, and they had fixed a plank cross the stream, and we ran across it to our camp, quite giddy with the brown tangled water running under it."[54]

It was a landscape within which both the Indians and the ruins were integral parts. "One of the Indian boys was painted with 'rain-drops' on his face to make it rain," Freire-Marreco wrote, "and they all sang rain-songs in the evening."[55] In the brief intermissions he allowed himself to take from work Harrington wrote poetry about the Rito that described the scene in an unabashedly romantic mode.

> Bye yonder bank where one can faintly hear
> The hollow rushing sounds, the chirping tones
> Of the smooth waters sliding o'er the stones
> The unnamed ruins of a village lie—
> A place of crumbling tufa old and queer
> and wondrous caved cliffs tow'ring to the sky.[56]

By the end of August the Rito camp was broken up, with Hewett and the core of his staff accompanying Hodge to the nearby valley of the Rio Jémez, where they conducted further fieldwork under the auspices of the Bureau until September 16. The others dispersed, with Freire-Marreco spending time at San Ildefonso and Santa Clara pueblos and Henderson returning to Boulder. Laudatory motions passed by the regents of the museum at their streamside conclave were published in the *New Mexican*. "I wish to underscore the profound impression made upon me by the scenes daily witnessed during my short visit to Frijoles Cañon," wrote Springer. "In archaeology I know of nothing like it."[57]

The intellectual promise of the summer session was recognized by some in the archaeological community, Hodge in particular. "I believe the result of last summer's work . . . will be far-reaching in effect," he wrote Kelsey, who monitored the situation from Ann Arbor.[58] A. V. Kidder, who with his new wife, Madeleine, arrived in Santa Fe for dissertation research after the session was over, took a more analytical view of the program. As a Harvard student with Southwest interests Kidder carefully negotiated the hostile terrain between Hewett and Tozzer and was used as a conduit of information by both men. Hewett was "much the same old Czar of the Rito," he wrote Tozzer, describing the multifaceted approach employed by the School as an interesting innovation. He feared, however, that the archaeological side, being under Hewett's direct authority, would be neglected.[59]

In his skepticism about the research value of the summer session, Kidder was largely correct. Freire-Marreco, Harrington, Henderson, and Robbins published substantial reports on the basis of their fieldwork, but these were not complemented by a similar study of the archaeology of the Rito from Hewett. Hewett's major discussion of Pajarito archaeology was not published until nearly a generation later, in 1938, and even then it consisted principally of quotations from his shorter articles.[60]

As in previous endeavors, the successes of the summer of 1910 contained within them the seeds of future difficulties. The public appeal Springer saw as the strength of the program was largely condemned by Hewett's professional colleagues. Boas, in particular, dismissed the effort. "The necessary subserviency to local interests," he wrote, "for which the Archaeological Institute has to thank Mr. Hewett . . . is, in my opinion, opposed to the best interests of science."[61] Boas's condemnatory remarks were not disinterested. He was deep in negotiations over an institution of his own devising that would compete directly with Hewett's operation, an International School of Archaeology to be headquartered in Mexico City. "I confess I do not see how such an establishment can strengthen the American work at present," Hewett wrote an ally; but the new plan was popular with members of the professional community who thought that Hewett had hijacked the school from the Institute and that a new effort would be more successful in training young professionals.[62]

Hewett scrupulously maintained his good relations with his local supporters, but at the end of the summer he offended someone who would ultimately cause him considerable grief. Bronson Cutting, scion of an influential New York family, came to Santa Fe with his sister, Justine Cabot Ward, in the summer of 1910 to seek relief from tuberculosis. The two quickly became prominent in Santa Fe society and were friendly with Bradford Prince and former governor Miguel Antonio Otero. Both men were Hewett opponents, and from the beginning Cutting was encouraged to take a negative view of the School's activities.[63] Rumors concerning Justine Ward and Hewett's artist, Karl Lotave, proved embarrassing to all, and a trip to the Rito at the end of the summer with Hewett as guide failed to mend the breach. Cutting "apparently expected to be met by a brass band," wrote Kidder, "and he also struck camp when they were short of grub and I guess he pretty well starved."[64] The antics of Cutting's guests, two Harvard students who scaled the cliffs of the Rito and told the newspaper that the drive up the mesa was arduous enough "to surpass crew work or the tactics of the gridiron,"[65] may not have endeared them to the local archaeologists. An aggrieved Cutting wrote friends at Harvard to complain about Hewett, allegations that made their way to higher levels.

Through Cutting's agency, links between Hewett's local opponents and his enemies among the professional archaeologists were established for the first time. While in previous years the conflict between Hewett and his adversaries had largely been behind closed doors, after 1910 it became increasingly open and personal. The price of developing a public agenda was public scrutiny, and Hewett was shortly to become aware that professional rivalries were only one form of the competition the success of the summer session had aroused.

Politics, Professionals, and the Shifting Public Agenda

In February 1911 Kelsey asked Hewett to respond to Boas's charges that, in appealing to a public audience, he was hindering the professional development of anthropology. "In practically every case where we have organized work it has been in response to local demand—the same demand that is causing the building of museums, libraries and colleges all over the United States," Hewett wrote. "There has been little trouble in 'providing for scientific work.' The people are providing for what they want and are getting it."[66]

Now that the School of American Archaeology was up and running, rhetoric could be distinguished from reality, and the public slant of the Rito project confirmed the suspicions of those who thought the School's programs should conform to a more professional model. Opposition to Hewett, previously confined to those who had particular grievances, became more widespread. His involvement in several controversies, such as a dispute between Boas and Smithsonian Secretary Walcott over alleged financial improprieties, did not enhance his reputation among his colleagues.[67] Alfred Tozzer in particular took the opportunity to oppose Hewett whenever it arose. Not all professional anthropologists were enthusiastic about such zealotry; Pliny Goddard wrote that he "wouldn't care to assist to bring all the Southwestern work to an end without further evidence," while Alice Fletcher commented derisively about "little Tozzer."[68] Holmes, Hodge, Fewkes, and other Smithsonian scientists continued to collaborate with the School, but government scholarship itself was on the wane in the face of the expansion of anthropology in the universities.

Ironically, the erosion of Hewett's professional standing in the conflict over archaeological rationales pushed him even further into the area of public programs. In his previous efforts Hewett had justified the importance of public education as a component of the professional development of anthropology. After 1910, however, he increasingly described public education as an end in itself.

In expanding the public programs of the School, Hewett found himself involved more deeply both in the councils of the Institute and in political skirmishes within Santa Fe itself. In the years the School had been establishing itself on the ground, what was generally known as the "Kelsey Program" was taking root in the parent organization. Working with members of the Institute who opposed the New England elite, such as Mitchell Carroll of the American University and Harry Wilson of Johns Hopkins, Kelsey expanded the role of the western societies within the organization and continued to promote activities that would raise the visibility of the Institute in the eyes of the public. The public lecture circuit, which had been in operation since before the turn of the century, was expanded, although American subjects continued to be rare. Kelsey's reforms produced strenuous objections on the part of the traditional leaders of the organization.[69] Controversy over the use of proxy votes from western societies swirled around the Institute's annual meeting in Baltimore in 1909, which, according to the local newspaper, was "unlike the usual staid meetings and akin to a legislature on the last day of a busy session."[70]

Since one of the original motivations for founding the School had been to mobilize the public in support of archaeology, Kelsey and his associates were steadfast in their backing of Hewett.[71] None of the results of the anti-Hewett maneuvers of professional anthropologists, such as the reduction of opportunities to teach young professionals or of the potential to conduct original research, were of particular concern to this group, which continued to see the western populace as a fertile source of funding for larger Institute projects. Instead, members of the Kelsey party within the Institute began to play greater personal roles in the School's activities. Lewis Bayles Paton, an Institute member from the Hartford Theological Seminary, lectured on "Palestine before the Hebrew Conquest" in Santa Fe in fall 1910 and was thereafter a regular participant in events at the School. Mitchell Carroll became close to Hewett as well, as did Harry Wilson and Henry Rushton Fairclough of Stanford. None of these people had expertise in American archaeology. American specialists such as Alice Fletcher and W. H. Holmes who were involved with the Managing Board seemed generally content to let Hewett chart his own course.

One unforeseen impact of Hewett's greater reliance on the Institute was a reduced role for American archaeology in the School's programs. As in the previous year, fieldwork for the 1911 summer program was conducted in the Rito, where effort continued to focus on clearing the ruins of Tyuonyi, with the participation of about fifty students and "auditors" over the course of the summer. Many of the principal contributors of 1910 were no longer involved with the School, so the excavation staff was made up of the permanent Santa Fe employees. Hewett, Chapman, and Harrington all lectured on American subjects, but they were joined by several others who spoke on their own non-American specialties. These included Carroll, whose topic was Greek archaeology, and Paton, whose lectures covered "the primitive Semitic literature, art, religion, and social organization."[72] An additional feature of the School was a special series of Sunday evening lectures in Santa Fe, of which not even Hewett's talk on "The Holy Cities of America" had significant southwestern content. When the summer session and the meeting of the Managing Committee were done Hewett and Hodge returned to the Jémez region for more joint fieldwork, but on the whole Southwest archaeology had served more as backdrop than as the center of action in 1911.

This trend was even more pronounced in 1912, when the summer session was divided between a two-week course of lectures in Santa Fe and a two-week encampment during which students could "witness" the Rito excavations. Lecture topics included heredity and evolution, Roman archaeology, historical epochs in art, shamanism, folklore, the Mayas, and the monuments of the Aztecs. Only Hewett's presentation on "The Ancient Pueblos and Cliff Dwellers" and lectures on the Indians of the Southwest delivered by T. Harmon Parkhurst had any local significance. The Sunday evening series in Santa Fe continued but was concerned entirely with Old World and Central American subjects.[73] A few of the students attracted to the School's events seem to have had intentions of going on to further anthropological training, but the audience was otherwise almost entirely avocational.[74] The slow pace of work at Tyuonyi, portions of which remained unexcavated even after four years of attention, was another indication that the Rito effort was now largely show. When Hodge, exasperated by Hewett's overcommitments, declined to continue supporting the late-season excavations in the Jémez, support was cobbled together from the Southwest Society and the Toronto Society of the Institute to continue the work. It was, however, more an effort to give the illusion of progress and entice new allies than a coordinated program of research such as had been advocated for the Rito project only two years before.

Another indicator of the gradual divergence of research and education at the School was the revival of Hewett's old network of western societies, once used to promote fieldwork but now functioning exclusively as part of an expanded educational program. In 1912 a summer session along the lines of that offered in Santa Fe was inaugurated in Colorado Springs under the sponsorship of the Colorado Society of the Institute. Similar sessions were held in San Diego and Los Angeles, with Wilson and other Institute figures presenting lectures. "The work here goes nicely and we seem to be stirring the town up somewhat," Wilson wrote Hewett from Colorado, "as our audience grows larger each day. Carroll and I had about fifty out this morning." Afterward the two men proceeded on to Santa Fe to lecture on similar topics.[75]

This vastly expanded summer session reached its peak in 1913, when sequential programs in three Colorado cities, San Diego, and Santa Fe spanned virtually the entire summer. The lecturers traveled from one venue to the next, presenting largely Old World topics but usually including Hewett amongst their number as well. Recruitment on behalf of the Institute was a component of the lecture series, and one of the results of the 1912 session was the establishment of an affiliated society in San Diego. The constant skirmishing between the Institute and the Southwest Society was brought to an end the same year by the dissolution of the Southwest Society and its replacement by a Los Angeles affiliate organized along more traditional lines. Later the same year, when ground was finally broken in Los Angeles for the Southwest Museum, it was an entirely separate institution, divorced for the time being from the promotion of Southwest research.[76] Only in Santa Fe was any effort made to correlate the lectures with ongoing archaeological activity, which by 1913 was largely perfunctory. At the meeting of the Managing Board that year resolutions were passed reasserting the School's "dual function of training field students in Archaeology, and of extending the knowledge of Archaeology among the public," with the promotion of research largely abandoned.[77]

The increasing dominance of the School's public programs and the incorporation of classical and other Old World themes made sense in light of the educational mission of the institution, but it did so at the expense of other elements of the agenda. The audience for the summer session programs was largely composed of westerners, but they heard comparatively little about western archaeology. Just a few years earlier this kind of focus on the Old World had been one of the points of new members' criticism of the Institute. In 1907 Byron Cummings had taken umbrage at a lecturer sent west to Salt Lake City. "We have had two lectures on classic subjects already this fall, and he [Kelsey] must realize that the Western societies are more interested in American archaeology at present at least."[78]

The local public's acquiescence to Hewett's deviation from their preferred southwestern subjects may have been due in part to his success drawing parallels between new and old world antiquity. Certainly lectures like "Paul at Athens" being delivered around the campfire in the Rito enhanced the aura of respectability of the ruins in the vicinity. In subsequent years Paton delivered Sunday sermons in the Ceremonial Cave (fig. 5.3).[79] A key weakness, however, was Hewett's reluctance to provide a stage for any New World specialist other than himself and some of his staff. Even Hewett's allies, such as Jesse Fewkes, never participated in the summer sessions, and it is safe to say that Hewett reserved comment on American archaeology as his own bailiwick. The absence from the Institute's programs of other scholars in the American field inevitably tilted the balance toward the more numerous classicists.

The accusation of bias in favor of classical scholarship, however, eventually fueled a backlash against Hewett from within his local audience, in the course of which the rhetoric of cultural nationalism he had used a few years earlier was employed against him. The controversy, which involved Hewett's former allies in the Santa Fe Chamber of Commerce and at the *New Mexican,* illustrated the complexities of the national-local debate over archaeology, professionalism, and the public.

The catalyst for the revolt against Hewett, ironically, was yet another Santa Fe promotional campaign, one sponsored by the Chamber of Commerce that identified Santa Fe as the oldest city in the United States.[80] Exactly why Hewett chose to make an issue of this propaganda is unclear, particularly since he had consistently drawn attention to the presence of an indigenous village on the site of Santa Fe predating the founding of the Spanish town, but he went so far as to elicit the opinions of a number of historians and used them publicly to disparage the claims of the Chamber and its president, Harry Dorman.

Figure 5.3   Lewis B. Paton speaking to students at Ceremonial Cave, Rito de los Frijoles, ca. 1916. (Courtesy Photo Archives, Fray Angélico Chávez
History Library, Palace of the Governors, Santa
Fe; neg. no. 42060)

What should have been a minor fracas quickly escalated into a confronta-
tion between Hewett and his antagonists both in the Santa Fe community and
within the profession. In 1912 Bronson Cutting bought the *New Mexican* from
Hewett's associate, Paul Walter, thereby ending the paper's favorable coverage of
the School. Dorman was an ally of Cutting, and when the "oldest city" controversy
broke the *New Mexican* attacked Hewett and his policies. The barrage of bad press
and the interest taken in the affair by average citizens caught the attention of Nels
Nelson, who passed through Santa Fe while finishing up his 1913 field season
and was startled by the public debate over museum affairs. "One hears people
talk about 'Dr.' H. on the street & in the Hotel," he wrote Wissler, "so that one
wonders what the poor devil has really done."[81]

The attack on Hewett mobilized his opponents, both professional and local.
Tozzer, always alert, sensed that the fray offered the potential for recapturing the
School as a center of professional training and rallied other academics to Dorman's side. In a letter published under the headline "Tozzer tells why students
stay away" he attacked Hewett's professional credentials and ridiculed the current
status of the School. "The 'school' has never been a school in the accepted sense of

the term. Hewett has had a lot of his personal friends lecturing on Palestine and Greece to a picnic crowd of women. His camp at the Rito de los Frijoles has had a shorter and shorter session as the years have gone by. No real work was done and great opportunities have been thrown away."[82] Letters from Boas and Dixon also appeared in the *New Mexican,* accentuating the rift between Hewett and the leaders of the profession.

As Tozzer publicly questioned Hewett's professional fitness, the *New Mexican* accused the School's director of failing to promote Southwest archaeology. "Should competent or incompetent Semitic, Egyptian, and Classical professors direct AMERICAN archaeology?" read one headline. The Managing Board was also criticized as not being sympathetic to western interests.[83] Hewett had recently been placed in charge of the Department of Anthropology at the Panama-Pacific Exposition in San Diego, raising concerns that the School would be transferred to the West Coast. These fears were fanned by Cutting's continued assault. Even local allies became concerned that Hewett would depart and take the School with him, and the Archaeological Society passed a resolution requesting that the Institute affirm that Santa Fe was the permanent home for the School.[84] The controversy was sufficiently intense for Tozzer to prepare a plan for the reorganization of the School along professional lines and without Hewett. At the annual meeting of the Institute on January 2, 1914, Dorman appeared before the Managing Committee of the School with the proposal for reorganization, backed by Tozzer, Boas, Dixon, and Goddard, along with a letter in opposition to Hewett signed by many prominent Santa Fe citizens.[85]

The Institute, however, had no intention of allowing its agenda for the School be railroaded by either professional or local opposition. As early as November Kelsey had recommended going over Tozzer's head to President Lowell of Harvard to ask "whether he thinks it either proper or dignified for members of the faculty in Harvard University to be engaging in petty strife in a case where opinion is at least divided," and the support of the Institute had been marshalled long before the meeting took place.[86] Dorman, whose character was thoroughly smeared by a letter from Paul Walter received the day of the meeting, came equipped with accusations but no hard evidence, leaving him exposed to what Hewett called Kelsey's "rapid fire-gun."[87] Action on the matter was tabled and, with Dorman sufficiently embarrassed to abscond with the transcripts of the meeting, the anti-Hewett forces collapsed amid general recrimination.[88]

As had been demonstrated in previous years, the Institute was sensitive to criticism of its American programs emanating from the anthropological community, and while Hewett continued as director of the School some effort was made to address the complaints. By this time the Managing Board of the School included several of the archaeologists associated with the Bureau and the U.S. National Museum, who nominally were Hewett allies but were also concerned with the overall advancement of American archaeology. In spring 1914 the growing rift between the educational and research agendas of the School was acknowledged by an attempt to "spin off" the summer session as an independent organization while reestablishing research as a priority of the School itself. The new entity also seems to have been conceived as a means to mend fences with the Santa Fe business community, and the cooperation of the Chamber of Commerce was solicited. The curriculum of what was first called the New Mexico Academy of Arts and Science and ultimately the New Mexico Institute of Science and Education was broadly conceived, including courses on psychology, pedagogy, "domestic science, manual training and agriculture" in addition to anthropological subjects.[89] Of the 150 lectures presented by the New Mexico Institute in the summer of 1914, only 30 were on archaeology, and there was no field component.[90] The attendance of three hundred at the Institute's program was apparently a disappointment, and by 1916 the School's summer session had been reinstated.

Despite the intentions of the Managing Board, the School's research program was not reinvigorated by the shedding of its educational program, largely because of Hewett's continued dalliance in San Diego. Suspicions that he intended to remove the School to the West Coast were not entirely unfounded, as he floated a plan during this period to establish what he called "the San Diego Anthropological Station," ostensibly to be a far western branch of the Santa Fe operation.[91] Desultory research was conducted in 1914 in the Jémez mountains and at the Salinas pueblo of Quarai, while Lucy Wilson's excavations the following summer at the Pajarito site of Otowi were conducted under the auspices of the School and with the assistance of School staff. All of these endeavors were opportunistic rather than part of a general plan. The mystery and allure of the ruins of the Rito and the educational offerings of the Museum continued to lure tourists, but they were no longer part of a larger program.

When Hewett was finally finished in San Diego and returned to Santa Fe to run the summer session in 1916, his horizons had narrowed considerably. The setting for the work was Puyé, to which he had brought Kidder and Morley nine years earlier. "We had the full number of students (20) to which the Summer School class at Puyé was limited," he wrote. "Not the best group we ever had nor the poorest. Just a fair average with a number of strong individuals who will go on."[92] This new crop of students, however, had little to do with the professional world

Figure 5.4 Excavations at Otowi Pueblo, August 1915. (Photograph by Lucy L. Wilson; courtesy Photo Archives, Fray Angélico Chávez History Library, Palace of the Governors, Santa Fe; neg. no. 82871)

of American archaeology. By 1916 Morley, Harrington, and other core members of Hewett's staff had departed and had been replaced by students with more local credentials who had few connections to the larger professional community. Springer, Lummis, and Fletcher were aging and unable to do more than passively support Hewett's plans. The Institute was no longer a reliable ally either, since Kelsey's chosen successor Harry Wilson had died after only a month in office. The compromise replacement, Frederick W. Shipley of St. Louis, was sympathetic to the Kelsey program but was perceived as a weak leader.[93]

In Santa Fe, the western archaeological agenda Hewett had helped to create continued on its own, fueled by tourism and local advocates. Thousands of people toured the museum facilities in the Palace annually, and it was thoroughly established as a hub of the town's cultural life. Resentment of Hewett faded as his detractors either ceased to play an active role in public life (e.g., Bradford Prince), or found other outlets for their political activities (e.g., Bronson Cutting). After a complex and bitter fight, the ruins of the Rito and other sites on the Pajarito Plateau were reserved as Bandelier National Monument in 1916.[94] In many ways the creation of the monument was the highest endorsement of the local archaeology program, since the preservation by the federal government of Tyuonyi and other sites, both excavated and unexcavated, was considered tacit acknowledgment of their national importance.

Hewett's experience in Santa Fe had taken his ambitions for a new model for American archaeology and shaped them in an entirely unexpected way. What had begun as a means to harness western enthusiasm in support of a national agenda had become a rationale for archaeology that was of greatest significance within the Southwest itself. Like many other agendas, that of the School of American Archaeology was long on conception but short on execution. But in its emphasis on place, on the relationships between people, landscape, and history, it provided a rationale for archaeology as a means of creating heritage. And in 1916 an outsider may have perceived that Hewett was secure in his Santa Fe niche promoting just such an agenda. Times were changing, however, and Hewett in particular was quick to adjust to shifting terrain. The Santa Fe of Prince and Springer, in which an interest in antiquities had grown up alongside a political drive for national recognition and legitimacy, was by the eve of World War I already being superseded. Archaeology in this new environment, in which even the insecurities of the late territorial days were fading, was to become a surprising synthesis of what had gone before: the animosities and ambitions of the previous generation were reconfigured into a paradigm for Southwest archaeology that would last fifty years.

6

Conclusion

The Making of
Southwest Archaeology

In 1917 Clark Wissler, Nels Nelson, Frank Springer, and Edgar Lee Hewett came together in Santa Fe for a ceremonial occasion that had significance for both the development of professional Southwest archaeology and the role of archaeology in the construction of southwestern identity. The event was the dedication of a gallery of art associated with the Museum of New Mexico, a building designed in a new southwestern style that immediately attracted attention as a harbinger of things to come in New Mexico's capital city. Springer had been the financial patron of the endeavor, and Wissler had seen the event as an opportunity to have a close look at an institutional rival. "Notwithstanding some of our personal antipathies to Hewett I feel it our duty to take some part in the celebration," he wrote Nelson, who obligingly took time off from his fieldwork to attend.[1] Hewett was, as usual, at center stage, but on this occasion his opening address focused on the esthetics of the southwestern environment rather than on its history. "The beauty of the Southwest is subtle, mysterious, elemental," he proclaimed. "We who live in it have long silently felt it—the eternal character of these vast spaces, silent but vibrant with life and color . . . on which man through the ages has wrought no change."[2]

The opening of the new art museum, sometimes referred to as the "cathedral in the desert," was a pivotal moment in the making of Southwest archaeology.[3] Despite the fact that many of the traditional supporters of the School of American Archaeology were present that afternoon, including Byron Cummings, Francis Kelsey, and Charles Lummis, there was a sense that the agenda had changed. The entry of America into World War I, the nation's changing demographics, and turbulence in the professional community all exerted influence on the study of southwestern antiquity. Unbeknownst to Wissler and Hewett, their presence on a Santa Fe stage that fall marked the moment when the competition between the social and intellectual traditions they represented gave way to a broad-based consensus on what Southwest archaeology should be.

The End of the Huntington Survey

Even as the chronological methods developed by Nelson and promoted by Wissler gained force within archaeology, the factors that would bring the project to a halt were rapidly coalescing. Institutional circumstances, developments within society at large, and the interpersonal dynamics of the members of the Huntington Survey ultimately produced conditions under which it was no longer possible for the project to function as it had since 1909.

First among the circumstances that undermined the survey were increasing financial constraints. Despite Wissler's repeated overtures to Osborn, and Osborn's sensitivity to the aggressive "claims of the Heye Museum,"[4] little additional internal funding was secured. No further support for anthropological projects was forthcoming from J. P. Morgan. "Having shown a willingness to contribute," wrote Nelson several years later, "they wanted to rope him in for something bigger" than archaeology.[5] Huntington, in fact, increased his donation to the American Museum, contributing $12,008.94 during 1917. Five thousand dollars of this was initially earmarked for Southwest research, but it seems originally to have been designated entirely for support of the Aztec excavations. Once the decision had been made to use Aztec as a showcase for the museum's Southwest work, investment in that part of the project necessarily took precedence over funds for Nelson's more abstract chronological studies.[6]

The incipient entry of the United States into World War I also had a drastic effect on conditions at the American Museum. The museum administration was concerned both to be perceived as making a contribution to the war effort and to curtail expenses. On the one hand this led to museum employees engaging in military drills on the grounds; on the other, significant effort was made to justify research activities as yielding useful results. One example of this shift in emphasis was the "Mandan corn" episode of 1917. A researcher affiliated with the Department of Anthropology, Gilbert A. Wilson, made headlines by suggesting that hardy strains of corn formerly used by Mandan people on the northern plains could be adopted for modern agriculture, increasing production during wartime. Even though the project failed to materialize, Wissler and Osborn saw Mandan corn as a demonstration of the value of the museum's research program, with a practical appeal archaeology could not hope to match.[7]

Staff also became vulnerable. In the winter of 1917 Wissler repeatedly found himself in conflict with the administration over personnel matters. "A short time ago," wrote director Lucas, "the museum was to lose the respect of anthropologists if it did not devote more money to explorations, now it will lose their respect if the salary of one member of the staff is not increased. All of which is somewhat irritating."[8] External relationships, such as those established with the University of Colorado, were curtailed. Younger researchers like Spier and Morris were eligible for the draft, making their availability for planned research questionable.[9] Morale within the Department of Anthropology plummeted.

Nelson observed the decline of the Southwest program with increasing disillusionment. He had never favored the Aztec excavations, which he saw as a betrayal of the survey's original mission. "[I] didn't exactly like the prospect of being tied down for several years to such a piece of work," he wrote Wissler. "I had 3–4 years of semi-intensive excavation and was beginning to believe that for a time at least I could contribute more of permanent value to the solution of the Southwest problem by some speedier method."[10] In a letter to Morris years later, his bitterness over Aztec was evident. "You have gotten something worth while out of it I hope. The Museum and American archaeology generally have been enriched, I am sure. For myself, I sometimes wish I had never seen the damn place."[11] Morris's response was conciliatory: "without realizing it, I have been the hog who not only put all four feet in the trough, but lay down in it as well."[12]

With a smaller staff Nelson's responsibilities for the archaeological collections grew increasingly burdensome, and time to write up the results of his fieldwork was scarce. Small, opportunistic projects that Wissler sent his way, such as a study of Florida shell mounds in May 1917, and work in Kentucky immediately thereafter, also kept him from analyzing his Southwest data.[13] Under such circumstances, chances that the Galisteo and Chaco fieldwork would ever be completed seemed remote.

Wissler was not, however, entirely prepared to let the Huntington Survey collapse, and despite a general consensus that the 1917 field season would be cancelled he forged ahead with new plans.[14] The Aztec excavations would continue. Permits were also in hand for Leslie Spier to expand his reconnaissance in the Zuñi region, where George Heye and Frederick Hodge were finally making good on their own permit to excavate at Hawikuh.[15] Wissler played on Osborn's proprietary instincts one last time, and early in July it was announced that the field season was on after all.[16]

Sensing that he would get no further opportunities, Nelson spent the 1917 season dashing from one end of the Southwest to the other. The first week in September found him in the Little Colorado River country of eastern Arizona, while three weeks and hundreds of miles later he was examining ruins near Mountainair in central New Mexico. In the process he was able to look into the Bureau of American Ethnology's excavations in Arizona, examine the distribution of diagnostic pottery types, and search for Chaco-related ruins near the modern pueblos of Acoma and Laguna. Next he headed southward, apparently conducting reconnaissance in the Pecos River drainage as far as Pecos, Texas, before returning up the Rio Grande, examining sites along its eastern side.[17]

The 1917 survey was, in fact, Nelson's last substantive contribution to Southwest archaeology. His reports for that year have an uncharacteristically frenetic tone, filled with ideas about the movement of Chaco-related peoples, various ceramic types, the purchase of artifact collections, and ruins seen in passing. There was very little evidence of the patient, empirical fieldwork he preferred. His last letter, written from the "Carrizozo eating house" in Carrizozo, New Mexico, ruefully acknowledged that the end of the season probably meant the end of his part of the project. Further north, Morris continued to unearth the secrets of the Aztec Ruin, but Nelson's future, to his clear dismay, was in New York.[18]

At the "scientific congress" that accompanied the opening of the Art Museum in Santa Fe, Nelson presented a paper entitled "The Archaeological Problem of the Southwest," which summed up his views on the Huntington Survey. A similar work, published shortly afterward, described the project as an attempt to take advantage of conditions in Southwest archaeology to pose questions applicable to the study of prehistoric people in general.[19] Nelson bluntly contrasted the work of the American Museum with that of its predecessors and competitors. "We have entered the field not so much to recover specimens as to solve problems," he wrote. The distribution of the Pueblo culture over time and space, an aspect of what anthropologists called the "age-area hypothesis," was the issue at hand, and faced with the overwhelming nature of the data only methodological rigor could hope to provide a solution. Nelson was modest in evaluating his success in cracking the chronological problem through the correlation of stylistic change in ceramics with stratigraphic relationships. In fact his conclusions are disappointingly vague. Over time populations had moved, and nomadic traits had gradually given way to sedentary lifestyles, but otherwise the details of prehistoric society were interpretations left to the ethnologists and linguists working among living peoples.

Ironically, in their efforts to gain chronological control of the southwestern past, the anthropological archaeologists of the American Museum contributed to the perception that the past was merely an older version of the present. In reducing archaeology to chronology Nelson and Wissler stripped southwestern antiquity of its nuances, leaving very little to be said. Such a minimal cultural framework contrasted dramatically with the high-flying rhetoric of the cultural nationalists, many of whom were listening to Nelson as he spoke.

After leaving Santa Fe at the end of the congress Nelson did not return to the Southwest until 1920, when he was put in charge of "The Mrs. L. P. Cartier Archaeological Expedition to Grand Gulch, Utah."[20] Typical of the short-term, patron-centered research projects that arose in the vacuum left when the chronological focus of the Huntington Survey faltered, the Cartier Expedition was promoted by none other than Talbot Hyde, who hoped that revisiting the sites from which his Grand Gulch collections had been collected in the 1890s would help him reconstitute the original notes. Kept on a short financial leash by his family, Hyde's final attempt to reenter the Southwest field was only made possible by the patronage of a friend and the indulgence of Osborn. No usable information came from the Cartier Expedition, and the only union of Hyde and Nelson in the field marked the last time either man was engaged in Southwest research.[21] "Out here," Nelson wrote Goddard, "one lives face to face with one problem, one set of facts, for weeks at a time; at home this attention is divided among '57' or more topics. How can the fog be cleared from any one?"[22]

The remodeled Huntington Survey, with the Aztec excavations its only component, persisted at least in name until 1921. In 1923 Archer Huntington gracefully declined further support for the southwestern work of the American Museum. His contributions in the support of the various projects had totalled $73,500, by Wissler's estimate.[23] Morris, who had effectively replaced Nelson as field representative in the Southwest, worked sporadically for the American Museum throughout the 1920s. Like the Cartier Expedition, however, these initiatives were driven by patron demand and were typically exploration trips made on behalf of wealthy sponsors such as Charles L. Bernheimer and Ogden Mills.[24] Other small projects were begun, but the theoretical rationale of the survey years had entirely vanished. "[Y]ou will be pleased to learn," Nelson wrote Kidder, "that on inquiring casually whether our Southwest Survey had 'fizzled out,' I was told 'No, it had been brought to a successful conclusion.'"[25]

Art and Archaeology

The establishment of Santa Fe as an art colony in the 1910s had a critical impact on the identity of the region and on the significance of local archaeology. Artists had been drawing inspiration from the Southwest since the time of John Mix Stanley and the Kern brothers in the late 1840s, but it was only at the turn of the century that they began to settle in the region to study the esthetics of southwestern peoples and landscapes in detail. The Taos Art Colony was established by 1900, and within ten years a similar group of expatriate artists had set itself up in Santa Fe.[26] The incorporation of art into the agenda of the Museum of New Mexico followed quite closely, particularly since Carlos Vierra and Kenneth Chapman, associates and employees of Hewett, were leaders in the growing artistic community. The archaeological work of the School also influenced the artists arriving in Santa Fe, and Warren Rollins's exhibition in the Palace in 1910 indicated Hewett's awareness of the importance of art in the public consciousness.[27]

From 1910 onward art, always a central component of the humanistic tradition of archaeology, was incorporated into Hewett's rationale for Southwest archaeology. The esthetic treatment of archaeological materials, such as ruins and Greek vases, was fundamental to classical archaeological thought, and Hewett presented conference papers on the Pajaritan culture in the same halls where the cultural merits of Roman architecture and Babylonian murals were being discussed. The appeal of art for Southwest identity was that it was infinitely adaptable and varied, but had the same roots in the landscape and heritage that Hewett and Springer had emphasized through archaeology. The close relationship between art, archaeological heritage, and southwestern identity was made explicit in Hewett's later writings.

> The deeper influences of climate and soil that produced the aboriginal Americans . . . must still exist and, to some degree, retain their potency over the minds of men. They are profoundly felt in the elemental conditions of the American Southwest, a region that man finds it difficult to possess and modify but, on the

contrary, finds himself possessed by and absorbed in. The noted development
of art in the Southwest in recent years may be a happy portent of something of
which those who are participating can hardly be aware: a movement that is obey-
ing the influences that formed the mind of the earliest Americans.[28]

Hewett's increasing interest in art was as a logical outcome of his view of both the
humanistic roots of archaeology and its relevance to issues of identity.

The planning for the Art Museum had begun early in 1915. After lengthy
discussion, efforts to acquire a prime piece of property across the street from the
main museum complex in the Palace went forward, and by spring 1916 Hewett
was able to announce to the managing committee that $30,000 had been donated
by Springer and a few associates to build the facility.[29] Springer, who shared
Hewett's views on the relationship between art, history, and the southwestern
landscape, funded research on ancient southwestern "art" as well. When Hewett
moved the summer session to Puyé in 1916 and 1917, Springer and Kenneth
Chapman continued to work in the Rito de los Frijoles, spending the summers
recording the faint motifs and designs that had been scratched into the sooty
walls of the caves.

The new museum building was to be notable not only for its contents but
for its design, an expression of a new "Santa Fe style" in architecture.[30] Based on
a structure built for the Panama-Pacific Exposition in San Diego, it incorporated
elements of colonial and indigenous architectural traditions. The building was
the first of many built upon similar lines that rapidly replaced the Victorian style
that had dominated downtown Santa Fe for decades. The new look reflected a
new security in southwestern identity, built in part on the same cultural nationalist rhetoric that had infused local archaeology.

In fact, even as the Art Museum was attracting public attention the promotion of archaeology as an aspect of Southwest tourism was reaching new
heights. The sense of cultural pride that had become associated with local cultural
resources became increasingly exaggerated. Santa Fe had become "the imperial
city of the artist, the student, the historian, and the traveler."[31] Springer's address
at the opening of the Art Museum, delivered to a crowd of 1,200 people, also
reflected great pride in the achievement of Southwest archaeology, and expressed
his hopes that the new facility would bring together the many threads of southwestern culture. From Springer's perspective, the School's work was central to
this emerging synthesis.

Thus may America begin to know herself. Depending no longer upon other
lands or times for inspiration to brush, to chisel, to trowel or to song, we shall

find at home the themes for boundless achievement, and our arts shall grow—as this temple has grown, and as all true and enduring Art must ever grow—straight from our own soil.

Thus while the Past may teach us, it is the Future that calls and beckons.[32]

By the time Springer spoke to the audience at the museum's dedication, however, the significance of archaeology as a source of local pride and identity was on the wane. Tourist maps of the Santa Fe area now included the homes of the most prominent members of the art colony, called the "Cinco Pintores," along with the Rito and other traditional destinations.[33] Over the next decade revivals of Indian art, the elaboration of local festivals such as the Santa Fe fiesta, and the proliferation of the Santa Fe Style in architecture all became active components of the community's efforts to define itself.

One reason for the waning symbolic value of southwestern antiquities was, paradoxically, rooted in the very success of the School and other programs of archaeology. Ruins and relics had been useful as sources of heritage for the Anglo-American population largely because of their ambiguity. As long as the southwestern past remained unknown it was possible to reconstruct that remote time along the classical lines promoted by cultural nationalists. As archaeological information about southwestern ruins accumulated, however, the direct relationship between ancient and modern Native Americans became clearer with every stroke of the spade. A. V. Kidder's *Introduction to the Study of Southwestern Archaeology* was published in 1924, for the first time bringing the fruits of thirty years of archaeology to the general public. "A review of the subject matter of Southwestern archaeology," Kidder wrote, "must necessarily begin with a consideration of the still-inhabited pueblos of New Mexico and Arizona."[34] Through the works of Kidder and others, the professional, anthropological perceptions of the ancient Southwest began to reach a broader audience. While pamphlets still referred to "relics of a vanished race," the romantic past conjured by such images increasingly gave way to the more accurate view that southwestern ruins were explicable in terms of Native American history.[35]

More accurate perceptions of the ancient Southwest did not necessarily invalidate it as a source of Anglo-American identity, since the image of the Pueblo people had itself undergone a renaissance during this period. Positive images of Native American culture, fueled in particular by a newfound appreciation of Pueblo art, attracted the attention of both residents and tourists. But the immediacy of living artists, Indian or otherwise, was precisely what ancient relics lacked. While the ruins of the Rito and Puyé, of Mesa Verde or Chaco Canyon, remained sources of visual inspiration, they could not have the same impact as dances in teeming pueblo plazas.[36]

Figure 6.1 Tourists at Pueblo Bonito in the 1920s. (Courtesy Museum of Indian Arts and Cultures, Museum of New Mexico)

In the aftermath of active archaeological programs in the Rito and other touristed locales, the restored ruins became, in many ways, akin to the natural landscape. With little to see that reflected the original life of the ancient villages and in the absence of participatory excavations, visitors observed walls of stone and inexplicable fragments of artifacts. These material forms took their place alongside cliffs, canyons, and ponderosa pine in an evolving southwestern esthetic. While to informed tourists ruins reflected the past of another culture, to more casual viewers they were completely dehistoricized, remote to understanding.

Bereft of the dynamism that had come from competing with the professional community over the rationale for Southwest archaeology, the work of the School became a largely formulaic affair. Within the American Institute of Archaeology, the rise of a new group of "New York men" who assumed control from those of Kelsey's generation soon broke up the close relationship between the School and the parent organization.[37] With few remaining allies on the national level Hewett invested more and more time in activities of local relevance, taking the School further from its original role. These shifts in purpose and allegiance were reflected in suggestions that the school be renamed, first to "The Institute of American Archaeology and Art at Santa Fe" and then, officially, to the "School of American

Research," the name it took in 1917 and still retains.[38] The summer sessions continued but had become, as Tozzer had predicted, little more than outings.

Nelson and Wissler, Springer and Hewett could not have been aware, as they met in Santa Fe in autumn 1917, that the competition they had engaged in over Southwest archaeology was largely finished. Humanistic and scientific models for archaeology had been laid out in stark contrast, formed by struggle between institutions and identities, patrons and scholars, and had between them revealed a framework for the ancient past of the Southwest that had significance for public and professional audiences. The coming generation of scholars, subject to a new set of influences and constraints, would occupy a remarkably consistent common ground, a new agenda, formed by the earlier conflict, that would persist until the 1960s.

The Rationale for Southwest Archaeology

In theoretical terms, the chronological archaeology of Nelson and Wissler set the tone for the next several decades of southwestern scholarship. Through dendrochronology, and then through statistical evaluation of ceramic style, the building of a temporal framework for the ancient Southwest dominated archaeological efforts. The leader in the field was A. V. Kidder, who had learned from both Hewett and from Tozzer and considered Nelson one of his principal influences.

Wissler's failure to integrate archaeology and ethnology into a common program was not unique. After the turn of the century the different intellectual roots of archaeology and ethnology were increasingly obvious, despite the fact that the two were linked by institutional structures. In the Southwest, the integrated vision developed by scholars like Bandelier and Cushing in the 1880s was largely forgotten. One impact of the divide between ethnology and archaeology was that archaeologists had less and less to do with subjects of ethnological interest, such as social structure, political organization, and ritual. As archaeologists ceded this ground to their colleagues, they fell back on a static view of ancient southwestern society as a direct analog of historic societies. Ironically, Wissler had devised the chronological program as a way to study culture change, but many of those who adopted the strategy tacitly viewed the past as unchanging.

The uncritical use of historic pueblo analogy as a model for the southwestern past resulted from the split between archaeology and ethnology and persisted into the 1970s.[39] Archaeologists were concerned with time, and temporal indicators such as ceramics, devoting little attention to other areas of culture. Complex phenomena, such as that represented by the enigmatic ruins of Chaco Canyon, were explained in ways that fit poorly with existing data. Some archaeologists understood that in their preoccupation with organizing, rather than interpreting, the archaeological record, they had let important opportunities pass by. "We have, it is true, been dealing with people long dead," wrote A. V. Kidder, looking back. "But we have made small effort to bring them back to life."[40]

By 1920 the eastern institutions had largely reestablished themselves as important players in Southwest archaeology. Kidder's excavations at Pecos and the National Geographic Society's Chaco Canyon project in the 1920s were two examples of the renewed vigor of professional research programs, a pattern established by the Huntington Survey. In contrast, the dilution of the cultural nationalist rationale for locally based archaeological research meant that the southwestern societies largely ceased to be influential. Although the fieldwork programs of the School of American Research and the Museum of New Mexico continued, their impact on the broader profession was muted.

Western influence remained critical, however, in two areas that reflected the educational legacy of the southwestern societies. Many of the scholars employed by the eastern institutions in their Southwest research from the 1910s onward were themselves born in the West or trained by westerners. Neil Judd, Jesse Nusbaum, Earl Morris, and Kidder himself fit this category. Practically the entire generation that controlled Southwest archaeology in the 1920s had passed through Hewett's field schools and summer sessions. While they largely adopted the chronological paradigm, these individuals also brought a detailed knowledge of the southwestern landscape and its antiquity to their eastern posts. While Hewett as an individual was largely repudiated by Judd and the rest, their experiences with the School and its activities exerted subtle influences on their careers. For example, the end-of-season information exchange launched by Kidder as the "Pecos Conference" reflected similar gatherings Hewett had hosted at the Rito that Kidder had attended twenty years earlier.

The tradition of field education is arguably the most lasting contribution of the southwestern rationale for archaeology. After a few false starts regional universities became involved in archaeological work in 1915, when Byron Cummings left Utah and joined the University of Arizona. Field schools were important to Cummings's program, and when Hewett later founded the Department of Anthropology at the University of New Mexico field education was central to the agenda developed there. In the 1920s archaeological field schools run by the School and the University of New Mexico at Chaco Canyon and in the Jémez valley trained dozens of new students.[41] Although the university setting of these new endeavors meant that the training of professionals was once again emphasized, field schools continued to offer opportunities to the general public. To the end of his life Hewett resisted a narrow professional agenda, sticking to his belief that participation in archaeological work and experiencing southwestern antiquity firsthand had value for all.

Despite certain shared general principles, an East-West divide remained in Southwest archaeology, continuing the rivalries of the turn of the century in a more polite form. Cummings and Hewett remained forces to be reckoned with or avoided well into the 1940s but played minor roles in professional councils. Many of their later students took positions in western institutions and guarded the tradition of regionally based research even after the original rationale for that approach had faded. Today differences of perspective between locally based archaeologists and their colleagues from elsewhere in the United States are one of the social realities of Southwest archaeology.

A final aspect of modern Southwest archaeology that emerged in the 1920s concerned the ruins themselves. Efforts to reconstruct prehistoric sites and interpret them for the public were begun by Jesse Fewkes and other representatives of government science, and antiquities preservation became central to the western strategy. Throughout the twentieth century, the preservation of ruins as "field museums" for touristic and educational purposes has been central in southwestern archaeology, an activity that on the basis of proximity alone was largely conducted by westerners. The sanction of national park and monument status for many of these locations added to their appeal, and while rarely conceived of as "heritage" in the sense that Hewett, Springer, and Lummis had intended, they are treated as cultural assets by the communities within which they are found.

Each of these aspects of Southwest archaeology in the twentieth century had its roots in the competitive conditions of a hundred years ago. The tension felt by the public over perceived scientific arrogance and by scholars over funding shortages and educational demands has continued to drive competing interests in southwestern antiquities. The debate, in many ways, remains the same, and in the pilgrimages of new-age tourists to "Anasazi" ruins can be seen echoes of earlier humanistic efforts to link ancient and modern lives. The search for meaning in antiquity, either in terms of scientific explanation or in terms of human experience, is fundamental to historical experience, and is the legacy of archaeology.

A. V. Kidder's grave is not the only place in the Southwest where archaeologists have been laid to rest in the settings they explored, surrounded by the material past they spent their lives deciphering. Hewett's ashes are interred within the walls of the Springers' art museum in Santa Fe, now known as the Museum of Fine Arts. Even the remains of Adolph Bandelier, who died in Spain in 1913, were eventually returned to New Mexico and scattered over the national monument that bears his name. In a small rincon, or bay, in the cliff behind Pueblo Bonito at Chaco Canyon, Richard Wetherill is buried within sight of the ruins he excavated for Talbot Hyde and the place where the American flag once flew over the outpost called "Putnam." Hyde's own material legacy in the modern Southwest is Hyde State Park, a picnic ground in the Sangre de Cristo mountains used by Santa Feans on weekends, donated to the state at Hyde's death for the promotion of nature education.

Not all of the pioneers of Southwest archaeology are commemorated in such concrete ways. By the time Nels Nelson died in 1964 he had outlived practically all his former colleagues and was largely forgotten. There is today no recollection of where in the vastness of New York's cemeteries he was laid to rest, and even the ruins he excavated are largely on private land and unvisited by the public.

Modern visitors can experience the monuments created by this earlier generation of explorers, but what cannot be reconstructed is the sense of excitement and discovery that, despite their conflicts, all seem to have shared. The Southwest was a place that changed them even as they sought to change the way it was seen by others. It was perhaps Pliny Goddard, writing to Kidder from his desk at the American Museum in 1926, never to see the western sunset again, who best expressed the feeling that he and his colleagues had shared:

> What should we have done all these years without the Southwest and you and Nelson to set it on fire?[42]

Notes

Note: A list of abbreviations used in the notes can be found at the beginning of the References Cited section below.

Introduction

1. I use the inadequate term "Anglo-American" here to indicate settlers from the United States as distinguished from the earlier Hispanic colonists of what became the American Southwest.
2. Lowenthal 1985:187.
3. Jackson 1980:101–102; Stewart 1984:133. See also Roth 1997.
4. Gjessing 1963; Schnapp 1996. For national archaeologies, see Diaz-Andreu and Champion 1996; Fowler 1987; Hudson 1981; Kristiansen 1985; Kehoe 1989, 1998; Kohl and Fawcett 1995; Patterson 1995; Trigger 1986, 1989. The origins

and development of the European tradition of archaeology are discussed in Jacks 1993; Marchand 1996; Parslow 1995; Ridley 1992; and Springer 1987.

5. Hinsley 1981.

6. Hinsley 1981; Stocking 1982; Fowler 1999. Fowler 2000 treats the subject of Southwest anthropology as a whole. For discussions of southwestern identity, see Byrkit 1992; Francaviglia 1994.

7. Miller 1970:61, 185.

8. Lears 1981:188.

9. Marchand 1996:96, 170.

10. There are notable exceptions, including Fagette 1996; Kidwell 1999; Lyon 1996; Snead 1999; Stocking 1982, 1992; Thoresen 1975; and Wilcox 1988.

11. For biology, see Appel 1988. Rainger (1990) provides a brief discussion of professionalizing trends in paleontology.

12. Haskell 1977:21; Russell 1983:220.

13. Haskell 1977:27; Ross 1991:160; Wiebe 1967:113.

14. Veysey 1979:65.

15. Griffiths 1996:1; Hinsley 1996a; Levine 1986; McKusick 1970. For classical archaeology, see Dyson 1998.

16. Dyson 1989; Silverberg 1970.

17. Parezo 1993.

18. Hinsley 1996c.

19. Hobsbawm 1983.

Chapter 1.   Relic Hunters and Museum Men

1. F. W. Putnam to C. M. Viets, 9 April 1891, 24 April 1891. HUG 1717.2.12, FWP.

2. Prescott 1843. For example, the Jesuit Eusebio Francisco Kino visited the Hohokam site later known as Casa Grande in 1694, and the ruins of Chaco Canyon were mentioned in the report of a Mexican military expedition in 1823. Clemensen 1992:11; Lister and Lister 1981:4. The writings of the eighteenth-century Jesuit Francisco Clavijero were particularly influential in Prescott's work. See Brading 1991:631.

3. William Becknell's mention of relics encountered in southwest Colorado in the winter of 1824 is one of the first Anglo-American references to southwestern antiquities from that region (Weber 1970:79). Accounts of southwestern ruins made by traders include Gregg 1844 and Wislizenus 1969. Of the soldiers and civil servants who discussed antiquities in their reports on the Southwest, the most notable are Lt. William H. Emory (1848, 1951), Lt. James H. Simpson (1850; McNitt 1964), Capt. Alonso Sitgreaves (1853), and John Russell Bartlett (1854).

4. Emory 1951:106, 130.

5. Hinsley (1996c:183–184) has noted a similar dichotomy between romance and utility

in William Henry Holmes's observation of southwestern ruins in the 1870s.

6. Kohlstedt (1988) discusses the role of college museum collections in the pre–Civil War period. An American tradition of classical archaeology was also developing during this period, albeit slowly (see Middleton 1997). For the general organization of American academic life during the nineteenth century, see Veysey 1965.

7. Bieder and Tax 1974:12; Mitra 1998 [1933]:65; Freeman 1967.

8. Hinsley 1981:35, 1993, 1996a; Meltzer 1985:250, 1998:15, 21.

9. Squier 1848:525. Regarding the military surveys of the West, see Goetzmann 1966; Bartlett 1962.

10. Simmel 1959 [1911]; Macaulay 1953; Zucker 1968; Roth 1997.

11. Macaulay 1953:1–2; Larson 1996:x; Silberman 1982; Wallach 1994; Traill 1995.

12. Meltzer (1998) presents the issues underlying the Mound Builder myth; more extensive discussions may be found in Silverberg (1986) and Williams (1991). Early reports of the Ohio mounds, such as those of Atwater (1973 [1820]) and Squier and Davis (1998 [1848]) provide contemporary archaeological perspectives. See also Bieder 1986:104–146. Regarding Mound Builder literature, see Mathews 1839, and William Cullen Bryant's "The Prairies" (Bryant 1840).

13. Goetzmann and Goetzmann 1986:38.

14. Weber 1985:87. Sweeney (1996) notes the relationship between Henry Cheever Pratt, who painted southwestern scenes while on John Russell Bartlett's boundary survey in the early 1850s, and Thomas Cole, whose use of the symbolism of ruins in landscape painting was highly influential in the mid-nineteenth century.

15. Loew 1879; Jackson 1879; Goetzmann 1966:356.

16. Hardacre 1878:266.

17. Rideing 1879. Ingersoll's book *The Crest of the Continent* (1889) went into at least thirty-eight printings. For Thomas Moran, see Kinsey 1992; Anderson 1997.

18. Parker 1956:155. For Putnam and the Peabody Museum, see Mark 1980; Hinsley 1985, 1992, 1996d.

19. Putnam 1879b:383.

20. Stegner 1953; Bartlett 1962; Judd 1967; Hinsley 1979. Following custom, I will refer to the Bureau as the "Bureau of American Ethnology" throughout. Former participants in the surveys on the Bureau's staff included William Henry Holmes, James Stevenson, and Cyrus Thomas.

21. Powell 1881:xv; Darnell 1998:24, 33; Noelke 1974:95.

22. Meltzer (1985) discusses the dichotomy between Powell and Baird. See also Parezo 1987:8; Darnell 1998:123. Powell's acquiescence may have been designed to build support for the Bureau's other programs in Congress, where archaeology had its proponents (Noelke 1974:187; Hinsley 1981:280).

23. Stevenson 1883a and b, 1884. See also Parezo (1993) for a discussion of Matilda Coxe Stevenson, and Green (1990:2–4) for an outline of Cushing's early career.

24. Norton 1880:22. The only major biography of Norton is Vanderbilt 1959.

25. Norton 1882:19. Dyson (1998:37–46) discusses Norton and the founding of the Archaeological Institute of America in some detail. See also Sheftel 1979; Dyson 1989.

26. Mark 1980:29.

27. Lange and Riley 1996:55. For the reports of the expedition, see Bandelier 1892. Bandelier's Southwest journals have been published as Lange and Riley 1966 and 1970, and Lange, Riley, and Lange 1975.

28. Recent research by Curtis Hinsley and David Wilcox has done much to resurrect the reputation of the Hemenway Expedition, which until recently was considered a near-total loss (Haury 1945). See Hinsley 1983; Hinsley and Wilcox 1995; Hinsley 1996b and c.

29. Brandes 1960:13. Early explorations of southwestern ruins by local settlers are described in Smith 1988; Lister and Lister 1990; and Clemensen 1992.

30. C. M. Landon to H. A. Ward, 1 May 1893. HUG 1717.2.1, FWP.

31. Prudden 1906:104.

32. Graves 1998:155. See also Wade 1985.

33. Lange and Riley 1966:74. Batkin (1999) provides an overview of the Santa Fe curio business.

34. Ingersoll 1889:86–87.

35. For example Lamar (1966:178) describes the career of Edmund G. Ross, who came to New Mexico as a merchant and took an interest in the establishment of cultural and educational institutions in his new home.

36. Lange and Riley 1966:409, 1970:332–334.

37. Walter 1932; Chauvenet 1983:67; J. McFie to E. L. Hewett, 17 January 1909. ELH. Prince's early political career in New Mexico is discussed in Donlon 1967.

38. The concern of southwestern Anglo-Americans over identity is discussed by Weigle and Fiore (1982:6) and Stensvaag (1980:293).

39. E. Montfort to L. B. Prince, 15 May 1895. File 18, LBP.

40. M. Prince to L. B. Prince, 5 March 1886. File 18, LBP.

41. A. H. Thompson to L. B. Prince, 14 December 1894; S. Hewlett to L. B. Prince, 16 December 1894; C. Darling to L. B. Prince, 24 May 1892. File 18, LBP.

42. Isaac H. Hall to L. B. Prince, 1 May 1890; E. Robinson to L. B. Prince, 11 November 1911; E. Halford to L. B. Prince, 14 February 1890; Secretary of the Interior to L. B. Prince, 17 February 1890. File 18, LBP.

43. L. B. Prince to J. W. Powell, 3 May 1890; L. B. Prince to W J McGee, 8 July 1899; R. Rathbun to L. B. Prince, 16 April 1903; E. Robinson to L. Prince, 11 November 1911. File 18, LBP.

44. E. L. Hewett later claimed to have seen the workshop where "Cleto Yulino" had manufactured many of the idols he sold to Prince. Photographs of the Prince Collection at the National Anthropological Archives are stored in a folder labeled "Frauds." Photo lot 40, box 9. See Lange, Riley, and Lange 1975:451–452 n. 602.

45. L. B. Prince to J. W. Powell, 22 July 1890. Note from Holmes, dated 30 July 1890, is on the reverse (emphasis in original). File 18, LBP.

46. Goldstein 1994.

47. Hinsley (1992:123–131) describes Putnam's network and attributes the origins of the Peabody network to Jeffries Wyman, who held the curatorship prior to Putnam. See also Hinsley 1985 and 1996d.

48. C. M. Viets to F. W. Putnam, 30 November 1888. Accession file 89–10, PM.

49. C. M. Viets to F. W. Putnam, 22 January 1889. Accession file 89–10, PM.

50. C. M. Viets to F. W Putnam, 28 January 1889; C. M. Viets to F. W Putnam, 26 May 1889; C. M. Viets to F. W Putnam, 10 August 1889; C. M. Viets to F. W Putnam, 31 December 1889; F. W. Putnam to C. M. Viets, 8 April 1890. Accession file 89–10, PM.

51. Gillmor and Wetherill 1934:1; Fletcher 1977:96.

52. John Wetherill, Nusbaum Questionnaire, 1930. File 89LA3.023.2, LOA.

53. *The Antiquarian* 1, no. 5 (1897): 128.

54. Fletcher 1977:181; Chapin 1892:155.

55. Daniels 1976:9; Fletcher 1977:125; Blackburn and Williamson 1997:22; Phillips 1993:107. C. M. Viets to F. W. Putnam, 26 May 1899. Accession file 89–10, PM.

56. McNitt 1957:328; Smith 1988:23; Harrell 1987.

57. Lister and Lister 1985:150; *The Antiquarian* 1, no. 9 (1897): 247.

58. Trachtenberg (1982:208–234) provides a cogent summary of the cultural issues surrounding the Chicago fair.

59. See Benedict 1983:27; Kasson 1978:11; Rydell 1984:40–41; Trennert 1987.

60. Dexter 1966:318.

61. Dexter 1966:315; Rydell 1984:56; Hinsley 1991:346.

62. Brown 1994:40; F. W. Putnam to F. C. Lowell, 7 January 1896. HUG 1717.2.1, FWP.

63. Fane 1993:160–162; Brown 1994:40; W. K. Moorehead to F. W. Putnam, 4 April 1892. HUG 1717.2.12, FWP; Phillips 1993:110.

64. *Report of the President to the Board of Directors of the World's Columbian Exposition,* 1898:183–185; Dexter 1966:323; Cole 1985:122.

65. Rydell 1984:40–41.

66. Fagin 1984.

67. Phillips 1993:109.

68. *Report. . . .* 1898:483. Cushing 1893:20.

69. Diamond and Olson 1991:53. The incident is discussed in McNitt 1957:43.

70. Agricultural Department, Colorado Exhibit, World's Columbian Exposition, 1893. The exhibit for San Juan County, New Mexico, where many significant ruins were located, focused entirely on fruit production (Women's Auxiliary Committee 1893).

71. Cushing 1893.

72. McNitt 1957:55.

73. R. Wetherill to F. W. Putnam, 12 November 1893; R. Wetherill to F. W. Putnam, 5 March 1894. HUG 1717.2.1, FWP.

74. Conn 1998:13–20.

75. Conn (1998) provides the most recent overview of natural history museums in the late nineteenth century. Many of these topics are discussed in the work of Sally Greg-

ory Kohlstedt (1979, 1980, 1988), who deals with both the institutional settings of natural history museums and their broader context. Lurie (1960) discusses Agassiz's Museum of Comparative Zoology at Harvard. For the commercial trade in natural history specimens, see also Benson 1988a. Deiss (1980) describes the acquisition strategy of Spencer Baird at the U.S. National Museum.

76. Kennedy (1968) provides the most detailed discussion of the American Museum, while Hellman (1968) is a more popular account. Osborn's (1911) history of the museum includes significant details of its early years.

77. Jesup's life is chronicled in Brown 1910. His supporters included J. P. Morgan and William E. Dodge (Lowitt 1954).

78. Brown 1910; Hammack 1982:57, 102.

79. *Annual Report, American Museum of Natural History,* 1894:10.

80. Kennedy 1968:134.

81. Darnell 1998:136.

82. Extract from the minutes of a special meeting of the Executive Committee, 16 April 1894, at the residence of Vice President Constable. Correspondence files, AMNH/ANTH. F. W. Putnam to J. H. Winser, 21 June 1894. HUG 1717.10, FWP. There is evidence that Putnam had been angling for a position at the American Museum for some time. He was instrumental in getting Marshall Saville appointed to a curatorial position at the museum in early 1894, and a letter from Franz Boas to Putnam on the occasion of his appointment makes veiled reference to earlier "plans." F. W. Putnam to M. Saville, 23 December 1893; F. Boas to F. W. Putnam, 4 May 1894. HUG 1717.2.1, FWP. It is also interesting that W. H. Holmes, rather than Putnam, had been Jesup's first choice, but the effort to get him appointed was unsuccessful. M. K. Jesup to A. Rogers, 13 January 1894. Administrative records, letterbooks, AMNH/CA. See also McVicker 1999.

83. F. W. Putnam to M. K. Jesup, 8 November 1894 [draft report]; M. K. Jesup to F. W. Putnam, 27 November 1894. Correspondence files, AMNH/ANTH. M. K. Jesup to H. J. Gould, 16 January 1895. Administrative files, letterbooks, AMNH/CA.

84. Darnell 1970; Winegrad 1993.

85. Holmes 1878:408.

Chapter 2. "Fires of Jealousy and Spite"

1. R. Wetherill to F. W. Putnam, 3 May 1894. HUG 1717.2.1, FWP.

2. *Dictionary of American Biography* 1:455.

3. Biographical notes derived from Ida Josephine Hyde Sexton, "Uncle Bennie—Naturalist," 1935. TM, and *Cyclopedia of American Biography* 30.

4. *Cyclopedia of American Biography* 26:196.

5. A. M. Tozzer to family, 3 August 1901. Box 1, 997–5, AMT.

6. Blackburn and Williamson 1997:47, 173; B. T. Hyde, Memorandum, 18 May 1930.

Accession file 1897–45, AMNH/ANTH. While Hyde's memorandum suggests that their visit to Mancos occurred in 1893, other evidence indicates that the trip actually took place the previous year. The world tour is described in correspondence such as F. E. Hyde Jr. to "Grandma," 25 November 1892. TM. B. T. Hyde to F. A. Lucas, 17 October 1918. Correspondence files, AMNH/CA.

7. R. Wetherill to B. T. Hyde, 6 January 1896. Accession file 1895–34, AMNH/ANTH.

8. W. H. French to J. Nusbaum, 22 November 1947; R. Wetherill to B. T. Hyde, n.d.; R. Wetherill to B. T. Hyde, 28 March 1894; R. Wetherill to B. T. Hyde, 11 April 1894. Accession file 1895–34, AMNH/ANTH. Daniels (1976) has published the journal of Charles Carey Graham, who excavated in the Grand Gulch with Charles McLoyd in the winter of 1890–1891. Phillips (1993), Hayes (1993), and Blackburn and Williamson (1997) discuss these and other relic hunters who worked the Grand Gulch district.

9. R. Wetherill to B. T. Hyde, 28 March 1894; B. T. Hyde to R. Wetherill, draft, 4 January 1894. Accession file 1895–34, AMNH/ANTH. In keeping with current usage, I use the term "Basketmaker" rather than "Basket Maker." The common assumption that Wetherill named the Basketmakers is incorrect. Ultimately it was T. Mitchell Prudden, another patron of the Wetherills, who introduced the Basketmakers to the public in his 1879 "An Elder Brother to the Cliff Dwellers."

10. R. Wetherill to F. W. Putnam, 3 May 1894. HUG 1717.2.1, FWP. B. T. Hyde, Memorandum, 18 May 1930. Accession file 1897–45, AMNH/ANTH.

11. Hayes 1993:126.

12. H. Alliot to S. Culin, 14 May 1894. Curatorial, American Section, Collections-Hazzard/Hearst, UPM.

13. *25th Annual Report, American Museum of Natural History,* 1893; *10th Annual Report, American Museum of Natural History,* 1878.

14. W. Pepper to C. C. Hazzard, 28 January 1896. Curatorial, American Section, Collections-Hazzard/Hearst, UPM.

15. F. W. Putnam to F. Boas, 7 March 1894. HUG 1717.2.1, FWP.

16. Fred Hyde attended classes at Harvard from 1893 through 1898. HUG 300, Harvard University Archives.

17. R. Wetherill to F. W. Putnam, 3 May 1894; M. H. Saville to F. W. Putnam, 29 July 1895. HUG 1717.2.1, FWP. J. C. Winser to F. W. Putnam, 27 May 1895. Correspondence files, AMNH/ANTH. Talbot Hyde's suggestion that they had planned their own museum came in a letter to Henry Fairfield Osborn (16 January 1909. OC 288, GHP).

18. *27th Annual Report, American Museum of Natural History,* 1895:18.

19. Richard Whitley has remarked that "the purpose to which professional skills are put is controlled, to varying degrees, by lay clients and employers. How the work is carried out is the preserve of the worker . . . but the selection and co-ordination of skills is often controlled by non-professionals" (1984:20).

20. M. Saville to F. W. Putnam, 15 February 1895; F. Boas to F. W. Putnam, 9 December 1895. HUG 1717.2.1, FWP.

21. J. Terry to G. H. Pepper, 6 February 1893. OC 204B, GHP. G. H. Pepper to F. W. Putnam, 9 October 1895. HUG 1717.2.1, FWP. F. W. Putnam to F. Boas, 7 April 1896. Correspondence files, AMNH/ANTH. B. T. Hyde, Nusbaum Questionnaire, 1930. LOA. The salary arrangement seems to have been a standard practice at the Museum, as even Boas was at first paid by his father-in-law. A. Jacobi to M. K. Jesup, 4 January 1895. Administrative files, AMNH/CA.

22. B. T. Hyde to R. Wetherill, n.d. (draft: following 1 October 1895); R. Wetherill to B. T. Hyde, 16 October 1894; R. Wetherill to B. T. Hyde, 3 June 1895; R. Wetherill to B. T. Hyde, 1 December 1895. Accession file 1895–34, AMNH/ANTH.

23. B. T. Hyde to R. Wetherill, n.d. (draft: following 1 October 1895); R. Wetherill to B. T. Hyde, 6 January 1896; R. Wetherill to B. T. Hyde, 1 December 1895. Accession file 1895–34, AMNH/ANTH. See also Lister and Lister 1981:17.

24. B. T. Hyde to F. E. Hyde Jr., 13 May 1896. File 89LA3.023.2, LOA.

25. J. Wortman to H. F. Osborn, 20 April 1892. Correspondence files, Department of Vertebrate Paleontology, American Museum of Natural History.

26. Pepper 1920.

27. G. Pepper to B. T. Hyde, 12 June 1896. Accession file 1897–45, AMNH/ANTH.

28. B. T. Hyde to F. W. Putnam, 4 October 1896. HUG 1717.2.1. Annual Report, Department of Anthropology, 25 April 1897; Quarterly Report, Department of Anthropology, 10 April 1896. HUG 1717.10. FWP.

29. R. Wetherill to B. T. Hyde, 31 October 1896 and 7 May 1897. Accession file 1895–34, AMNH/ANTH. Little is know of George Bowles, the Harvard student, or his tutor, C. E. Whitmore, although Wetherill's report on the expedition (in the same accession file) is an important baseline for scholarship in the Grand Gulch area.

30. G. H. Pepper to B. T. Hyde, 9 August 1897. Accession file 1897–45, AMNH/ANTH.

31. "You see," Wetherill wrote Hyde, "I am horribly in debt here through my efforts to help all." R. Wetherill to B. T. Hyde, 16 February 1898; R. Wetherill to B. T. Hyde, 3 July 1898. Accession file 1895–34, AMNH/ANTH. See also B. T. Hyde Memorandum, n.d., TM; J. R. Swanton to F. W. Putnam, 12 June 1898. HUG 1717.2.1, FWP.

32. Gabriel 1992:109; H. Schweizer to J. Nusbaum, 19 April 1930; J. Wetherill to J. Nusbaum, 1 April 1930. 89LA3.043.2, LOA.

33. R. Wetherill to B. T. Hyde, 17 April 1901. Accession file 1895–34, AMNH/ANTH. See also McNitt 1957:194, 210; Fletcher 1977:271.

34. R. Wetherill to B. T. Hyde, 17 April 1901. Accession file 1895–34, AMNH/ANTH. B. T. Hyde, questionnaire, 5 April 1930. 89LA3.023.2, LOA.

35. B. T. Hyde, questionnaire, 5 April 1930. 89LA3.023.2, LOA. See also Brugge 1980:160. Aleš Hrdlička, in a letter to Putnam dated 28 September 1899, wrote that "the mounds that Mr. Weatherill [sic] spoke of did not yield anything, they were ransacked by the Navahoes [sic]." HUG 1717.2.1, FWP.

36. R. Wetherill to B. T. Hyde, 28 October 1901; T. Hyde Memorandum, n.d. TM.

37. J. R. Swanton to F. W. Putnam, 16 July 1898. HUG 1717.2.1, FWP. J. R. Swanton, "Notes," 17. MS 4651, NAA.

38. F. W. Russell to F. W. Putnam, 22 September 1898. HUG 1717.2.1, FWP.

39. R. E. Dodge to F. W. Putnam, 5 January 1900; 2 November 1900. Accession file 1895–34, AMNH/ANTH. Talbot Hyde was a trustee of Teacher's College, and it was he who introduced Dodge to Putnam. T. Hyde, memorandum, n.d. TM.

40. Farabee Report on Excavations at Chaco Canyon, 1901. Accession file 01–32, Collections Department, PM.

41. B. T. Hyde to F. W. Putnam, 10 May 1899. HUG 1717.2.1, FWP.

42. Pueblo Bonito/Hyde Expedition Photographs, 99–22. Photo archives, PM. Frederick W. Putnam to Franz Boas, 10 August 1899. Correspondence files, AMNH/ANTH.

43. *American Museum of Natural History, Annual Report*, 1899:15.

44. Hrdlička and Vorhees notebook. Miscellaneous files, AMNH/ANTH. A. Hrdlička to F. W. Putnam, 28 September 1899. HUG 1717.2.1, FWP. See Hrdlička 1908.

45. Matthews 1902; *Annual Report, American Museum of Natural History*, 1901, 1902. Washington Matthews was a friend of Putnam's and is considered the initiator of ethnographic research on the Navajos (Young 1983:399). Efforts to publish other southwestern ethnographies under Hyde patronage, such as the works of Hopi trader Thomas Keam, were unsuccessful. F. W. Putnam to W. Matthews, 3 August 1900. HUG 1717.2.1, FWP.

46. For Marietta Wetherill's recollections of life at Pueblo Bonito, see Gabriel 1992.

47. Aleš Hrdlička, "American Southwest 1899–1917," n.d., 194. MJ-4-27, NAA.

48. Alfred M. Tozzer to family, 2 August 1901 and 6 August 1901. Box 1, 997–5, AMT.

49. Alfred M. Tozzer to family, 3 October 1901 and 19 October 1901. Box 1, 997–5, AMT.

50. Alfred M. Tozzer to family, 19 October 1901. Box 1, 997–5, AMT.

51. *New York Times*, 31 May 1896.

52. Fewkes 1896; Judd 1967:64; Hinsley 1983, 1996c:191. F. W. Putnam to M. K. Jesup, 10 May 1897. HUG 1717.10, FWP. G. H. Pepper to R. Wetherill, 14 January 1897 [transcript]. Frank McNitt Papers, New Mexico State Records Center and Archives.

53. Moorehead 1906:53; *The Antiquarian* 1, no. 7 (1897):ii.

54. Kroeber 1943; Weizner n.d.:12; *New York Times*, 14 March 1897.

55. Annual Report, Department of Anthropology, 12 January 1898. HUG 1717.10, FWP.

56. J. H. Winser to M. K. Jesup, 30 July 1896; J. H. Winser to F. W. Putnam, 16 January 1895; J. H. Winser to F. W. Putnam, 20 July 1898. Administrative files, Letterbooks, AMNH/CA.

57. F. Boas to M. K. Jesup, 7 November 1896, 28 May 1898. Correspondence files, AMNH/CA. See also Jacknis 1985.

58. George H. Pepper, lecture notebook. OC 87, GHP.

59. Lister 1997:6; Wilcox 1987:16; Smith 1988:46; Hobbs 1946a:87.

60. Lister 1997:7; Chauvenet 1983:40; Hobbs 1946a:87.

61. Smith 1988:17, 42.

62. Hewett's background is presented by Bloom (1939) and Chauvenet (1983); Hobbs (1946a) reviews his early archaeological work, although the details of this activity remain obscure. For the lecture series, see Hewett 1900–1901.

63. *Santa Fe New Mexican*, 30 April 1900.

64. *Santa Fe New Mexican*, 1 May 1900.

65. M. Pracht to B. Hermann, 8 May 1900. Transcript of file in National Archives; File 655b, CC.

66. M. Pracht to B. Hermann, 16 May 1900. Transcript of file in National Archives; File 655b, CC.

67. G. H. Pepper to F. W. Putnam, 6 June 1900. HUG 1717.2.1, FWP; F. W. Putnam to Commissioner of Indian Affairs, 24 July 1900. Record Group 75, 11E3/6/7/6, box 1812 no. 36336, National Archives, Washington. A. C. Tonner to F. W. Putnam, 31 July 1900. HUG 1717.2.1, FWP.

68. F. Russell to F. W. Putnam, 3 August 1900, 13 August 1900; F. W. Putnam to W. Matthews, 3 August 1900. HUG 1717.2.1, FWP. See Artifact Inventories, 1900, Accession file 00–23, Collections Department, PM. There are murkier aspects to the Russell affair. A permit for archaeological research for the same area and time as requested for Russell had been issued to George Dorsey at the Field Columbian Museum. This suggests the possibility that political influence was being brought to bear on the General Land Office in support of Dorsey and his patron, Chicago industrialist Stanley McCormick. Sec., Dept. of the Interior, 27 January 1900. Owen, Chas. Stanley McCormick Southwest Exp. Folder 1899–04. FM.

69. R. E. Dodge to B. T. Hyde, 27 August 1900. 89LA3.043.2, LOA.

70. G. H. Pepper to F. W. Putnam, 6 June 1900; R. Wetherill to F. W. Putnam, 25 October 1900. HUG 1717.2.1, FWP. Holsinger Report, 73. Copy on file, AMNH/ANTH.

71. T. Wilson to F. W. Putnam, 14 May 1900. HUG 1717.2.1, FWP. Tozzer was under the impression that both Putnam and Pepper had a financial stake in the Hyde Expedition, and Putnam's nephew John Clarke was by that time working as an employee of the business. A. M. Tozzer to family, 6 August 1900. Box 1, 997–5, AMT. B. T. Hyde memorandum, n.d. TM. See also Lee 1970.

72. Hobbs 1946a:86; Twitchell 1912:524.

73. *Santa Fe New Mexican*, 19 November 1900.

74. S. Holsinger to B. Hermann, 21 December 1900. Transcript of file in National Archives; File 655b, CC.

75. L.B. Prince to B. Hermann, 6 February 1901; C. McHenry to L. B. Prince, 20 December 1900; G. Pradt to L. B. Prince, 12 January 1901; L. B. Prince to B. Hermann, 6 February 1901. File 1, LBP.

76. S. Holsinger to L. B. Prince, 8 May 1901. File 1, LBP.

77. Holsinger Report, 70, 74. Copy on file, AMNH/ANTH.

78. Holsinger Report, 2. Copy on file, AMNH/ANTH.

79. *Santa Fe New Mexican*, 17 November 1911.

80. Lister and Lister 1981:56.

81. G. H. Pepper, Annual Report, 1901. HUG 1717.10, FWP.

82. Hewett 1904. In December 1903 Hewett visited the American Museum in New York;

the following March he made an oblique proposal that the Hydes sponsor his own plans, under Pepper's direction, to conduct a full-scale archaeological survey of the Pajarito Plateau. E. L. Hewett to G. H. Pepper, 4 March 1904. OC 289, GHP.

83. McNary 1956:33; McNary 1902.

84. M. K. Jesup to F. W. Putnam, 13 February 1897. Administrative files, letterbooks, AMNH/CA. Membership records, Century Club, New York.

85. F. W. Putnam to M. K. Jesup, 10 December 1903. HUG 1717.10, FWP.

86. Mark 1980:44.

87. B. T. Hyde to F. W. Putnam, 15 January 1902. HUG 1717.2.1, FWP.

88. R. Wetherill to F. E. Hyde Jr., 21 March 1902. Accession file 1895–34, AMNH/ANTH. New Mexico State Corporation Commission, SCC 0033241. A store was set up in Albuquerque and co-managed by Putnam's nephew John Clarke, who seems to have shared some of Fred Hyde's philanthropic ideals, but despite Putnam's interest in it Clarke's business was not successful. H. Schweizer to J. Nusbaum, 19 April 1930.89LA3.023.2, LOA. F. W. Putnam to G. H. Pepper, n.d. OC 288, GHP.

89. R. Wetherill to B. T. Hyde, 26 January 1903; J. W. Benham to Commissioner, GLO, 10 September 1904 [both transcripts]. File 655b, CC. Benham underlined portions of the letter that he thought indicated illicit activities and passed it on to the Land Office.

90. B. T. Hyde to M. K. Jesup, 29 January 1900. Administrative files, AMNH/CA.

91. Bumpus 1947:56; Kennedy 1968:152; Osborn 1911:40. Bumpus also revived the Department of Public Instruction at the American Museum.

92. F. Boas to H. C. Bumpus, 21 February 1902; B. T. Hyde to F. Boas, 9 May 1904. Correspondence files, AMNH/ANTH.

93. Hotel Astor Indian Hall, Brochure, n.d. General Catalog, New York Public Library.

94. Darnell 1998:138; Howard 1996; Pardue 1996.

95. Mason 1958; Wallace 1960; G. G. Heye to G. H. Pepper, 2 July 1904. OC 87, GHP. G. G. Heye to G. H. Pepper, 10 August 1904. OC 289, GHP.

96. G. G. Heye to G. H. Pepper, 22 November 1904. OC 289, GHP.

97. B. T. Hyde to F. W. Putnam, 11 February 1905. HUG 1717.2.1, FWP.

98. F. Boas to H. C. Bumpus, 21 February 1905. Correspondence files, AMNH/ANTH.

99. F. Boas to C. Wissler, 6 May 1905; F. Boas to M. K. Jesup, 23 May 1905. Correspondence files, AMNH/ANTH.

100. C. Wissler to B. T. Hyde, 16 November 1906; C. Wissler to G. H. Pepper, 24 May 1906. Correspondence files, AMNH/CA.

101. G. H. Pepper to C. Wissler, 30 April 1907. Correspondence files, AMNH/ANTH. B. T. Hyde to F. W. Putnam, 16 May 1908. HUG 1717.2.1, FWP.

102. B. T. Hyde to F. W. Putnam, 19 December 1905. HUG 1717.2.1, FWP.

103. Rainger 1991; Kennedy 1968:163.

104. Contract between G. B. Gordon and G. G. Heye, 5 April 1907. Curatorial, American Section, Collections-Heye, UPM.

105. G. B. Gordon to G. G. Heye, 20 October 1908. Curatorial, American Section, Collections-Heye, UPM; B. T. Hyde to F. W. Putnam, 16 May 1908. HUG 1717.2.1, FWP.

106. G. H. Pepper to C. Wissler, 22 December 1908. Correspondence files, AMNH/ANTH.
107. H. C. Bumpus to H. F. Osborn, 13 January 1909. Correspondence files, AMNH/CA.
108. Memorandum of Conference between B. T. Hyde and H. F. Osborn, 13 January 1909. Correspondence file 125, AMNH/ANTH; B. T. Hyde to H. F. Osborn, 16 January 1909. OC 288, GHP.
109. Memorandum of 23 August 1909, "Bumpus List." Correspondence file 125, AMNH/ANTH. G. G. Heye to G. B. Gordon, 12 June 1909; G. G. Heye to G. B. Gordon, 26 August n.d. [1909]. Curatorial, American Section, Collections-Heye, UPM.
110. G. B. Gordon to G. G. Heye, 20 October 1908; B. T. Hyde to G. B. Gordon, 16 November 1910; B. T. Hyde to G. B. Gordon, 16 November 1910. Curatorial, American Section, Collections-Heye, UPM.
111. G. H. Sherwood to J. Choate, 21 December 1910. Correspondence files, AMNH/CA. G. G. Heye to C. C. Harrison, 25 January 1914. Curatorial, American Section, Collections-Heye, UPM.
112. B. T. Hyde to C. J. Harrison, 21 August 1914. Curatorial, American Section, Collections-Heye, UPM. A copy of the bill of sale, derived from an unspecified file at the National Museum of the American Indian, is archived at AMNH/ANTH. See also Phillips 1993:117.
113. Blackburn and Williamson 1997.
114. Pepper 1920.
115. *Santa Fe New Mexican,* 24 June 1910.

Chapter 3. The "Western Idea"

1. Springer n.d. Some of the following discussion is based on Snead 2000.
2. Lamar 1966:176.
3. Weigle and Fiore (1982) argue that this urge to reproduce American institutions in the Southwest originated with long-term residents, while more recent immigrants took a greater interest in local sources of identity. As I have indicated here, however, local interest in antiquities dating from the 1880s prefigured subsequent developments. See also Stensvaag 1980.
4. Twitchell 1912.
5. *Santa Fe New Mexican,* 7 November 1900.
6. The historian Michael Kammen has described the close relationship between regionalism and nationalism in the construction of American heritage, noting that local identity requires the validation of a national audience (1991:141).
7. Norton 1880.
8. Archaeological Institute of America 1889:28.
9. Hinsley 1986; Archaeological Institute of America 1890:56.
10. Dyson 1998:43–44. W. Thomas to J. W. White, 3 October 1902; F. W. Kelsey, 23 April 1903. Box 10.9, AIA.
11. F. W. Kelsey to T. D. Seymour, 11 May 1904. Box 11.4, AIA.

12. The best source on Charles Lummis's life remains Fiske and Lummis 1975. See also Gordon 1972, Houlihan and Houlihan 1986, and, most recently, Wilson and Falkenstein-Doyle 1999. For an example of critical scholarship on Lummis and his work, see Paget 1995.

13. Fiske and Lummis 1975:21. Lummis's complex relationship with Bandelier is treated in Lange and Lange 1992.

14. Lummis 1895; emphasis in original.

15. C. F. Lummis to T. D. Seymour, 27 February 1904, 24 August 1905. Box 11.8, AIA.

16. Lummis n.d.; Lummis 1905; C. F. Lummis to T. D. Seymour, 27 February 1904. Box 11.8, AIA.

17. C. F. Lummis to T. D. Seymour, 18 August 1904. Box 11.8, AIA.

18. Lummis 1910.

19. C. F. Lummis to F. M. Coulter, 21 January 1904. Box 13.5, UA.

20. Hinsley 1984:64G.

21. S. E. Platner to F. W. Kelsey, 17 December 1904. Box 11.5, AIA. F. W. Kelsey to T. D. Seymour, 31 May 1905. Box 12.5, AIA.

22. Palmer 1905.

23. Fewkes 1896; Hough 1903:357. Hough astutely observed that the publicity surrounding Fewkes's excavations directly stimulated the commercial trade in antiquities.

24. G. A. Dorsey to S. McCormick, 23 March 1901. Accession file 745, FM. The representative of the Brooklyn Museum was Stuart Culin. C. F. Lummis to T. D. Seymour, 18 August 1904. Box 11.8, AIA.

25. The failure of the Board of the Normal School to renew Hewett's contract has been variously attributed to his progressive teaching strategy (Chauvenet 1983:47) and to a flap over Sunday sporting events (McNary 1956:37). Frank Springer, who himself resigned from the Board of Trustees over the flap, attributed Hewett's ouster to the machinations of a local newspaper that had failed to win a contract for the printing business of the Normal School (Springer Scrapbook, New Mexico State Records Center and Archives).

26. E. L. Hewett to W. H. Holmes, 28 November 1903. Letters received, BAE. Hobbs 1946b:177.

27. Kroeber 1970; Thoresen 1975.

28. F. W. Kelsey to A. L. Kroeber, 13 November 1905. Box 10.9, AIA.

29. J. Peterson to A. L. Kroeber, 3 February 1906. CU-23, box 15, BANC. Palmer 1905. See also Jacknis 1999.

30. C. F. Larabee to Secretary of the Interior, 29 July 1905; C. F. Lummis to T. D. Seymour, 14 August 1905. Box 11.8, AIA.

31. W. H. Holmes to R. Rathbun, 13 September 1905. Box 15 (Southwest Museum), AAP. C. F. Larabee to W. H. Holmes, 3 October 1905. MS 1.1.21IIA, SWM.

32. Lummis 1907:22.

33. See Pinsky 1992.

34. F. W. Putnam to F. W. Kelsey, 8 November 1906. Box 12.10, AIA.

35. Quoted in Mark 1988:302.

36. See Frank Hamilton Cushing, "Itinerary of Reconnaissance to Casa Grande Ruins, December 31, 1887 to January 4, 1888," in Hinsley and Wilcox 1995. See also Lears 1981; Runte 1987; Hinsley 1989:191.

37. Smith 1988:46; *Santa Fe New Mexican*, 7 November 1900. The failure of McClurg's negotiations over Mesa Verde related to federal law concerning reservation lands rather than to a lack of enthusiasm on the part of the participants.

38. Governmental involvement in the preservation of antiquities in the late nineteenth and early twentieth centuries has generated a considerable body of scholarship. In addition to Lee 1970 and Rothman 1989, see also Wilson 1976; Unrau and Williss 1987; and Righter 1989. Administrative histories of specific national monuments provide detailed information about individual cases (e.g., Rothman 1988, 1992). A good comparison is found in the British case, discussed in Chippindale 1983; Murray 1989; and Evans 1994.

39. Lee 1970:20; Rothman 1989. T. D. Seymour to F. W. Kelsey, 15 June 1904. Box 11.3, AIA.

40. Kelsey testified that the United States was "at a great disadvantage in dealing with this question [preservation] when compared with the countries of Europe." Transcript of Hearing before the subcommittee of the public lands of the U.S. Senate, 58th Congress, 2nd Session. Document no. 314. "Preservation of Historic and Prehistoric Ruins, etc." Concerns Bill s. 4127, introduced by Senator Cullom, and s. 5603, introduced by Senator Lodge.

41. E. L. Hewett to W. H. Holmes, approx. 24 July 1905. Letters received, BAE.

42. E. L. Hewett to W. McKinley, 26 Oct. 1900. Letters received, BAE.

43. Bandelier 1892; Lange and Riley 1966. James Stevenson's Smithsonian party had preceded Bandelier by a month. See Stevenson 1883b:431; J. Stevenson to J. W. Powell, 27 October 1880. Letters received, BAE. Other visitors included Charles Lummis, who joined Bandelier on a later trip across the Pajarito Plateau. Bradford Prince published an account of his own explorations in the area. See Lange and Lange 1992; Prince 1903.

44. According to the Hewett-Holmes correspondence, excavations were conducted at Otowi, Tsankawi, the Rito de los Frijoles, and at the site of Perage near the Rio Grande, where for the first time Hewett encountered Native American resistance to his activities. In keeping with his peripatetic style he also examined sites in the more northerly Chama Valley, and was prepared to extend explorations westward into the Jémez mountains when funding ran out. See, for example, E. L. Hewett to W. H. Holmes, 20 June 1905. Letters received, BAE.

45. E. L. Hewett to W. H. Holmes, 15 December 1905. Letters received, BAE.

46. Hinsley 1986:220.

47. W. H. Holmes to Thomas Ryan, 27 February 1906. Letters received, BAE. E. L. Hewett to F. W. Kelsey, 14 March 1906. Box 13.2, AIA.

48. Minutes, Santa Fe Archaeological Society, 23 April 1906. SFAS scrapbook, box B-2 91ASP.000, LOA.

49. Cummings n.d.:55; Utah Society of the AIA to Senators Smoot and Sutherland, 10 May 1906. Box 12.21, AIA.

50. F. W. Kelsey to C. P. Bowditch, 1 June 1906. Box 12.15, AIA.

51. E. L. Hewett to F. W. Kelsey, 19 May 1906. Box 12.17, AIA.

52. C. F. Lummis to E. L. Hewett, 8 June 1906; E. L. Hewett to C. F. Lummis, 20 June 1906. MS 1.1.2032, SWM.

53. Palmer, Southwest Society Report, 1906. Box 15 (Southwest Museum), AAP.

54. Lee 1970:77, 80.

55. E. L. Hewett to W. H. Holmes, n.d. [probably 3 July 1906]. Letters received, BAE.

56. A. L. Kroeber to Sec. of the Interior, 27 June 1906. Box 5 (California, University of), AAP. A. L. Kroeber to J. Peterson, 27 June 1906. CU-23, vol. 6, BANC.

57. B. Cummings to T. D. Seymour, 20 July 1906. Box 12.14, AIA. Cummings n.d.:55. This expedition, to Utah's Green River, was intended to establish the northern boundary of the "cliff dwellers."

58. E. L. Hewett to F. W. Kelsey, 3 February 1906. Box 13.2, AIA.

59. Smith 1988:58. Peabody had been a vice president of the Colorado Society since its founding in 1904, but had previously maintained a foothold in both organizations. Minutes of the First Meeting of the Colorado Society of the Archaeological Institute of America, 22 April 1904. Box 12.14, AIA.

60. Cummings n.d.:40. In his memoir Cummings conflates different visits by officials of the Institute, but describes the anti-Mormon animosity that complicated efforts to organize the local society.

61. A. Fletcher to F. W. Kelsey, 20 December 1906. Box 12.10, AIA. For Fletcher's life, see Mark 1988.

62. A. Fletcher to the AIA American Committee, 3 January 1907. Box 12.10, AIA.

63. Byron Cummings to E. L. Hewett, 14 March 1907. Box 39, ELH.

64. Reynolds was a political supporter of William McKinley, and Hewett had used his name in his 1900 letter to the president. E. L. Hewett to W. McKinley, 26 October 1900. Letters received, BAE.

65. E. L. Hewett to A. L. Kroeber, 31 May 1907. Filed under Archaeological Institute of America, BANC MSS C-B 925, box 8, BANC.

66. F. W. Putnam to E. L. Hewett, 19 July 1907. Box 21, ELH. E. L. Hewett to B. Cummings, 16 May 1907. Box 39, ELH.

67. Givens 1992:11–24.

68. Hewett 1944:153; Sylvanus Morley Diary, July 1907. Carnegie Institute of Washington Records 58–34, PM.

69. Hewett 1907:52. The area to which the team devoted its attention would subsequently become Natural Bridges National Monument.

70. B. Cummings to T. D. Seymour, August 1906. Box 12.14, AIA. Utah Society 1906.

71. E. L. Hewett to B. Cummings, 16 May 1907. Box 39, ELH.

72. Sylvanus Morley diary, 25 July 1907. Carnegie Institute of Washington Records 58–34, PM.

73. L. E. Peabody to E. L. Hewett, 12 August 1907. Box 21, ELH.

74. C. F. Lummis to E. L. Hewett, 26 April 1907. MS 1.1.2032B, SWM.

75. E. L. Hewett to C. F. Lummis, 23 July 1907. MS 1.1.2032C, SWM.

76. Santa Fe Archaeological Society, Minutes, 5 July 1907. SFAS scrapbook, box B-2 91ASP.000, LOA.

77. E. L. Hewett to J. M. McFie, 17 May 1907. Box 21, ELH.

78. C. F. Lummis to E. L. Hewett, 2 August 1907. MS 1.1.2032C, SWM. E. L. Hewett to C. F. Lummis, 15 August 1907. MS 1.1.2032C, SWM.

79. Lange, Riley, and Lange 1975:159.

80. *Santa Fe New Mexican*, 7 November 1900. E. L. Hewett to C. F. Lummis, 31 August 1907. MS 1.1.2032C, SWM. Rothman (1997:66) notes that Hewett made an unsuccessful attempt to stop Cole and his associates.

81. E. L. Hewett to C. F. Lummis, 21 August 1907. MS 1.1.2032C, SWM. S. Naranjo to E. L. Hewett, 28 March 1916. Box 25, ELH. Hewett 1944:15.

82. E. L. Hewett to C. F. Lummis, 21 August 1907. MS 1.1.2032C, SWM.

83. Lange, Riley, and Lange 1975:261.

84. Sylvanus Morley Diary, 22 August 1907. HP.

85. Parsons 1929:62–63.

86. E. L. Hewett to C. F. Lummis, 21 August 1907. MS 1.1.2032C, SWM.

87. E. L. Hewett to C. F. Lummis, 10 August 1907 [should be 10 September]. MS 1.1.2032C, SWM. E. L. Hewett to C. F. Lummis, 19 September 1907. MS 1.1.2032D, SWM. Morley 1910.

88. E. L. Hewett to F. W. Kelsey, 23 September 1907. Box 14.5, AIA.

89. Santa Fe Archaeological Society, Minutes, 18 October 1907. SFAS scrapbook, box B-2 91ASP.000, LOA.

90. C. F. Lummis to E. L. Hewett, 30 September 1907. MS 1.1.2032D, SWM.

91. F. W. Palmer to W. H. Holmes, December 1906. Box 15 (Southwest Museum), AAP. C. F. Lummis, undated memorandum, post-18 January 1909. Box 13.6, UA.

92. C. F. Lummis, "Answer by Lummis." Box 13.6, UA.

93. E. L. Hewett to F. W. Kelsey, 24 April 1906. Box 13.2, AIA.

94. C. P. Bowditch to F. W. Kelsey, 9 November 1906; F. W. Kelsey to C. P. Bowditch, 17 November 1906; C. P. Bowditch to F. W. Kelsey, 6 May 1907. Box 13.5, AIA. F. W. Kelsey to M. Carroll, 7 July 1906. Box 13.2, AIA.

95. E. L. Hewett to F. W. Kelsey, 24 April 1906. Box 13.2, AIA. C. F. Lummis to C. P. Bowditch, 3 February 1907. Box 11.8, AIA.

96. J. R. McFie, W. E. Garrison, and P. Walter to F. W. Kelsey, 22 December 1906. Box 12.16, AIA. H. J. Hagerman to F. W. Kelsey, 2 January 1907. Box 12.17, AIA.

97. F. W. Kelsey to E. L. Hewett, 23 January 1907. Box 13.1, AIA.

98. F. W. Putnam to F. W. Kelsey, 8 November 1906. Box 12.10, AIA.

99. E. L. Hewett to C. F. Lummis, 22 March 1907. MS I.I.2032B, SWM. E. L. Hewett to R. McFie, 17 May 1907. Box 21, ELH.

100. E. L. Hewett to C. F. Lummis, 3 October 1907. MS I.I.2032D, SWM. W. C. Tight to E. L. Hewett, 22 February 1907. Box 21, ELH.

101. E. L. Hewett to C. F. Lummis, 2 January 1908. MS I.I.2032E, SWM.

102. F. W. Kelsey Diary, 1 January 1907. FWK.

103. C. F. Lummis to the Southwest Society, 17 January 1908. Box 13.6, UA.

104. Santa Fe Archaeological Society, Minutes, 3 February 1908. SFAS scrapbook, box B-2 9IASP.000, LOA.

105. E. L. Hewett to V. McClurg, 13 November 1909. Box 22, ELH.

106. Colorado Society of the Archaeological Institute of America, 1908.

107. A. M. Tozzer to F. W. Putnam, 20 August 1908. HUG 1717.2.I, FWP.

108. *Santa Fe New Mexican,* 7 November 1908.

109. E. L. Hewett to C. F. Lummis, 1 December 1908. MS I.I.2032F, SWM.

110. Hewett 1908.

Chapter 4. Archaeology as Anthropology

1. C. Wissler to N. C. Nelson, 8 January 1912. Correspondence files, AMNH/ANTH. These circumstances will be examined further in a planned publication.

2. Darnell (1969:240) lists Holmes, Fewkes, and Max Uhle as the archaeologists of the period to whom Boas accorded respect.

3. Veysey 1965.

4. Boas, also at the defense, was the only ethnologist present, although he had supervised Swanton's research on the subject of the "Chinook verb." Russell, whom Swanton described as the "first real teacher" of anthropology at Harvard, died of tuberculosis in 1903. Swanton, "Notes," 10, 22. MS 4651, NAA.

5. Pepper made a trip to the Southwest in 1903 on behalf of patron Emily DeForest, but it was more a buying trip than an expedition. G. H. Pepper to F. W. Putnam, 25 June 1903. OC 288, GHP.

6. G. A. Dorsey to S. McCormick, 20 August 1904. Charles Owen Papers, Stanley McCormick Southwest Exp. 1899–04, FM.

7. The biographical data on Clark Wissler used here are derived largely from Freed and Freed 1983 and 1992. Concerning the 1902 expedition, which was originally assigned to Boas's student Montgomery Schuyler, see F. Boas to H. C. Bumpus, 16 May 1902. Correspondence files, AMNH/ANTH.

8. Freed and Freed 1983:812.

9. Clark Wissler to Hermon C. Bumpus, 24 December 1909. Correspondence files, AMNH/CA.

10. C. Wissler to H. C. Bumpus, 2 January 1909; 23 January 1909. Correspondence files, AMNH/CA.

11. In a 1907 quarterly report, Wissler noted that the Museum's financial support of the department had steadily declined since its high point in 1903. C. Wissler to H. C. Bumpus, 2 December 1907. Correspondence files, AMNH/CA.

12. Proske 1963.

13. Ultimately these three institutions, as well as the Museum of the American Indian, were to be housed on Audubon Terrace at Broadway and 155th Street, Manhattan, an intellectual center funded and inspired by Huntington.

14. After his father's death in 1900 Archer Huntington had stepped in, providing support for the California work through 1903. F. Boas to H. C. Bumpus, 29 April 1901. Administrative files, AMNH/CA.

15. H. F. Osborn to A. M. Huntington, 2 March 1909; Hermon C. Bumpus to Clark Wissler, 6 March 1909; Archer M. Huntington, subscriptions. Correspondence files, AMNH/CA.

16. C. Wissler to H. C. Bumpus, 2 January 1909; C. Wissler to H. J. Spinden, 1 September 1909. Correspondence files, AMNH/ANTH.

17. Report of Committees on Primitive Peoples of the Southwest, Annual Meeting of Board of Trustees, 14 February 1910. Correspondence files, AMNH/CA.

18. See Lange and Riley 1996; Hinsley and Wilcox 1995.

19. Freed and Freed 1983:803.

20. Huntington appears to have inspected the collections obtained with his funds on only a few occasions, despite invitations and an offer to set aside of one of the rooms of the museum for the use of the project and himself. H. F. Osborn to A. M. Huntington, 23 November 1910. Archives, Hispanic Society of America.

21. See Howard 1996.

22. C. Wissler to H. C. Bumpus, 12 May 1910. Correspondence files, AMNH/CA. One of Wissler's notable successes, however, was acquiring part of the Voth collection of Hopi artifacts from the Fred Harvey store at the Grand Canyon. He purchased the material for a relatively low price when the local manager was elsewhere, much to the company's later regret. J. F. Huckel to H. R. Voth, 13 May 1910. Voth Mixed Expedition Collections, FM.

23. Clark Wissler to Hermon C. Bumpus, n.d. [January 1910]. Correspondence files, AMNH/CA.

24. Putnam, Holmes, and Aleš Hrdlička all played critical roles in the controversy, which was more central to their professional careers than was their involvement in the Southwest. See, for example, Grayson 1983, Meltzer 1983.

25. The most famous of these was Laufer 1913.

26. C. Wissler to H. C. Bumpus, 24 December 1909. Correspondence files, AMNH/CA. Note that this comment precedes by several years Laufer's published remarks on the same topic.

27. Uhle's chronological work on the shell mounds of San Francisco Bay was done during a brief interval between the Peruvian projects that were the principal focus of his attention. See Rowe 1954.

28. "Work among the Primitive Peoples of the Southwest," 1910. Correspondence files, AMNH/CA. C. Wissler to H. C. Bumpus, 24 December 1909.

29. C. Wissler to H. C. Bumpus, 2 August 1909. AMNH/CA.

30. Newspaper accounts of Bumpus's departure suggest that his efforts to popularize the museum had led to his downfall, but internal sources indicate that he accused President Osborn of financial impropriety and was repudiated by the Board of Trustees. Undated newspaper clipping, Bumpus biographical file, AMNH/CA; Kennedy 1968:171.

31. In the first phase of the Huntington Survey, for instance, Wissler had attempted to hire John Peabody Harrington and Edward Sapir before settling on Spinden. C. Wissler to H. C. Bumpus, n.d. (received 3 June 1909), AMNH/CA.

32. Data on Nelson's early life are derived from Barton 1941. While Nelson's own personal files are archived in the American Museum of Natural History, he edited them severely in the 1940s, apparently discarding all but a selection of the material bearing on his career prior to his involvement with the museum.

33. N. C. Nelson to E. M. Wilbur, 4 July 1907. AMNH/NCN. Junius Bird Oral History. AMNH/ANTH.

34. N. C. Nelson to J. C. Merriam, 4 January 1906. MSSC-B 970, box 11, BANC; Rowe 1954:8; Wallace and Lathrap 1975:3. While it has been suggested that Nelson worked with Uhle (i.e., Praetzellis 1993:73), Uhle had departed Berkeley for Peru in 1903, years before Nelson's arrival at the university.

35. For examples, see Nelson 1910; Broughton 1996.

36. J. C. Merriam to P. E. Goddard, 13 February 1911. MSS C-B 970, box 2.

37. Nels C. Nelson to Pliny E. Goddard, 29 November 1911; Clark Wissler to Nels Nelson, 12 December 1911. Correspondence files, AMNH/ANTH.

38. Clark Wissler to Nels Nelson, 8 January 1912. Correspondence files, AMNH/ANTH.

39. C. Wissler to N. C. Nelson, 12 March 1912. Accession file 1912–52, AMNH/ANTH.

40. H. J. Spinden to C. Wissler, 6 October 1911. Correspondence files, AMNH/ANTH.

41. N. C. Nelson Field Journal, 1912. AMNH/NCN.

42. N. C. Nelson Field Journal, 1912. AMNH/NCN.

43. N. C. Nelson to A. L. Kroeber, 26 August 1912. AMNH/NCN. C. Wissler to N. C. Nelson, 12 July 1912. Accession file 1912–52, AMNH/ANTH.

44. N. C. Nelson Field Journal, 1912. AMNH/NCN. N. C. Nelson to P. E. Goddard, 6 August 1912, 25 August 1912. Accession file 1912–52, AMNH/ANTH.

45. N. C. Nelson to P. E. Goddard, 6 August 1912. Accession file 1912–52, AMNH/ANTH.

46. N. C. Nelson to P. E. Goddard, 8 September 1912. Accession file 1912–52, AMNH/ANTH.

47. Givens (1992:40) indicates that Kidder collected potsherds from a variety of sites in the region in 1911. See Kidder 1915.

48. Museum Notes, *American Museum Journal* 12, no. 6:221; Breuil and Obermaier 1912, 1913.

49. N. C. Nelson to C. Wissler, 14 June 1913. Correspondence files, AMNH/ANTH.

50. N. C. Nelson to C. Wissler, 19 May 1913, 7 July 1913. Correspondence files, AMNH/ANTH. In addition to Obermaier and Breuil, other participants included Hermilio Alcalde del Rio, Pierre Teilhard de Chardin, and Miles Burkitt.

51. See, for example, Grayson 1983; Meltzer 1983.

52. N. C. Nelson to C. Wissler, 21 April 1917. Correspondence files, AMNH/ANTH. A number of recent studies have discussed the relationship between archaeology, anthropology, and chronology, the most prominent of which are Praetzellis 1993; Browman and Givens 1996; and Lyman, O'Brien, and Dunnell 1997.

53. N. C. Nelson to C. Wissler, 19 May 1913. Correspondence files, AMNH/ANTH.

54. Nelson, late in life, suggested that the Castillo stratigraphy was much clearer than is indicated in his writings at the time. See Woodbury 1960a, 1960b. Interestingly, scholars working at Castillo Cave in recent years have credited Nelson for providing much of the stratigraphic information that exists from the 1913 excavations. See Cabrera Valdes 1984:31.

55. N. C. Nelson Field Journal, 1913. AMNH/NCN.

56. N. C. Nelson to C. Wissler, 26 November 1914. Correspondence files, AMNH/ANTH.

57. Nelson 1916; A. V. Kidder to N. C. Nelson, 16 February 1915. AMNH/NCN.

58. C. Wissler to A. M. Huntington, 28 January 1915. Correspondence files, AMNH/ANTH.

59. C. Wissler to L. Farrand, 10 February 1915. Correspondence files, AMNH/ANTH. Kroeber 1970:90; Lowie 1959:67; C. Wissler to A. L. Kroeber, 23 January 1915. AMNH/NCN. For a detailed discussion of the evolution of dendrochronology, see Nash 1999.

60. N. C. Nelson Field Journal, 1915. AMNH/NCN. For Morris, see Lister and Lister 1968. Despite the distractions, Nelson accomplished a great deal in 1915. In addition to San Marcos, he also excavated at Ojito de Cañoncito, Los Aguajes, La Ciénega (which Nelson called "Pueblo Mesita"), and Cieneguilla, all along or near the Santa Fe river. After returning from Zuñi at the end of the season Nelson worked at the site of Arroyo Hondo Pueblo.

61. A. L. Kroeber to C. Wissler, 11 February 1915, 4 August 1915. Correspondence files, AMNH/ANTH.

62. Kroeber 1916.

63. C. Wissler to N. C. Nelson, 23 August 1915; C. Wissler to A. L. Kroeber, 2 September 1915. Correspondence files, AMNH/ANTH.

64. Kidder 1958; C. Wissler to N. C. Nelson, 6 October 1915. Correspondence files, AMNH/ANTH.

65. C. Wissler to H. F. Osborn, 20 December 1915. Correspondence files, AMNH/CA.

66. C. Wissler to F. W. Hodge, 4 February 1916; F. W. Hodge to C. Wissler, 5 February 1916. Box 2 (American Museum of Natural History 1907–1925), AAP. N. C. Nelson to C. Wissler, 10 December 1915. AMNH/ANTH.

67. C. Wissler to H. F. Osborn, 24 December 1915. Correspondence files, AMNH/CA.

68. Lister and Lister 1990:6. Morris had, in fact, been excavating a residential site in the vicinity of Aztec in 1915, sponsored by the St. Louis Society of the Archaeological Institute of America. Earl H. Morris to Nels C. Nelson, 23 August 1915. Nels Nelson Papers, Archives, Department of Anthropology, American Museum of Natural History.

69. C. Wissler to H. F. Osborn, 24 December 1915. Correspondence files, AMNH/CA.

70. F. A. Lucas to C. Wissler, 3 May 1916. Correspondence files, AMNH/ANTH.

71. C. Wissler to H. D. Abrams, 1 April 1916. Correspondence files, AMNH/ANTH.

72. N. C. Nelson, Field Journal, 1915. AMNH/NCN.

73. C. Wissler to N. C. Nelson, 17 July 1915. AMNH/NCN. C. Wissler to H. F. Osborn, 26 February 1916. Correspondence files, AMNH/CA. Undated summary of Antiquities Permits, 1906–1927, AAP.

74. B. T. Hyde to F. W. Hodge, 1 June 1916. Box 18 (Chaco Canyon), AAP.

75. C. Wissler to Sec. of the Interior, 2 June 1916. Box 18 (Chaco Canyon), AAP.

76. N. C. Nelson Field Journal, 1916. AMNH/NCN. That the trash mound was a constructed feature, rather than a simple accumulation of debris as those at San Cristóbal had been, was not anticipated at the time. The unusual characteristics of Chacoan trash mounds are discussed in Stein and Lekson 1992.

77. N. C. Nelson to C. Wissler, 23 July 1916. Correspondence files, AMNH/ANTH.

78. C. Wissler to N. C. Nelson, 15 April 1916; H. F. Osborn to C. Wissler, 5 July 1917. Correspondence files, AMNH/ANTH. N. C. Nelson to C. Wissler, n.d. [July 1916]. AMNH/NCN.

79. P. E. Goddard to N. C. Nelson, 6 November 1916. Correspondence files, AMNH/ANTH.

80. P. E. Goddard to N. C. Nelson, 8 December 1916; N. C. Nelson to P. E. Goddard, 15 December 1916. Correspondence files, AMNH/ANTH.

81. N. C. Nelson to A. L. Kroeber, 24 April 1914. AMNH/NCN.

82. H. F. Osborn to C. Wissler, 23 January 1917. Correspondence files, AMNH/CA.

Chapter 5. Archaeology as Heritage

1. *Santa Fe New Mexican*, 20 August 1910. Portions of this chapter are derived from Snead in press.

2. Lamar 1966:491; Larson 1968.

3. New Mexico Bureau of Immigration 1909.

4. Discussion of the creation of identity in California, as well as the Lummis quotation, is derived from Starr (1973:400). Thomas (1991) discusses the relationship between literature, archaeology, and mission revival architecture. See also Hobsbawm 1983.

5. The biographical information on Frank Springer presented here was derived from several sources, in particular Schuchert (1928) and Twitchell (n.d.)

6. Springer 1917:16–17.

7. Fiske and Lummis 1975:72; Hewett 1916a:259.

8. Trennert 1987:139; Dilworth 1996.

9. "Era of Cliff Dwellers," New York *Sun*, 4 June 1900; N. M. Judd to E. L. Hewett, 28 November 1909. Box 22, ELH.

10. Lummis 1893:145; Prince 1903:7.

11. Underwood 1916.

12. Hewett 1916b:324.

13. Hewett 1916a:257.

14. *Santa Fe New Mexican*, 5 July 1910.

15. Bandelier 1916; Lummis 1893.

16. Hewett 1906:12–13.

17. Hewett 1909:342–343.

18. New Mexico Bureau of Immigration 1900:82–83; Passenger Traffic Department 1907:5.

19. United States Department of Agriculture 1925:1. See also Santa Fe Guide Service n.d.; Santa Fe 1915:214.

20. Passenger Traffic Department 1907:5.

21. J. R. McFie to E. L. Hewett, 6 April 1907. Box 21, ELH. J. R. McFie to E. L. Hewett, 14 January 1909. Box 22, ELH.

22. Chauvenet 1983:68.

23. F. Springer to A. Fletcher, 25 August 1909. Box 21, ELH.

24. E. L. Hewett to Charles D. Walcott, 1 February 1910. Box 17.6, AIA. The collection referred to was probably that made by Hewett while working for the Bureau in 1905.

25. F. Springer to A. C. Fletcher, 25 August 1909. Box 21, ELH.

26. Hobbs 1946c:208.

27. *Santa Fe New Mexican*, 8 June 1910, 4 June 1910. A notice that appeared in the paper on July 6 indicated that the codex exhibit had been postponed, and it is not clear whether the facsimile codices were ever displayed.

28. *Santa Fe New Mexican*, 1 August 1910, 13 August 1910. Another contributor to the preparation of the exhibit rooms was the Women's Board of Trade.

29. *Santa Fe New Mexican*, 22 August 1910.

30. *Santa Fe New Mexican*, 20 August 1910.

31. Report of the Director of American Archaeology, 1909. Box 21, ELH.

32. Lange, Riley, and Lange 1975:76.

33. A. J. Abbott to E. L. Hewett, 12 March 1909. Box 22, ELH; Rothman 1997:95.

34. Director's Statement on the School of American Archaeology's Activities during the first half of 1908. Box 21, ELH. School of American Archaeology, Annual Report, 1908. Woodbury (1993:15) discusses the origins of the Pecos Conference, of which Kidder late in life had only vague recollections.

35. E. L. Hewett to F. W. Kelsey, 19 August 1909. Box 16.14, AIA.

36. Springer 1910a:624.

37. Schuchert 1928; Springer 1910b; Lurie 1960, 1974. Other summer schools included Annisquam, established by Alphaeus Hyatt in 1879; the Summer School of the Peabody Institute of Science; and the Marine Biological Laboratory at Woods Hole. See Benson 1988b; Pauly 1988.

38. N. H. Hammond to E. L. Hewett, 22 February 1909. Box 16.14, AIA. Report by the Director of American Archaeology, 1909. Box 21, ELH. Bandelier's stipend was provided by Mrs. John Hays Hammond.

39. Director's Statement on the School of American Archaeology's Activities during the first half of 1908. Box 21, ELH. A. R. Priest to J. P. Harrington, 2 March 1910. Box 22, ELH.

40. Petch 1998:21; Babcock and Parezo 1988:21; B. Freire-Marreco to E. L. Hewett, 8 December 1909. Box 22, ELH. *Santa Fe New Mexican,* 10 June 1910.

41. J. Henderson to E. L. Hewett, 15 June 1910; G. Morlin to E. L. Hewett, 12 February 1909; N. M. Judd to E. L. Hewett, 28 November 1909, 14 May 1910. Box 22, ELH. E. L. Hewett to D. Beauregard, 5 May 1910. Box 37, ELH.

42. Judd 1967:25.

43. E. L. Hewett to F. W. Hodge, 22 January 1910. Box 22, ELH. E. L. Hewett to C. D. Walcott, 1 February 1910. Box 17.6, AIA.

44. R. B. Dixon to E. L. Hewett, 4 January 1909. Box 22, ELH. Fowler 1999.

45. E. L. Hewett to A. L. Kroeber, 9 July 1909. Box 22, ELH.

46. Notes pertaining to these various participants appeared in the *Santa Fe New Mexican* throughout the duration of the summer session.

47. *Santa Fe New Mexican,* 16 July 1910.

48. S. G. Morley, "Journal Rio Grande Expedition 1910." Box 528, ELH. N. M. Judd to E. L. Hewett, 12 September 1910. Box 22, ELH. Judd's 1968 memoir suggests that the Chama project occurred after the summer school, but this is not borne out by correspondence written at the time. Like many similar accounts, Judd's version of the 1910 season is colorful but conflates events that actually occurred at different times.

49. Rothman 1997; Judd 1968:139; *Santa Fe New Mexican,* 29 August 1910.

50. J. Henderson to E. L. Hewett, 5 November 1910. Box 22, ELH. Judd 1968:140.

51. Hewett 1908; *Santa Fe New Mexican,* 29 August 1910.

52. *Santa Fe New Mexican,* 30 July 1910, 29 August 1910; Springer 1910a:622–623.

53. The estimate of attendance was made by F. W. Hodge. F. W. Hodge to F. W. Kelsey, 15 October 1910. Box 17.25, AIA.

54. Freire-Marreco 1911:61.

55. Freire-Marreco 1911:61.

56. *Santa Fe New Mexican,* 29 August 1910.

57. *Santa Fe New Mexican,* 15 September 1910.

58. F. W. Hodge to F. W. Kelsey, 15 October 1910. Box 17.25, AIA.

59. A. V. Kidder to A. M. Tozzer, n.d. Walcott File, box 1, 997–5, AMT.

60. Harrington 1916; Henderson and Harrington 1914; Hewett, Henderson, and Robbins 1913; Robbins, Harrington, and Freire-Marreco 1914; Hewett 1953.

61. F. Boas to F. W. Kelsey, 16 December 1910. Box 17, AIA.
62. E. L. Hewett to G. G. MacCurdy, 1 September 1910. Box 22, ELH.
63. Otero was governor during the controversy over the Normal School that resulted in Hewett's ouster, and played a role in the affair. See Chauvenet 1983.
64. Lowitt (1992:46) and Chauvenet (1983:97) provide contrasting perspectives on the Lotave affair, but neither refers to the Rito trip mentioned in the *Santa Fe New Mexican*, 2 September 1910, and in Kidder's correspondence; A. V. Kidder to A. M. Tozzer, n.d. Walcott File, box 1, 997–5, AMT.
65. *Santa Fe New Mexican*, 7 September 1910.
66. E. L. Hewett to F. W. Kelsey, 1 February 1911. Box 19.4, AIA.
67. Boas 1910; E. L. Hewett to F. W. Kelsey, 20 January n.d. Box 17.6, AIA.
68. P. E. Goddard to A. M. Tozzer, 22 December 1910. Walcott File, box 1, 997–5, AMT. A. Fletcher to F. W. Kelsey, 15 March 1910. Box 18, AIA.
69. N. M. Judd to E. L. Hewett, 15 January 1911. Box 23, ELH.
70. The *Baltimore Sun*, 1 January 1909. The specific issue concerned the use of proxies in the votes of the Council, which increased the influence of the Western societies since their members were less likely to attend the meetings.
71. Hinsley 1986.
72. The School of American Archaeology 1911.
73. Hewett 1912. The most unusual of these lectures, on shamanism, was presented by Lummis.
74. One of the exceptions was a student named Elizabeth Deuel, who went on to take graduate courses from Frederick Starr and George Dorsey in Chicago. E. Deuel to E. L. Hewett, 5 May 1913. Box 24, ELH.
75. H. L. Wilson to E. L. Hewett, 18 July 1912, 22 July 1912. Box 23, ELH.
76. The San Diego Society of the American Institute of Archaeology 1916; H. Alliot to F. W. Kelsey, 15 September 1912. Box 19, AIA.
77. Minutes of the 6th Annual Meeting of the Executive Committee of the SAA, 14–16 August 1913. Box 21, ELH.
78. B. Cummings to E. L. Hewett, 11 December 1907. Box 39, ELH.
79. Denver and Rio Grande Railroad 1916.
80. Chauvenet (1983:110) discusses the affair in detail.
81. N. C. Nelson to C. Wissler, 16 November 1913. Correspondence files, AMNH/ANTH.
82. *Santa Fe New Mexican*, late October 1913.
83. *Santa Fe New Mexican*, 12 November 1913; Chauvenet 1983:116.
84. *Santa Fe Eagle*, 15 November 1913.
85. Fowler 1999; Secretary, Managing Committee, School of American Archaeology, to J. R. McFie, 3 January 1913 [should be 1914]. Box 52.2, FWK.
86. F. W. Kelsey to M. Carroll, 24 November 1913; M. Carroll to F. W. Kelsey, 1 December 1913. Box 6.3, FWK.
87. P. A. Walter to E. L. Hewett, 2 January 1914. Box 52.2, FWK. E. L. Hewett to J. R. McFie, 3 January 1914. Box 25, ELH.

88. Secretary, Managing Committee, School of American Archaeology, to J. R. McFie, 3 January 1913 [should be 1914]. Box 52.2, FWK.

89. E. L. Hewett to H. B. Peairs, 9 April 1914. Box 24, ELH.

90. New Mexico Institute of Science and Education, 1914. Summer School Marked Success 1914.

91. E. L. Hewett to W. H. Holmes, 24 May 1915. Box 25, ELH.

92. E. L. Hewett to C. Peabody, 20 October 1916. Box 25, ELH.

93. M. Carroll to F. W. Kelsey, 1 May 1913. Box 6.1, FWK.

94. Rothman 1988:18.

Chapter 6. Conclusion

1. C. Wissler to N. C. Nelson, 2 October 1917. Correspondence files, AMNH/ANTH.

2. Hewett 1918:50.

3. Shishkin 1968.

4. H. F. Osborn to G. H. Sherwood, 28 February 1917. Correspondence files, AMNH/CA.

5. N. C. Nelson to E. H. Morris, 1 May 1922. AMNH/NCN.

6. A. M. Huntington, subscriptions, 22 January 1922. Correspondence files, AMNH/CA. Morris, however, was also working with A. E. Douglass on the tree ring studies that would play a central role in the next wave of chronological research. A. E. Douglass to Earl H. Morris, 21 March 1916. AMNH/NCN.

7. F. A. Lucas to C. Wissler, 14 February 1917. Correspondence files, AMNH/CA.

8. F. A. Lucas to H. F. Osborn, 15 February 1917. Correspondence files, AMNH/CA.

9. C. Wissler to A. L. Kroeber, 10 November 1916. Correspondence files, AMNH/ANTH. N. C. Nelson to A. V. Kidder, n.d. [1917]. AMNH/NCN. The collections that were derived from the collaboration with the University of Colorado remained in Boulder and were never divided, although Morris (1939:iii) noted that the AMNH contribution to the project was refunded in the 1920s.

10. N. C. Nelson to C. Wissler, 21 April 1917. Correspondence files, AMNH/ANTH.

11. N. C. Nelson to E. H. Morris, 1 May 1922. AMNH/NCN.

12. E. H. Morris to N. C. Nelson, 16 May 1922. AMNH/NCN.

13. C. Wissler to N. C. Nelson, 19 April 1917. AMNH/NCN.

14. H. F. Osborn to N. C. Nelson, 20 April 1917. AMNH/NCN.

15. E. C. Bradley to P. E. Goddard, 11 May 1917. Box 1a, American Museum of Natural History, AAP. F. W. Hodge, Excavations at the Zuni Pueblo of Hawikuh in 1917, n.d. Box 1a (American Museum–Heye Foundation), AAP.

16. H. F. Osborn to C. Wissler, 5 July 1917. Correspondence files, AMNH/ANTH.

17. N. C. Nelson to P. E. Goddard, 3 September 1917, 23 September 1917; N. C. Nelson to C. Wissler, 8 October 1917. Correspondence files, AMNH/ANTH.

18. N. C. Nelson to C. Wissler, 4 November 1917. Correspondence files, AMNH/ANTH.

19. Nelson 1919.

20. P. E. Goddard to L. P. Cartier, 9 September 1920. Accession file 1920–71, AMNH/ANTH.

21. N. C. Nelson to P. E. Goddard, n.d. [November 1920]. Correspondence files, AMNH/ANTH.

22. N. C. Nelson to P. E. Goddard, 16 December 1920. Correspondence files, AMNH/ANTH. Nelson made a brief stop at San Cristóbal a few years later, to arrange for some excavations to supply skeletons for the Museum's comparative collection. N. C. Nelson to E. H. Morris, 12 July 1923. AMNH/NCN.

23. C. Wissler to H. F. Osborn, 19 December 1923. Correspondence files, AMNH/CA. Wissler (1917) provides a brief discussion of his sense of the impact of the Huntington Survey on American anthropology.

24. Lister and Lister 1968:106.

25. N. C. Nelson to A. V. Kidder, 19 April 1921. AMNH/NCN.

26. Gibson 1983:31.

27. Gibson 1983:44; Goetzmann and Goetzmann 1986:360.

28. Hewett 1944:95.

29. J. R. McFie to E. L. Hewett, 19 April 1915. Box 25, ELH. E. L. Hewett to L. B. Paton, 17 April 1916. Box 21, ELH.

30. Wilson 1997:135.

31. Santa Fe 1915:214.

32. Springer 1917:7.

33. Santa Fe Guide Service n.d.

34. Kidder 1924:143.

35. United States Department of Agriculture 1925.

36. Mullin 1992; Dilworth 1996.

37. F. W. Kelsey to E. L. Hewett, 11 November 1919. Box 16.3, FWK.

38. E. L. Hewett to L. B. Paton, 13 October 1916. Box 25, ELH.

39. See Cordell and Plog 1979.

40. Kidder 1958:130.

41. Gifford and Morris 1985; Joiner 1992; Mathien 1992.

42. P. E. Goddard to A. V. Kidder, 11 January 1926. Correspondence files, AMNH/ANTH.

References Cited

Abbreviations for Collected Papers, Manuscripts, and Archives

AAP   American Antiquities Permit Files, National Anthropological Archives, National Museum of Natural History, Smithsonian Institution, Washington, D.C.

AIA   Archaeological Institute of America Papers, Stone Science Library, Boston University, Boston, Mass.

AMNH/ANTH   American Museum of Natural History, Division of Anthropology Archives, New York, N.Y.

AMNH/CA   American Museum of Natural History, Central Archives, New York, N.Y.

AMNH/NCN   Nels C. Nelson Papers, American Museum of Natural History, Division of Anthropology Archives, New York, N.Y.

AMT   Alfred Marston Tozzer Papers, Peabody Museum of Archaeology and Ethnology, Harvard University, Cambridge, Mass.

BAE   Bureau of American Ethnology Papers, National Anthropological Archives, National Museum of Natural History, Smithsonian Institution, Washington, D.C.

BANC   Bancroft Library, University of California, Berkeley, Calif.

CC   National Park Service, Chaco Culture NHP, Museum Collection Archive, VA 655b, Albuquerque, N.M.

ELH   Edgar Lee Hewett Papers, Fray Angélico Chávez History Library, Palace of the Governors, Santa Fe, N.M.

FM   Department of Anthropology, Field Museum of Natural History, Chicago, Ill.

FWK   Francis W. Kelsey Papers, Bentley Historical Library, University of Michigan, Ann Arbor, Mich.

FWP   Frederic W. Putnam Papers, Harvard University Archives, Cambridge, Mass.

GHP   George H. Pepper Correspondence, National Museum of the American Indian, Archives, Washington, D.C.

LBP   Governor L. Bradford Prince Papers, Historical Notes and Events, New Mexico State Records and Archives, Santa Fe, N.M.

LOA   Laboratory of Anthropology, Museum of Indian Arts and Cultures, Archives, Museum of New Mexico, Santa Fe, N.M.

NAA   National Anthropological Archives, National Museum of Natural History, Smithsonian Institution, Washington, D.C.

PM   Peabody Museum of Archaeology and Ethnology, Archives, Harvard University, Cambridge, Mass.

SWM   Charles F. Lummis Papers, Southwest Museum, Los Angeles, Calif.

TM   Archives, Trailside Museum, Bear Mountain, N.Y.

UA   Charles F. Lummis Papers, Special Collections, University of Arizona Library, Tucson, Ariz.

UPM   Archives, University of Pennsylvania Museum, Philadelphia, Pa.

Published Works

Abert, James W. 1962. *Abert's New Mexico Report, 1846–47.* Albuquerque, N.M.: Horn & Wallace.

Agricultural Department, Colorado Exhibit, World's Columbian Exposition. 1893. *The Resources, Wealth, and Industrial Development of Colorado.* Chicago: G. M. Collier Press.

Alexander, Edward P. 1979. *Museums in Motion.* Nashville, Tenn.: American Association for State and Local History.

Allen, Rebecca. 1990. The History of the University Museum's Southwestern Pottery Collection. In J. J. Brody, *Beauty from the Earth: Pueblo Indian Pottery from the Univer-*

sity Museum of Archaeology and Anthropology, 61–88. Philadelphia: University of Pennsylvania Museum.

Anderson, Nancy K. 1997. *Thomas Moran*. New Haven, Conn.: Yale University Press.

Appel, Toby A. 1988. Organizing Biology: The American Society of Naturalists and its "Affiliated Societies," 1883–1923. In *The American Development of Biology*, ed. Ronald Rainger, Keith R. Benson, and Jane Maienschein, 87–120. Philadelphia: University of Pennsylvania Press.

Archaeological Institute of America. 1889. *Tenth Annual Report: 1888–89*. Cambridge, Mass.: John Wilson and Son.

———. 1890. *Eleventh Annual Report: 1889–90*. Cambridge, Mass.: John Wilson and Son.

Atwater, Caleb. 1973 [1820]. *Description of Antiquities Discovered in the State Of Ohio and Other Western States*. New York: AMS Press.

Austin, Mary. 1924. *Land of Journey's Ending*. New York: The Century Co.

Babcock, Barbara A., and Nancy J. Parezo. 1988. *Daughters of the Desert: Women Anthropologists and the Native American Southwest, 1880–1980*. Albuquerque: University of New Mexico Press.

Bandelier, Adolf F. 1892. *Final Report of Investigations among the Indians of the Southwestern United States, Carried on Mainly in the Years from 1880 to 1885*. Part II. Papers of the Archaeological Institute of America, American Series, 4. Cambridge: John Wilson and Son.

———. 1916. *The Delight Makers*. 2d ed. New York: Dodd, Mead, and Co.

Bartlett, John Russell. 1854. *Personal Narrative of Explorations and Incidents in Texas, New Mexico, California, Sonora, and Chihuahua, Connected with the United States and Mexican Boundary Commission, During the Years 1850, '51, '52, and '53*. New York: D. Appleton & Co.

Bartlett, Richard A. 1962. *Great Surveys of the American West*. Norman: University of Oklahoma Press.

Barton, D. R. 1941. Mud, Stones, and History. *Natural History* 47 (5): 293–303.

Batkin, Jonathan. 1999. Tourism Is Overrated: Pueblo Pottery and the Early Curio Trade, 1880–1910. In *Unpacking Culture: Art and Commodity in Colonial and Postcolonial Worlds*, ed. Ruth B. Phillips and Christopher B. Steiner, 282–97. Berkeley: University of California Press.

Benedict, Burton. 1983. The Anthropology of World's Fairs. In Benedict, *The Anthropology of World's Fairs*, 1–65. Berkeley: Scholar Press.

Benson, Keith R. 1988a. From Museum Research to Laboratory Research: The Transformation of Natural History into Academic Biology. In *The American Development of Biology*, ed. Ronald Rainger, Keith R. Benson, and Jane Maienschein, 49–83. Philadelphia: University of Pennsylvania Press.

———. 1988b. Laboratories on the New England Shore: The 'Somewhat Different Direction' of American Marine Biology. *New England Quarterly* 61 (1): 55–78.

Berkhofer, Robert F., Jr. 1978. *The White Man's Indian: Images of the American Indian from Columbus to the Present*. New York: Alfred A. Knopf.

Bieder, Robert E. 1986. *Science Encounters the Indian, 1820–1880.* Norman: University of Oklahoma Press.

Bieder, Robert E., and Thomas G. Tax. 1974. From Ethnologists to Anthropologists: A Brief History of the American Ethnological Society. In *American Anthropology: The Early Years*, ed. John V. Murra, 11–12. *Proceedings of the American Anthropological Society*, 1974.

Blackburn, Fred M., and Ray A. Williamson. 1997. *Cowboys and Cave Dwellers: Basketmaker Archaeology in Utah's Grand Gulch.* Santa Fe, N.M.: School of American Research Press.

Bloom, Lansing B. 1939. Edgar Lee Hewett: His Biography and Writings to Date. In *So Live the Works of Men*, ed. Donald D. Brand and Fred E. Harvey, 13–34. Albuquerque: University of New Mexico Press.

Boas, Franz. 1910. *Transcripts of Letters between Franz Boas and Charles D. Walcott.* Privately published. Copy on file, AMT.

Brading, D. A. 1991. *The First America: The Spanish Monarchy, Creole Patriots and the Liberal State, 1492–1867.* Cambridge: Cambridge University Press.

Brandes, Ray. 1960. Archaeological Awareness of the Southwest as Illustrated in Literature to 1890. *Arizona and the West* 2 (1): 6–25.

Breuil, Abbe Henri, and Hugo Obermaier. 1912. Les premiers travaux de l'Institut de Paleontologie Humaine. *L'Anthropologie* 23: 1–27.

———. 1913. Travaux executés en 1912. *L'Anthropologie* 24: 1–16.

———. 1914. Travaux de l'année 1913, ii. Travaux en Espagne. *L'Anthropologie* 25: 233–62.

Broughton, Jack M., ed. 1996. *Excavation of the Emeryville Shellmound, 1906: Nels C. Nelson's Final Report, transcribed and prefaced by Jack M. Broughton.* Contributions of the University of California Archaeological Research Facility, no. 54.

Browman, David L., and Douglas R. Givens. 1996. Stratigraphic Excavation: The First "New Archaeology." *American Anthropologist* 98 (1): 80–95.

Brown, Julie K. 1994. *Contesting Images: Photography and the World's Columbian Exhibition.* Tucson: The University of Arizona Press.

Brown, William A. 1910. *Morris Ketchum Jesup: A Character Sketch.* New York: Charles Scribner's Sons.

Brugge, David M. 1980. *A History of the Chaco Navajos.* Reports of the Chaco Center 4. Albuquerque, N.M.: National Park Service.

Bryant, William Cullen. 1840. *Poems.* 6th ed. New York: Harper & Brothers.

Byrkit, James. 1992. The Southwest Defined. *Journal of the Southwest* 34 (3).

Cabrera Valdes, Victoria. 1984. *El Yacimiento de la Cueva de "El Castillo."* Consejo Superior de Investigaciones Cientificas, Insituto Español de Prehistoria.

Chapin, Frederick H. 1892. *The Land of the Cliff Dwellers.* Boston: W. B. Clarke and Co.

Chauvenet, Beatrice. 1983. *Hewett and Friends: A Biography of Santa Fe's Vibrant Era.* Santa Fe: Museum of New Mexico Press.

Chippindale, Christopher. 1983. The Making of the First Ancient Monuments Act, 1882, and Its Administration under General Pitt-Rivers. *Journal of the British Archaeo-*

logical Association 136: 1–55.

Clemensen, A. Berle. 1992. *Casa Grande Ruins National Monument, Arizona: A Centennial History of the First Prehistoric Reserve 1892–1992*. Washington, D.C.: United States Department of the Interior, National Park Service.

Cole, Douglas. 1985. *Captured Heritage: The Scramble for Northwest Coast Artifacts*. Norman: University of Oklahoma Press.

Colorado Society of the Archaeological Institute of America. 1908. *Announcement of Fieldwork*. Printed brochure.

———. 1913. Course of Summer Lectures. Printed brochure.

Conn, Steven. 1998. *Museums and American Intellectual Life, 1876–1926*. Chicago: University of Chicago Press.

Cordell, Linda S., and Fred Plog. 1979. Escaping the Confines of Normative Thought: A Reevaluation of Puebloan Prehistory. *American Antiquity* 44 (3): 405–29.

Cummings, Byron. n.d. Trodden Trails. Manuscript on file, Byron Cummings Papers, Box 6, file 73, Arizona Historical Society, Tucson, Ariz.

Cushing, Frank H. 1893. Diaries for 1893. Transcribed by David R. Wilcox. Manuscript on file, Library, Museum of Northern Arizona, Flagstaff. Original in National Anthropological Archives, Smithsonian Institution, Washington, D.C.

Daniels, Helen S. 1976. *Adventures with the Anasazi of Falls Creek*. Occasional Papers of the Center of Southwest Studies, 3. Durango, Colo.: Fort Lewis College.

Darnell, Regna D. 1969. The Development of American Anthropology 1879–1920: From the Bureau of American Ethnology to Franz Boas. Ph.D. dissertation, University of Pennsylvania. Ann Arbor, Mich.: University Microfilms.

———. 1970. The Emergence of Academic Anthropology at the University of Pennsylvania. *Journal of the History of the Behavioral Sciences* 6 (1): 80–91.

———. 1998. *And Along Came Boas: Continuity and Revolution in Americanist Anthropology*. Amsterdam: John Benjamins Publishing Co.

Deiss, William A. 1980. Spencer F. Baird and His Collectors. *Journal of the Society for the Bibliography of Natural History* 9 (4): 635–745.

Denver and Rio Grande Railroad. 1916. *In Pajarito Park, Amidst the Prehistoric Aboriginal Ruins of Northern New Mexico, Bandelier National Monument*. Printed brochure.

Dexter, Ralph W. 1966. Putnam's Problems in Popularizing Anthropology. *American Scientist* 54: 315–32.

———. 1974. The Role of F. W. Putnam in Developing Anthropology at the American Museum of Natural History. *Curator* 19 (4): 303–310.

Diamond, Irving L., and Daniel M. Olson, eds. 1991. *Letters of Gustaf Nordenskiold*. Mesa Verde, Colo.: Mesa Verde Museum Association, Mesa Verde National Park.

Diaz-Andreu, Magarita, and Timothy Champion, eds. 1996. *Nationalism and Archaeology in Europe*. Boulder, Colo.: Westview Press.

Dilworth, Leah. 1996. *Imagining Indians in the Southwest: Persistent Vision of a Primitive Past*. Washington, D.C.: Smithsonian Institution Press.

Donlon, Walter John. 1967. LeBaron Bradford Prince, Chief Justice and Governor of New

Mexico Territory, 1879–1893. Ph.D. dissertation, University of New Mexico. Ann Arbor, Mich.: University Microfilms.

Dyson, Stephen L. 1989. The Role of Ideology and Institutions in Shaping Classical Archaeology in the Nineteenth and Twentieth Centuries. In *Tracing Archaeology's Past: The Historiography of Archaeology,* ed. Andrew L. Christenson, 127–35. Carbondale: Southern Illinois University Press.

———. 1998. *Ancient Marbles to American Shores: Classical Archaeology in the United States.* Philadelphia: University of Pennsylvania Press.

Emory, William H. 1848. *Notes of a Military Reconnaissance from Fort Leavenworth, Missouri, to San Diego, in California, Including Parts of the Arkansas, Del Norte, and Gila Rivers.* 30th Cong., 1st sess., Senate Ex. Doc. no. 7.

———. 1951. *Lieutenant Emory Reports: A Reprint of Lieutenant W. H. Emory's Notes of a Military Reconnaissance.* Albuquerque: University of New Mexico Press.

Evans, Christopher. 1994. Natural Wonders and National Monuments: A Meditation upon the Fate of the Tolmen. *Antiquity* 68: 200–208.

Fagette, Paul. 1996. *Digging for Dollars: American Archaeology and the New Deal.* Albuquerque: University of New Mexico Press.

Fagin, Nancy. 1984. Closed Collections and Open Appeals: The Two Anthropology Exhibits at the Chicago World's Columbian Exhibition of 1893. *Curator* 27 (4): 249–64.

Fane, Diana. 1993. Reproducing the Pre-Columbian Past: Casts and Models in Exhibitions of Ancient America, 1824–1935. In *Collecting the Pre-Columbian Past,* ed. Elizabeth Boone, 141–76. Washington, D.C.: Dumbarton Oaks.

Fewkes, Jesse W. 1896. Archaeological Expedition to Arizona in 1895. *Annual Report of the Bureau of American Ethnology, 1895–1896,* 519–744. Washington, D.C.: U.S. Government Printing Office.

Fiske, Turbese Lummis, and Keith Lummis. 1975. *Charles F. Lummis: The Man and His West.* Norman: University of Oklahoma Press.

Fletcher, Maurine S., ed. 1977. *The Wetherills of the Mesa Verde: Autobiography of Benjamin Alfred Wetherill.* Lincoln: University of Nebraska Press.

Force, Roland W. 1999. Politics and the Museum of the American Indian: The Heye and the Mighty. Honolulu: Mechas Press.

Fowler, Don D. 1987. Uses of the Past: Archaeology in the Service of the State. *American Antiquity* 52 (2): 229–48.

———. 1999. Harvard versus Hewett: The Contest for Control of Southwestern Archaeology, 1904–1930. In *Assembling the Past: Studies in the Professionalization of Archaeology,* ed. Alice B. Kehoe and Mary Beth Emmerichs, 165–212. Albuquerque: University of New Mexico Press.

———. 2000. *A Laboratory for Anthropology: Science and Romanticism in the American Southwest, 1846–1930.* Albuquerque: University of New Mexico Press.

Francaviglia, Richard. 1994. Elusive Land: Changing Geographic Images of the Southwest. In *Essays on the Changing Images of the Southwest,* ed. Richard Francaviglia and David Narrett, 8–39. College Station: Texas A&M University Press.

References Cited

Freed, Stanley A., and Ruth S. Freed. 1983. Clark Wissler and the Development of Anthropology in the United States. *American Anthropologist* 85 (4): 800–825.

———. 1992. Clark Wissler. In *Biographical Memoirs*, vol. 61, 469–96. New York: National
Academy of Sciences.

Freeman, John F. 1967. The American Philosophical Society in American Anthropology.
In *The Philadelphia Anthropological Society: Papers Presented on Its Golden Anniversary*, ed. Jacob W. Gruber, 32–46. New York: Columbia University Press.

Freire-Marreco, Barbara. 1911. From My Diary in New Mexico. In *Brown Book 1911*, Lady
Margaret Hall, Somerville College, Oxford.

Fuller, Henry. 1893. *The Cliff Dwellers*. New York: Harper & Brothers.

Gabriel, Kathryn, ed. 1992. *Marietta Wetherill: Reflections on Life with the Navahos in Chaco
Canyon*. Boulder, Colo.: Johnson Books.

Gibson, Arrell Morgan. 1983. *The Santa Fe and Taos Colonies*. Norman: University of Oklahoma Press.

Gifford, Carol A., and Elizabeth A. Morris. 1985. Digging for Credit: Early Archaeological
Field Schools in the American Southwest. *American Antiquity* 50 (2): 395–411.

Gillmor, Frances, and Louisa Wade Wetherill. 1934. *Traders to the Navahos: The Story of the
Wetherills of Kayenta*. Boston: Houghton Mifflin Co.

Givens, Douglas R. 1992. *Alfred Vincent Kidder and the Development of Americanist Archaeology*. Albuquerque: University of New Mexico Press.

Gjessing, Gutorm. 1963. Archaeology, Nationalism, and Society. In *The Teaching of Anthropology*, ed. David G. Mandelbaum, Gabriel W. Lasker, and Ethel M. Albert. *American Anthropological Association Memoir* 94, 261–67.

Goetzmann, William H. 1966. *Exploration and Empire: The Explorer and the Scientist in the
Winning of the American West*. New York: H. Knopf and Son.

Goetzmann, William H., and William N. Goetzmann. 1986. *The West of the Imagination*.
New York: W. W. Norton.

Goldstein, Daniel. 1994. "Yours for Science": The Smithsonian Institution's Correspondents and the Shape of Scientific Community in Nineteenth-Century America.
Isis 85 (4): 573–99.

Gordon, Dudley. 1972. *Crusader in Corduroy*. Los Angeles, Calif.: Cultural Assets Press.

Graves, Laura. 1998. *Thomas Varker Keam: Indian Trader*. Norman: University of Oklahoma
Press.

Grayson, Donald K. 1983. *The Establishment of Human Antiquity*. New York: Academic
Press.

Green, Jesse, ed. 1990. *Cushing at Zuni: The Correspondence and Journals of Frank Hamilton
Cushing, 1879–1884*. Albuquerque: University of New Mexico Press.

Gregg, Josiah. 1844. *Commerce of the Prairies*, vol 1. New York: Henry G. Langley.

Griffiths, Tom. 1996. *Hunters and Collectors: The Antiquarian Imagination in Australia*.
Cambridge: Cambridge University Press.

Hammack, David C. 1982. *Power and Society: Greater New York at the Turn of the Century*.
New York: Russell Sage Foundation.

Hardacre, Emma C. 1878. The Cliff-Dwellers. *Scribner's Monthly* 17 (2): 266–76.

Harrell, David. 1987. "We Contacted Smithsonian": The Wetherills at Mesa Verde. *New Mexico Historical Review* 62 (3): 229–48.

Harrington, John P. 1916. The Ethnogeography of the Tewa Indians. *29th Annual Report of the Bureau of American Ethnology, 1907–1908*. Washington, D.C.: U.S. Government Printing Office.

Haskell, Thomas L. 1977. *The Emergence of Professional Social Science: The American Social Science Association and the Nineteenth-Century Crisis of Authority*. Urbana: University of Illinois Press.

Haury, Emil W. 1945. *The Excavations of Los Muertos and Neighboring Ruins in the Salt River Valley, Southern Arizona*. Papers of the Peabody Museum of American Archaeology and Ethnology 24 (1).

Hayes, Ann. 1993. The Chicago Connection: 100 Years in the Life of the C. H. Green Collection. In *Anasazi Basketmaker: Papers from the 1990 Wetherill-Grand Gulch Symposium*, ed. Victoria M. Atkins, 121–41. Cultural Resources Series 24. Salt Lake City, Utah: United States Department of the Interior, Bureau of Land Management.

Hellman, Geoffrey. 1968. *Bankers, Bones and Beetles: The First Century of the American Museum of Natural History*. Garden City, N.Y.: The Natural History Press.

Henderson, Junius, and John P. Harrington. 1914. *Ethnozoology of the Tewa Indians*. Bureau of American Ethnology Bulletin 56. Washington, D.C.: U.S. Government Printing Office.

Hewett, Edgar L. 1900–1901. Announcement of Anthropology/Archaeology Courses, New Mexico Normal University, Las Vegas.

———. 1904. *Circular Relating to Historic and Prehistoric Ruins of the Southwest and Their Preservation*. Washington, D.C.: Department of the Interior, General Land Office.

———. 1906. *Antiquities of the Jemez Plateau, New Mexico*. Bureau of American Ethnology Bulletin 32. Washington, D.C.: U.S. Government Printing Office.

———. 1907. Report of the Director. *American Journal of Archaeology*, Second Series, 11 (Supplement): 51–60.

———. 1908. Report of the Director. *American Journal of Archaeology*, Second Series, 12 (supplement): 48–54.

———. 1909. The Pajaritan Culture. *American Journal of Archaeology*, Second Series, 13 (3): 334–44.

———. 1912. Report of the Director. *5th Annual Report of the Managing Committee of the School of American Archaeology, 1911–12*. Boston: Archaeological Institute of America.

———. 1916a. America's Archaeological Heritage. *Art and Archaeology* 4 (6): 257–66.

———. 1916b. The School of American Archaeology. *Art and Archaeology* 4 (6): 317–29.

———. 1918. On the Opening of the Art Galleries. *Art and Archaeology* 7 (1–2): 50–52.

———. 1944. *Man in the Pageant of the Ages*. Albuquerque: University of New Mexico Press.

References Cited

———. 1953. *Pajarito Plateau and Its Ancient People.* 2d ed. Revised by Bertha P. Dutton. Albuquerque: School of American Research and University of New Mexico Press.

Hewett, Edgar L., Junius Henderson, and Wilfred W. Robbins. 1913. *The Physiography of the Rio Grande Valley, New Mexico, in Relation to Pueblo Culture.* Bureau of American Ethnology Bulletin 54. Washington, D.C.: U.S. Government Printing Office.

Hinsley, Curtis M., Jr. 1979. Anthropology as Science and Politics: The Dilemmas of the Bureau of American Ethnology, 1879 to 1904. In *The Uses of Anthropology,* ed. Walter W. Goldschmidt, 15–32. Washington, D.C.: American Anthropological Association.

———. 1981. *The Smithsonian and the American Indian: Making a Moral Anthropology in Victorian America.* Washington, D.C.: Smithsonian Institution Press.

———. 1983. Ethnographic Charisma and Scientific Routine: Cushing and Fewkes in the American Southwest. In *Observers Observed: Essays on Ethnographic Fieldwork,* ed. George W. Stocking Jr., 53–69. Madison: University of Wisconsin Press.

———. 1984. Wanted: One Good Man to Discover Central American History. *Harvard Magazine* 87 (2): 64B–64H.

———. 1985. From Shell-Heaps to Stelae: Early Anthropology at the Peabody Museum. In *Objects and Others: Essays on Museums and Material Culture,* ed. George W. Stocking Jr., 49–74. Madison: University of Wisconsin Press.

———. 1986. Edgar Lee Hewett and the School of American Archaeology in Santa Fe, 1906–1912. In *American Archaeology Past And Future,* ed. David J. Meltzer, Don L. Fowler, and Jeremy A. Sabloff, 217–36. Washington, D.C.: Smithsonian Institution Press.

———. 1989. Zunis and Brahmins: Cultural Ambivalence in the Gilded Age. In *Romantic Motives: Essays on Anthropological Sensibility,* ed. George W. Stocking Jr., 169–207. Madison: University of Wisconsin Press.

———. 1991. The World as Marketplace: Commodification of the Exotic at the World's Columbian Exposition, Chicago, 1893. In *Exhibiting Cultures: The Poetics and Politics of Museum Display,* ed. Ivan Karp and Steven D. Lavine, 344–65. Washington, D.C.: Smithsonian Institution Press.

———. 1992. The Museum Origins of Harvard Anthropology 1866–1915. In *Science at Harvard University: Historical Perspectives,* ed. Clark A. Elliott and Margaret W. Rossiter, 121–45. Bethlehem, Pa.: Lehigh University Press.

———. 1993. In Search of the New World Classical. In *Collecting the Pre-Columbian Past: A Symposium at Dumbarton Oaks,* ed. Elizabeth Boone, 105–121. Washington, D.C.. Dumbarton Oaks.

———. 1996a. Digging for Identity: Reflections on the Cultural Background of Collecting. *The American Indian Quarterly* 20: 180–96.

———. 1996b. Boston Meets the Southwest: The World of Frank Hamilton Cushing and Sylvester Baxter. In *The Southwest in the American Imagination: The Writings of Sylvester Baxter, 1889–1889,* ed. Curtis M. Hinsley and David Wilcox, 3–36. Tucson: University of Arizona Press.

———. 1996c. The Promise of the Southwest: A Humanized Landscape. In *The South-west in the American Imagination: The Writings of Sylvester Baxter, 1889–1889,* ed. Curtis M. Hinsley and David Wilcox, 181–206. Tucson: University of Arizona Press.

———. 1996d. Frederic Ward Putnam, 1839–1915. Unpublished manuscript in possession of the author.

Hinsley, Curtis M. Jr., and David Wilcox, eds. 1995. A Hemenway Portfolio. *Journal of the Southwest* 37 (4).

Hobbs, Hulda R. 1946a. The Story of the Archaeological Society, I. Prologue: The Awakening of Interest. *El Palacio* 53 (4): 79–88.

———. 1946b. The Story of the Archaeological Society, II. The First Thirteen Years. *El Palacio* 53 (7): 175–86.

———. 1946c. The Story of the Archaeological Society, II. The First Thirteen Years (Concluded). *El Palacio* 53 (8): 203–11.

Hobsbawm, Eric. 1983. Introduction: Inventing Traditions. In *The Invention of Tradition,* ed. Eric Hobsbawm and Terence Ranger, 1–14. Cambridge: Cambridge University Press.

Holmes, William H. 1878. Report on the Ancient Ruins of Southwestern Colorado, Examined during the Summers of 1875 and 1876. In *10th Annual Report of the United States Geological and Geographical Survey of the Territories,* 383–408. Washington, D.C.: U.S. Government Printing Office.

Hough, Walter. 1903. Archaeological Field Work in North-Eastern Arizona. The Museum-Gates Expedition of 1901. In *U.S. National Museum Annual Report,* 287–358. Washington, D.C.: U.S. Government Printing Office.

Houlihan, Patrick T., and Betsey E. Houlihan. 1986. *Lummis in the Pueblos.* Flagstaff, Ariz.: Northland Press.

Howard, Kathleen L. 1996. "A Most Remarkable Success": Herman Schweizer and the Fred Harvey Indian Department. In *The Great Southwest of the Fred Harvey Company and the Santa Fe Railway,* ed. Marta Weigle and Barbara A. Babcock, 87–101. Phoenix, Ariz.: The Heard Museum.

Hrdlička, Aleš. 1908. *Physiological and Medical Observations among the Indians of Southwestern United States and Northern Mexico.* Bureau of American Ethnology Bulletin 34. Washington, D.C.: U.S. Government Printing Office.

Hudson, Kenneth. 1981. *A Social History of Archaeology: The British Experience.* London: Macmillan.

Ingersoll, Ernest. 1889. *The Crest of the Continent: A Record of a Summer's Ramble in the Rocky Mountains and Beyond.* 36th ed. Chicago: R. R. Donnelley & Sons.

Jacknis, Ira. 1985. Franz Boas and Exhibits: On the Limitations of the Museum Method in Anthropology. In *Objects and Others: Essays on Museums and Material Culture,* ed. George W. Stocking Jr., 75–111. Madison: University of Wisconsin Press.

———. 1999. Patrons, Potters, and Painters: Phoebe Hearst's Collections from the American Southwest. In *Collecting Native America, 1870–1960,* ed. Shepard Krech III and Barbara A. Hail, 139–171. Washington, D.C.: Smithsonian Institution Press.

References Cited

Jacks, Philip. 1993. *The Antiquarian and the Myth of Antiquity: The Origins of Rome in Renaissance Thought.* Cambridge: Cambridge University Press.

Jackson, John B. 1980. *The Necessity for Ruins, and Other Topics.* Amherst: University of Massachusetts Press.

Jackson, William H. 1879. Report on the Ancient Ruins Examined in 1875 and 1877. In *10th Annual Report of the United States Geological and Geographical Survey of the Territories,* 411–30. Washington, D.C.: U.S. Government Printing Office.

Joiner, Carol. 1992. The Boys and Girls of Summer: The University of New Mexico Archaeological Field School in Chaco Canyon. *Journal of Anthropological Research* 48 (1): 49–68.

Judd, Neil M. 1967. *The Bureau of American Ethnology: A Partial History.* Norman: University of Oklahoma Press.

———. 1968. *Men Met along the Trail.* Norman: University of Oklahoma Press.

Kammen, Michael. 1991. *Mystic Chords of Memory: The Transformation of Tradition in American Culture.* New York: Alfred A. Knopf.

Kasson, John F. 1978. *Amusing the Million: Coney Island at the Turn of the Century.* New York: Hill & Wang.

Kehoe, Alice B. 1989. Contextualizing Archaeology. In *Tracing Archaeology's Past: The Historiography of Archaeology,* ed. Andrew L. Christenson, 97–106. Carbondale: Southern Illinois University Press.

———. 1998. *The Land of Prehistory: A Critical History of American Archaeology.* New York: Routledge.

Kennedy, John M. 1968. Philanthropy and Science in New York City: The American Museum of Natural History, 1868–1968. Ph.D. dissertation, Yale University. Ann Arbor, Mich.: University Microfilms.

Kidder, Alfred V. 1915. *Pottery of the Pajarito Plateau and of Some Adjacent Regions in New Mexico.* Memoirs of the American Anthropological Association 12.

———. 1924. *An Introduction to the Study of Southwestern Archaeology.* New Haven, Conn.: Yale University Press.

———. 1958. *Pecos, New Mexico: Archaeological Notes.* Papers of the Robert S. Peabody Foundation for Archaeology 5. Andover, Mass.: Phillips Academy.

Kidwell, Clara S. 1999. Every Last Dishcloth: The Prodigious Collecting of George Gustav Heye. In *Collecting Native America, 1870–1960,* ed. Shepard Krech III and Barbara A. Hail, 232–258. Washington, D.C.: Smithsonian Institution Press.

Kinsey, Joni L. 1992. *Thomas Moran and the Surveying of the American West.* Washington, D.C.: Smithsonian Institution Press.

Kohl, Philip L., and Clare Fawcett, eds. 1995. *Nationalism, Politics, and the Practice of Archaeology.* Cambridge: Cambridge University Press.

Kohlstedt, Sally Gregory. 1979. From Learned Society to Public Museum: The Boston Society of Natural History. In *The Organization of Knowledge in America,* ed. Alexandra Oleson and John Voss, 386–406. Baltimore, Md.: The Johns Hopkins University Press.

———. 1980. Henry A. Ward: The Merchant Naturalist and American Museum Development. *Journal of the Society for the Bibliography of Natural History* 9: 647–61.

———. 1988. Museums on Campus: A Tradition of Inquiry and Teaching. In *The American Development of Biology,* ed. Ronald Rainger, Keith R. Benson, and Jane Maienschein, 15–47. Philadelphia: University of Pennsylvania Press.

Kristiansen, Kristian. 1985. A Social History of Danish Archaeology. In *Towards a History of Archaeology,* ed. Glyn Daniel, 20–44. London: Thames and Hudson.

Kroeber, Alfred L. 1916. Zuni Potsherds. In *Anthropological Papers of the American Museum of Natural History* 18, 1–38. New York.

———. 1943. Franz Boas: The Man. *American Anthropologist,* n.s., 45 (3), pt. 2: 5–26.

Kroeber, Theodora. 1970. *Alfred Kroeber: A Personal Configuration.* Berkeley: University of California Press.

Lamar, Howard. 1966. *The Far Southwest, 1846–1912: A Territorial History.* New Haven, Conn.: Yale University Press.

Lange, Charles H., and Patricia Fogelman Lange. 1992. Adolph F. Bandelier and Charles F. Lummis. In *Archaeology, Art, and Anthropology: Papers in Honor of J. J. Brody,* ed. Meliha H. Duran and David T. Kirkpatrick, 99–109. Papers of the Archaeological Society of New Mexico 18. Albuquerque: University of New Mexico Press.

Lange, Charles H., and Carroll L. Riley. 1966. *The Southwest Journals of Adolph F. Bandelier, 1880–1882.* Albuquerque: University of New Mexico Press.

———. 1970. *The Southwest Journals of Adolph F. Bandelier, 1883–1884.* Albuquerque: University of New Mexico Press.

———. 1996. *Bandelier: The Life and Times of Adolf Bandelier.* Salt Lake City: University of Utah Press.

Lange, Charles H., Carroll L. Riley, and Elizabeth M. Lange. 1975. *The Southwest Journals of Adolph F. Bandelier, 1885–1888.* Albuquerque: University of New Mexico Press.

Larson, Mogens Trolle. 1996. *The Conquest of Assyria: Excavations in an Antique Land.* London: Oxford University Press.

Larson, Robert W. 1968. *New Mexico's Quest for Statehood, 1846–1912.* Albuquerque: University of New Mexico Press.

Laufer, Berthold. 1913. Remarks. *American Anthropologist* 15 (4): 573–577.

Lears, T. J. Jackson. 1981. *No Place of Grace: Antimodernism and the Transformation of American Culture, 1870–1916.* New York: Pantheon Books.

Lee, Ronald F. 1970. *The Antiquities Act of 1906.* Washington, D.C.: National Park Service, Office of History and Historic Architecture, Eastern Service Center.

Levine, Philippa. 1986. *The Amateur and the Professional: Antiquarians, Historians, and Archaeologists in Victorian England, 1838–1886.* Cambridge: Cambridge University Press.

Lister, Florence C. 1997. *Prehistory in Peril: The Worst and Best of Durango Archaeology.* Niwot, Colo.: University Press of Colorado.

Lister, Robert H., and Florence C. Lister. 1968. *Earl Morris & Southwestern Archaeology.* Albuquerque: University of New Mexico Press.

———. 1981. *Chaco Canyon: Archaeology and Archaeologists*. Albuquerque: University of New Mexico Press.

———. 1985. The Wetherills: Vandals, Pothunters, or Archaeologists. In *Prehistory and History of the Southwest: Papers in Honor of Alden C. Hayes*, ed. Nancy C. Fox, 147–53. Albuquerque: Archaeological Society of New Mexico.

———. 1990. *Aztec Ruins National Monument: Administrative History of an Archaeological Preserve*. Southwest Cultural Resources Center Professional Papers no. 24. Santa Fe, N.M.: National Park Service.

Loew, Oscar. 1879. Report on the Ruins in New Mexico. In *Reports upon Archaeology and Ethnological Collections from Vicinity of Santa Barbara, California, and from Ruined Pueblos of Arizona and New Mexico, and Certain Interior Tribes*, ed. Frederic W. Putnam, 337–345. *Report of the United States Geographical Surveys West of the One Hundredth Meridian*, vol. 7: *Archaeology*. Washington, D.C.: U.S. Government Printing Office. [Abstracted from the *Annual Report of the Chief of Engineers for 1875*, Appendix LL.]

Lowenthal, David. 1985. *The Past Is a Foreign Country*. Cambridge: Cambridge University Press.

Lowie, Robert H. 1959. *Robert H. Lowie, Ethnologist: A Personal Record*. Berkeley: University of California Press.

Lowitt, Richard. 1954. *A Merchant Prince of the Nineteenth Century: William E. Dodge*. New York: Columbia University Press.

———. 1992. *Bronson M. Cutting: Progressive Politician*. Albuquerque: University of New Mexico Press.

Lummis, Charles F. n.d. *The Southwest Museum*. Undated brochure.

———. 1893. *Land of Poco Tiempo*. New York: Charles Scribner's Sons.

———. 1895. Editorial. *Land of Sunshine* 2 (3): 53.

———. 1905. Catching Our Archaeology Alive. *Second Bulletin, The Southwest Society of the Archaeological Institute of America*, 3–15.

———. 1907. The Southwest Museum. *Third Bulletin, The Southwest Society of the Archaeological Institute of America*, 3–32.

———. 1910. Sixth Annual Report. *Fifth Bulletin, The Southwest Society of the Archaeological Institute of America*.

Lurie, Edward. 1960. *Louis Agassiz: A Life in Science*. Chicago: University of Chicago Press.

———. 1974. *Nature and the American Mind: Louis Agassiz and the Culture of Science*. New York: Science History Publications.

Lyman, R. Lee, Michael J. O'Brien, and Robert C. Dunnell. 1997. *The Rise and Fall of Culture History*. New York: Plenum Press.

Lyon, Edwin A. 1996. *A New Deal for Southeastern Archaeology*. Tuscaloosa: University of Alabama Press.

Macaulay, Rose. 1953. *The Pleasure of Ruins*. London: Weidenfeld and Nicolson.

Marchand, Suzanne. 1996. *Down from Olympus: Archaeology and Philhellenism in Germany,*

1750–1970. Princeton, N.J.: Princeton University Press.

Mark, Joan. 1980. *Four Anthropologists: An American Science in Its Early Years*. New York: Science History Publications.

———. 1988. *A Stranger in Her Native Land: Alice Fletcher and the American Indians*. Lincoln: University of Nebraska Press.

Mason, J. Alden. 1958. *George G. Heye, 1874–1957*. Leaflets of the Museum of the American Indian, no. 6.

Mathews, Cornelius. 1839. *Behemoth: A Legend of the Mound-Builders*. New York: J. & J. G. Langley.

Mathien, Frances J. 1992. Women of Chaco: Then and Now. In *Rediscovering Our Past: Essays on the History of American Archaeology*, ed. Jonathan E. Reyman, 103–130. Avebury, U.K.: Aldershot.

Matthews, Washington. 1902. *The Night Chant: A Navaho Ceremony*. Memoirs of the American Museum of Natural History 6. New York.

McKusick, Marshall. 1970. *The Davenport Conspiracy*. Report #1, Iowa City, Iowa: Office the State Archaeologist.

McNary, James. 1956. *This Is My Life*. Albuquerque: University of New Mexico Press.

McNary, Margaretta M. 1902. Chaco Canyon Trip Diary by Margaretta M. McNary, July 1 to August 23, 1902. Unpublished manuscript in possession of the author.

McNitt, Frank. 1957. *Richard Wetherill: Anasazi*. Albuquerque: University of New Mexico Press.

———. 1964. *Navaho Expedition: Journal of a Military Reconnaissance from Santa Fe, New Mexico to the Navaho Country Made in 1849 by Lieutenant James H. Simpson*. Norman: University of Oklahoma Press.

McVicker, Donald. 1999. Buying a Curator: Establishing Anthropology at Field Columbian Museum. In *Assembling the Past: Studies in the Professionalization of Archaeology*, ed. Alice B. Kehoe and Mary Beth Emmerichs, 37–52. Albuquerque: University of New Mexico Press.

Meltzer, David J. 1983. The Antiquity of Man and the Development of American Archaeology. In *Advances in Archaeological Method and Theory*, vol. 6, ed. Michael B. Schiffer, 1–51. New York: Academic Press.

———. 1985. North American Archaeology and Archaeologists 1879–1934. *American Antiquity* 50 (2): 249–60.

———. 1998. Introduction: Ephraim Squier, Edwin Davis, and the Making of an American Archaeological Classic. In *Ancient Monuments of the Mississippi Valley*, by Ephraim G. Squier and Edwin H. Davis, 1–95. Washington, D.C.: Smithsonian Institution Press.

Middleton, John Izard. 1997. *The Roman Remains: John Izard Middleton's Visual Souvenirs*. Columbia: University of South Carolina Press.

Miller, Howard S. 1970. *Dollars for Research: Science and Its Patrons in Nineteenth-Century America*. Seattle: University of Washington Press.

Mindeleff, Victor. 1989 [1900]. *A Study of Pueblo Architecture in Tusayan and Cibola*. Washington, D.C.: Smithsonian Institution Press.

References Cited

Mitra, Panchanan. 1998 [1933]. *A History of American Anthropology*. Santa Fe, N.M.: Lower Mississippi Survey.

Moorehead, Warren K. 1906. *A Narrative of Explorations in New Mexico, Arizona, Indiana, etc.* Department of Archaeology Bulletin III. Andover, Mass.: Phillips Academy.

Morley, Sylvanus G. 1910. *The South House, Puye.* Sixth Bulletin, The Southwest Society of the American Institute of Archaeology.

Morris, Earl H. 1939. *Archaeological Studies in the La Plata District, Southwestern Colorado and Northwestern New Mexico.* Carnegie Institution of Washington Publication 519. Washington, D.C.: Carnegie Institution.

Mullin, Molly. 1992. The Patronage of Difference: Making Indian Art "Art, not Ethnology." *Cultural Anthropology* 7 (4): 395–424.

Murray, Tim. 1989. The History, Philosophy and Sociology of Archaeology: The Case of the Ancient Monuments Protection Act (1882). In *Critical Traditions in Contemporary Archaeology*, ed. Valerie Pinsky and Alison Wylie, 55–66. Cambridge: Cambridge University Press.

Nash, Stephen E. 1999. *Time, Trees, and Prehistory: Tree-Ring Dating and the Development of North American Archaeology, 1914–1950.* Salt Lake City: The University of Utah Press.

Nelson, Nels C. 1910. The Ellis Landing Shellmound. *University of California Publications in Archaeology and Ethnology* 7 (5): 357–426.

———. 1913. Ruins of Prehistoric New Mexico. *The American Museum Journal*, 13.

———. 1914. Pueblo Ruins of the Galisteo Basin, New Mexico. *Anthropological Papers of the American Museum of Natural History* 15, 1–124. New York.

———. 1916. Chronology of the Tano Ruins. *American Anthropologist* 18 (2): 159–80.

———. 1919. The Archaeology of the Southwest: A Preliminary Report. *Proceedings of the National Academy of Sciences* 5 (4): 114–20.

New Mexico Bureau of Immigration. 1900. *Climate Is Fate: New Mexico, the Health Resort of the Continent.* Brochure.

———. 1909. *Farming in New Mexico, the Land of Sunshine, the Land of Opportunity.* Brochure.

New Mexico Institute of Science and Education. 1914. Program of the Summer Session, August 3–28.

Noelke, Virginia H. 1974. The Origin and Early History of the Bureau of American Ethnology, 1879–1910. Ph.D. dissertation, University of Texas, Austin.

Norton, Charles Eliot. 1880. To the Members of the Archaeological Institute of America. *Annual Report, Archaeological Institute of America* 1, 13–26.

———. 1882. *Annual Report, Archaeological Institute of America* 3. Cambridge: John Wilson and Son.

Osborn, Henry F. 1911. *The American Museum of Natural History.* 2d ed. New York: The Irving Press.

Paget, Martin. 1995. Travel, Exoticism and the Writing of Region: Charles Fletcher Lummis and the "Creation" of the Southwest. *Journal of the Southwest* 37 (3): 421–49.

Palmer, Frank M. 1905. A Land of Mystery. *Out West* 23 (6): 525–38.

Pardue, Diana F. 1996. Marketing Ethnography: The Fred Harvey Indian Department and George A. Dorsey. In *The Great Southwest of the Fred Harvey Company and the Santa Fe Railway*, ed. Marta Weigle and Barbara A. Babcock, 102–9. Phoenix, Ariz.: The Heard Museum.

Parezo, Nancy J. 1987. The Formation of Ethnographic Collections: The Smithsonian Institution in the American Southwest. *Advances in Archaeological Method and Theory* 10, 1–47.

———. 1993. Matilda Cox Stevenson: Pioneer Ethnologist. In *Hidden Scholars: Women Anthropologists and the Native American Southwest*, ed. Nancy J. Parezo, 38–62. Albuquerque: University of New Mexico Press.

Parker, Franklin. 1956. *George Peabody: A Biography*. Nashville, Tenn.: Vanderbilt University Press.

Parslow, Christopher C. 1995. *Rediscovering Antiquity: Karl Weber and the Excavation of Herculaneum, Pompeii, and Stabiae*. Cambridge: Cambridge University Press.

Parsons, Elsie Clews. 1929. The Social Organization of the Tewa of New Mexico. In *Memoirs of the American Anthropological Association* 36. Menasha, Wisc.: American Anthropological Association.

Passenger Traffic Department. 1907. *New Mexico, the Land of Sunshine*. Rock Island Lines.

Patterson, T. 1995. *Toward a Social History of Archaeology in the United States*. New York: Harcourt, Brace, & Co.

Pauly, Philip J. 1988. Summer Resort and Scientific Discipline: Woods Hole and the Structure of American Biology, 1882–1925. In *The American Development of Biology*, ed. Ronald Rainger, Keith R. Benson, and Jane Maienschein, 121–50. Philadelphia: University of Pennsylvania Press.

Pepper, George H. 1920. Pueblo Bonito. *Anthropological Papers of the American Museum of Natural History* 27.

Petch, Alison. 1998. *Collectors 2: Collecting for the Pitt Rivers Museum*. Oxford: Pitt Rivers Museum.

Phillips, Ann. 1993. Archaeological Expeditions into Southeastern Utah and Southwestern Colorado between 1888 and 1898 and the Dispersal of the Collections. In *Anasazi Basketmaker: Papers from the 1990 Wetherill-Grand Gulch Symposium*, ed. Victoria M. Atkins, 103–18. Cultural Resources Series 24. Salt Lake City, Utah: United States Department of the Interior, Bureau of Land Management.

Pinsky, Valerie. 1992. Archaeology, Politics, and Boundary-Formation: The Boas Censure (1919) and the Development of American Archaeology during the Inter-War Years. In *Rediscovering Our Past: Essays on the History of American Archaeology*, ed. Jonathan E. Reyman, 162–89. Avebury, U.K.: Aldershot.

Powell, John W. 1881. Introductory. In *First Annual Report of the Bureau of Ethnology*, xi–xxxiii. Washington, D.C.: U.S. Government Printing Office.

Praetzellis, Adrian. 1993. The Limits of Arbitrary Excavation. In *Practices of Archaeological Stratigraphy*, ed. Edward C. Harris, Marley R. Brown III, and Gregory J. Brown, 68–86. San Diego, Calif.: Academic Press.

Prescott, William H. 1843. *History of the Conquest of Mexico, with a Preliminary View of the*

Ancient Mexican Civilization, and the Life of the Conqueror Hernando Cortés. New York: Harper.

Prince, L. Bradford. 1903. *The Stone Lions of Cochiti.* Santa Fe, N.M.: The New Mexican Printing Company.

Proske, Beatrice G. 1963. *Archer Milton Huntington.* New York: Hispanic Society of America.

Prudden, T. Mitchell. 1906. *On the Great American Plateau: Wanderings among Canyons and Buttes, in the Land of the Cliff-Dweller, and the Indian of To-Day.* New York: G. P. Putnam's Sons.

Putnam, Frederic W. 1879a. Introduction. In *Reports upon Archaeology and Ethnological Collections from Vicinity of Santa Barbara, California, and from Ruined Pueblos of Arizona and New Mexico, and Certain Interior Tribes,* ed. F. W. Putnam. *Report of the United States Geographical Surveys West of the One Hundredth Meridian,* vol. 8: *Archaeology.* Washington, D.C.: U.S. Government Printing Office.

———. 1879b. Notes on the Implements of Stone, Pottery, and Other Objects Obtained in New Mexico and Arizona. In *Reports upon Archaeology and Ethnological Collections from Vicinity of Santa Barbara, California, and from Ruined Pueblos of Arizona and New Mexico, and Certain Interior Tribes,* ed. F. W. Putnam. *Report of the United States Geographical Surveys West of the One Hundredth Meridian,* vol. 7: *Archaeology.* Washington, D.C.: U.S. Government Printing Office.

Rainger, Ronald. 1990. Collectors and Entrepreneurs: Hatcher, Wortman, and the Structure of American Vertebrate Paleontology circa 1900. *Earth Sciences History* 9 (1): 14–21.

———. 1991. *An Agenda for Antiquity: Henry Fairfield Osborne and Vertebrate Paleontology at the American Museum of Natural History, 1890–1935.* Tuscaloosa: University of Alabama Press.

Report of the President to the Board of Directors of the World's Columbian Exposition. 1898. Chicago: Rand McNally & Co.

Rideing, William H. 1879. *A-Saddle in the Wild West.* New York: D. Appleton and Co.

Ridley, Ronald T. 1992. *The Eagle and the Spade: Archaeology in Rome during the Napoleonic Era.* Cambridge: Cambridge University Press.

Righter, Robert W. 1989. National Monuments to National Parks: The Use of the Antiquities Act of 1906. *Western Historical Quarterly* 20 (3): 281–301.

Robbins, Wilfred W., John P. Harrington, and Barbara Freire-Marreco. 1914. *Ethnobotany of the Tewa Indians.* Bureau of American Ethnology Bulletin 55. Washington, D.C.: U.S. Government Printing Office.

Ross, Dorothy. 1991. *The Origins of American Social Science.* Cambridge: Cambridge University Press.

Roth, Michael S. 1997. Irresistible Decay: Ruins Reclaimed. In *Irresistible Decay: Ruins Reclaimed,* ed. Michael S. Roth with Claire Lyons and Charles Merewether, 1–24. Los Angeles, Calif.: Getty Research Institute for the History of Art and the Humanities.

Rothman, Hal. 1988. *Bandelier National Monument: An Administrative History.* Southwest

Cultural Resources Center Professional Papers 14. Santa Fe, N.M.: National Park Service.

———. 1989. *Preserving Different Pasts: The American National Monuments*. Urbana: University of Illinois Press.

———. 1992. *Navajo National Monument: A Place and Its People, an Administrative History*. Southwest Cultural Resources Center Professional Papers 40. Santa Fe, N.M.: National Park Service.

———. 1997. *On Rims and Ridges: The Los Alamos Area since 1880*. Lincoln: University of Nebraska Press.

Rowe, John Howland. 1954. *Max Uhle, 1856–1944: A Memoir of the Father of Peruvian Archaeology*. University of California Publications in American Archaeology and Ethnology 46 (1).

Runte, Alfred. 1987. *National Parks: The American Experience*. Lincoln: University of Nebraska Press.

Russell, Colin A. 1983. *Science and Social Change, 1700–1900*. London: Macmillan.

Rydell, Robert W. 1984. *All the World's a Fair: Visions of Empire at American International Expositions, 1876–1916*. Chicago: University of Chicago Press.

San Diego Society of the American Institute of Archaeology. 1916. Yearbook.

Santa Fe. 1915. *New Mexico, The Land of Opportunity. Official Souvenir of the State of New Mexico at Panama-California Exposition San Diego 1915*, 214–16. Albuquerque: Albuquerque Morning Journal Press.

Santa Fe Guide Service. n.d. *Map of the Most Interesting 50 Mile Square in America*. Brochure.

Schnapp, Alain. 1996. *The Discovery of the Past*. New York: Harry N. Abrams.

Schuchert, Charles. 1928. Memorial of Frank Springer. *Bulletin of the Geological Society of New Mexico* 39, 65–80.

The School of American Archaeology. 1911. *Science* 34 (874): 401.

Sheftel, Phoebe S. 1979. The AIA 1879–1979: A Centennial Review. *American Journal of Archaeology* 83 (1): 3–17.

Shishkin, J. K. 1968. *"The New Museum is a Wonder . . . ": An Early History of the Museum of New Mexico Fine Arts Building*. Santa Fe: Museum of New Mexico Press.

Silberman, Neil A. 1982. *Digging for God and Country: Exploration, Archaeology, and the Secret Struggle for the Holy Land, 1799–1917*. New York: Alfred A. Knopf.

Silverberg, Robert. 1986. *The Mound Builders*. Athens: Ohio University Press.

Simmel, Georg. 1959 [1911]. The Ruin. In *Georg Simmel, 1858–1911: A Collection of Essays, with Translations and a Bibliography*, ed. Kurt H. Wolff, 259–68. Columbus: The Ohio State University Press.

Simpson, James W. 1850. *Journal of a Military Reconnaissance from Santa Fé, New Mexico, to the Navajo Country in 1849*. U.S. Senate Executive Document 64. 31st Cong., 1st sess., Washington, D.C.

Sitgreaves, Lorenzo. 1853. *Report of an Expedition down the Zuni and Colorado Rivers.*

U.S. Senate, Executive Document 59. 32nd Cong., 2nd Sess. Robert Armstrong, Public Printer, Washington, D.C.

Smith, Duane A. 1988. *Mesa Verde National Park: Shadows of the Centuries.* Lawrence: University Press of Kansas.

Snead, James E. 1999. Science, Commerce, and Control: Patronage and the Development of Anthropological Archaeology in the Americas. *American Anthropologist* 101 (2): 256–71.

———. 2000. The AIA and the "Western Idea" in American Archaeology. In *Excavating Our Past: Perspectives on the History of the Archaeological Institute of America,* ed. Susan Heuck Allen. Boston: Archaeological Institute of America, in press.

———. In press. Lessons of the Ages: Archaeology and the Construction of Cultural Identity in the American Southwest. *Journal of the Southwest.*

Springer, Carolyn. 1987. *The Marble Wilderness: Ruins and Representation in Italian Romanticism, 1775–1850.* Cambridge: Cambridge University Press.

Springer, Frank. n.d. Commencement Address, Colorado State Normal School, 1902. In *Legal, Literary, and Scientific Activities of Frank Springer,* ed. R. E. Twitchell. Santa Fe, N.M.: Privately published.

———. 1910a. The Field Session of the School of American Archaeology. *Science,* n.s., 23 (827): 622–24.

———. 1910b. The Summer Session of the School of American Archaeology. *Santa Fe New Mexican,* 24 September.

———. 1917. Opening Remarks. *El Palacio* 4 (4): 1–18.

Squier, Ephraim G. 1848. New Mexico and California. *The American Review,* n.s., 2 (5): 503–28.

Squier, Ephraim G., and Edwin H. Davis. 1998 [1848]. *Ancient Monuments of the Mississippi Valley.* Washington, D.C.: Smithsonian Institution Press.

Starr, Kevin. 1973. *Americans and the California Dream, 1850–1915.* New York: Oxford University Press.

Stein, John R., and Stephen H. Lekson. 1992. Anasazi Ritual Landscapes. In *Anasazi Regional Organization and the Chaco System,* ed. David E. Doyel, 87–100. Anthropological Paper 5. Albuquerque: Maxwell Museum of Anthropology.

Stegner, Wallace. 1953. *Beyond the Hundredth Meridian.* Boston: Houghton Mifflin.

Stensvaag, James T. 1980. Clio on the Frontier: The Intellectual Evolution of the Historical Society of New Mexico, 1859–1925. *New Mexico Historical Review* 55: 294.

Stevenson, James. 1883a. Illustrated Catalog of the Collections Obtained from the Indians of New Mexico and Arizona in 1879. In *Second Annual Report of the Bureau of Ethnology,* 307–422. Washington, D.C.: U.S. Government Printing Office.

———. 1883b. Illustrated Catalog of the Collections Obtained from the Indians of New Mexico and Arizona in 1880. In *Second Annual Report of the Bureau of Ethnology,* 423–65. Washington, D.C.: U.S. Government Printing Office.

———. 1884. Illustrated Catalog of the Collections Obtained from the Pueblos of Zuñi,

New Mexico, and Wolpi, Arizona, in 1881. In *Third Annual Report of the Bureau of Ethnology*, 511–94. Washington, D.C.: U.S. Government Printing Office.

Stewart, Susan. 1984. *On Longing: Narratives of the Miniature, the Gigantic, the Souvenir, the Collection*. Baltimore, Md.: Johns Hopkins University Press.

Stocking, George W., Jr. 1982. The Santa Fe Style in American Anthropology: Regional Interest, Academic Initiative, and Philanthropic Policy in the First Two Decades of the Laboratory of Anthropology, Inc. *Journal of the History of the Behavioral Sciences* 18: 3–19.

———. 1992. Philanthropoids and Vanishing Cultures: Rockefeller Funding and the End of the Museum Era in Anglo-American Anthropology. In *The Ethnographer's Magic and Other Essays*, ed. George W. Stocking, 178–211. Madison: University of Wisconsin Press.

Summer School Marked Success. 1914. *El Palacio* 2 (1): 2.

Sweeney, Gray. 1996. Drawing Borders: Art and the Cultural Politics of the U.S.–Mexico Boundary Survey 1850–1853. In *Drawing the Borderline: Artist-Explorers and the U.S.–Mexico Boundary Survey*, Exhibit Catalog, 23–77. Albuquerque, N.M.: Albuquerque Museum.

Thomas, David H. 1991. Harvesting Ramona's Garden: Life in California's Mythical Past. In *The Spanish Borderlands in Pan-American Perspective*, ed. David H. Thomas, 119–60. Columbian Consequences 3. Washington, D.C.: Smithsonian Institution Press.

Thoresen, Timothy H. H. 1975. Paying the Piper and Calling the Tune: The Beginnings of Academic Anthropology in California. *Journal of the History of the Behavioral Sciences* 11 (3): 257–75.

Trachtenberg, Alan. 1982. *The Incorporation of America: Culture & Society in the Gilded Age*. New York: Hill & Wang.

Traill, David A. 1995. *Schliemann of Troy: Treasure and Deceit*. New York: St. Martin's Press.

Trennert, Robert A. 1987. Fairs, Expositions, and the Changing Image of Southwestern Indians, 1876–1904. *New Mexico Historical Review* 62 (2): 127–50.

Trigger, Bruce G. 1986. Prehistoric Archaeology and American Society. In *American Archaeology Past and Future*, ed. David J. Meltzer, Don L. Fowler, and Jeremy A. Sabloff, 187–215. Washington, D.C.: Smithsonian Institution Press.

———. 1989. *A History of Archaeological Thought*. Cambridge: Cambridge University Press.

Twitchell, Ralph E. n.d. *Legal, Literary, and Scientific Activities of Frank Springer*. Santa Fe, N.M.: privately published.

———. 1912. *The Leading Facts of New Mexico History* II. Cedar Rapids, Iowa: The Torch Press.

Underwood, John H. 1916. Tsan-Ka-Wi. *El Palacio* 4 (3): 9.

United States Department of Agriculture. 1925. *In the Land of the Ancient Cliff Dweller: Bandelier National Monument, Santa Fe National Forest, New Mexico*. USDA Miscellaneous Circular no. 5.

References Cited

Unrau, Harlan D., and G. Frank Williss. 1987. To Preserve the Nation's Past: The Growth of Historic Preservation in the National Park Service during the 1930s. *Public Historian* 9 (2): 19–49.

Utah Society, Archaeological Institute of America. 1906. *Program for 1906–7*. Brochure.

Vanderbilt, Kermit. 1959. *Charles Eliot Norton; Apostle of Culture in a Democracy*. Cambridge: Belknap Press of Harvard University Press.

Van Keuren, David K. 1989. Cabinets and Culture: Victorian Anthropology and the Museum Context. *Journal of the History of the Behavioral Sciences* 25: 26–39.

Veysey, Laurence R. 1965. *The Emergence of the American University*. Chicago: University of Chicago Press.

———. 1979. The Plural Organized Worlds of the Humanities. In *The Organization of Knowledge in America*, ed. Alexandra Oleson and John Voss, 51–106. Baltimore, Md.: The Johns Hopkins University Press.

Wade, Edwin L. 1985. The Ethnic Art Market in the American Southwest, 1880–1980. In *Objects and Others: Essays on Museums and Material Culture*, ed. George W. Stocking Jr., 167–91. Madison: University of Wisconsin Press.

Wallace, Kevin. 1960. Slim Shin's Monument. *The New Yorker*, 19 November.

Wallace, William J., and Donald W. Lathrap. 1975. *West Berkeley (CA-ALA-307): A Culturally Stratified Shell Mound on the East Shore of San Francisco Bay*. Contributions of the University of California Archaeological Research Facility 29.

Wallach, Alan. 1994. Thomas Cole: Landscape and the Course of American Empire. In *Thomas Cole: Landscape into History*, ed. William H. Truetter and Alan Wallach, 23–112. New Haven, Conn.: Yale University Press.

Walter, Paul A. F. 1932. Ten Years After. *New Mexico Historical Review* 7 (4): 371–76.

Weber, David J. 1970. *The Taos Trappers: The Fur Trade in the Far Southwest, 1540–1846*. Norman: University of Oklahoma Press.

———. 1985. *Richard H. Kern: Expeditionary Artist in the Far Southwest, 1848–1853*. Albuquerque: University of New Mexico Press.

Weigle, Marta, and Kyle Fiore. 1982. *Santa Fe and Taos: The Writer's Era, 1916–1941*. Santa Fe, N.M.: Ancient City Press.

Weizner, Bella. n.d. A Year-by-Year Summary of the Department of Anthropology. Manuscript on file, Department of Anthropology, American Museum of Natural History, New York.

Whitley, Richard. 1984. *The Intellectual and Social Organization of the Sciences*. Oxford: Clarendon Press.

Wiebe, Robert H. 1967. *The Search for Order, 1877–1920*. Westport, Conn.: Greenwood Press.

Wilcox, David R. 1987. *Frank Midvale's Investigation of La Ciudad*. Arizona State University Office of Cultural Resource Management Anthropological Field Studies 19.

———. 1988. The Changing Context of Support for Archaeology and the Work of Erich F. Schmidt. In *Erich F. Schmidt's Investigations of Salado Sites in Central Arizona: The Mrs. W. B. Thompson Archaeological Expedition of the American Museum of Natural*

History, ed. John W. Hohmann and Linda B. Kelley, 11–27. Museum of Northern Arizona Bulletin 56. Flagstaff: Museum of Northern Arizona.

Williams, Stephen. 1991. *Fantastic Archaeology: The Wild Side of North American Prehistory.* Philadelphia: University of Pennsylvania Press.

Wilson, Chris. 1997. *The Myth of Santa Fe: Creating a Modern Regional Tradition.* Albuquerque: University of New Mexico Press.

Wilson, Raymond. 1976. Establishing Canyon de Chelly National Monument: A Study in Navajo and Government Relations. *New Mexico Historical Review* 51 (2): 109–120.

Wilson, Thomas H., and Cheri Falkenstein-Doyle. 1999. Charles Fletcher Lummis and the Origins of the Southwest Museum. In *Collecting Native America, 1870–1960,* ed. Shepard Krech III and Barbara A. Hail, 74–104. Washington, D.C.: Smithsonian Institution Press.

Winegrad, Dilys P. 1993. *Through Time, across Continents: A Hundred Years of Archaeology and Anthropology at the University Museum.* Philadelphia: The University Museum, University of Pennsylvania.

Wislizenus, Adolph. 1969. *Memoir of a Tour to Northern Mexico Connected with Colonel Doniphan's Expedition in 1846 and 1847.* Albuquerque, N.M.: Calvin Horn Publisher.

Wissler, Clark. 1917. The New Archaeology. *The American Museum Journal* 17 (2): 100–101.

Woman's Auxiliary Committee, World's Columbian Exposition for San Juan County. 1893. *San Juan County, New Mexico.* Chicago: Rand, McNally & Co. Printers.

Woodbury, Richard B. 1960a. Nels C. Nelson and Chronological Archaeology. *American Antiquity* 25 (3): 400–401.

———. 1960b. Nelson's Stratigraphy. *American Antiquity* 36 (1): 98–99.

———. 1993. *Sixty Years of Southwestern Archaeology: A History of the Pecos Conference.* Albuquerque: University of New Mexico Press.

Young, Robert W. 1983. Apachean Languages. In *Handbook of North American Indians.* Vol. 10: *Southwest,* ed. Alfonso Ortiz, 393–400. Washington, D.C.: Smithsonian Institution.

Zucker, Paul. 1968. *Fascination of Decay: Ruins: Relic-Symbol-Ornament.* Ridgewood, N.J.: The Gregg Press.

Index

About the Author

James E. Snead was raised in Santa Fe, New Mexico, and attended Beloit College before going on to graduate school in the Department of Anthropology at UCLA. His dissertation, based on a study of fourteenth-century Ancestral Pueblo communities in the northern Rio Grande region, was completed in 1995, and he continues to pursue fieldwork in the American Southwest. He has held research fellowships at the School of American Research, the American Museum of Natural History, and the Clements Center for Southwest Studies at Southern Methodist University. He has taught at UCLA and the University of Arizona, and is presently Assistant Professor at George Mason University in Fairfax, Virginia. Among his recent publications is "Science, Commerce, and Control: Patronage and the History of Anthropological Archaeology in the Americas" (*American Anthropologist* 101, no. 2, 1999), which won the Gordon R. Willey award for the best archaeology article in *American Anthropologist* that year. Other publications include "Lessons of the Ages: Archaeology and the Construction of Cultural Identity in the American Southwest" (*Journal of the Southwest* 44, no. 1, 2002), and "Ancestral Pueblo Trails and the Cultural Landscape of the Pajarito Plateau, New Mexico" (*Antiquity* 76, 2002).